A GEOGRAPHY OF
PAKISTAN

ENVIRONMENT, PEOPLE AND ECONOMY

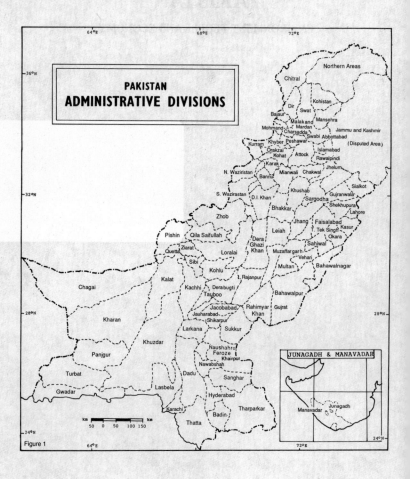

Figure 1

A GEOGRAPHY OF
PAKISTAN

ENVIRONMENT, PEOPLE AND ECONOMY

FAZLE KARIM KHAN

M. A. (Aligarh)
Ph. D. (Louisiana State University)

KARACHI

OXFORD UNIVERSITY PRESS

OXFORD   NEW YORK

Oxford University Press
OXFORD NEW YORK
TORONTO MELBOURNE AUCKLAND
KUALA LUMPUR SINGAPORE HONG KONG TOKYO
DELHI BOMBAY CALCUTTA MADRAS KARACHI
NAIROBI DAR ES SALAAM CAPE TOWN
and associates in
BERLIN IBADAN

OXFORD is a trade mark of Oxford University Press

First Edition, 1991

Second Impression, 1992

ISBN 0 19 577411 6

Printed at
Mueid Packages, Karachi
Published by
Oxford University Press
5-Bangalore Town, Sharae Faisal
P.O. Box 13033, Karachi-75350, Pakistan.

Contents

page

List of Photographs   x
List of Figures   xv
List of Tables   xiv
Preface   xv

PART I: THE CREATION OF PAKISTAN

1 Introduction   3

2 The Emergence of Pakistan   6
The Ancient Times *6*   The Aryans *6*   The Muslims *8*
The British *8*   The States *13*

PART II: ENVIRONMENT

3 Physiography   19
Western Highlands *19*   The Indus Plains *26*

4 Climate   31
Temperature *32*   Rainfall *38*   Climatic Regions *42*

5 Soils   52
Factors of Soil Formation in Pakistan *52*
Soil Classification *54*   Soil Erosion *59*

6 Environmental Challenge   61
Topographic Constraints *62*   Climatic Constraints *63*
Floods *64*   Desertification *64*   Earthquakes *65*
Population Growth and Resources *66*
Salinity and Waterlogging *67*
Urban Growth and Environmental Problems *68*
Air Pollution *69*   Water Pollution *69*

PART III: THE PEOPLE

7 Population: Growth and Distribution   75
The Growth of Population *75*   Urbanization *77*   Distribution
of Urban Places *82*   Distribution of Rural Places *84*

page

8 Population Composition 89
Age Composition *89* Labour Force *91* Languages *93*
Literacy *97* Religion *97*

PART IV: THE ECONOMY

9 Fishing 101
The Marine Fisheries *101* Inland Fisheries *102*
Fishing Craft *102* Fishermen *103* Local Consumption and
Export of Fish *104*

10 Forests 105
Forest Types and Distribution *105* Forest Products *110*
Forest Cover and Soil Erosion *111*

11 Agriculture: Problems and Solutions 112
Irrigation to Combat Aridity *113* Indus Water Treaty *121*
Waterlogging and Salinity *125* Improved Seeds *127*
Fertilizer *128* Plant Protection *129* Mechanization *130*
Farm Size and Fragmentation of Holdings *131*
Land Tenure and Land Reform *134*

12 Agriculture: Crops and Livestock 138
Agricultural Land Use *138* Crops *139* Livestock *159*

13 Minerals and Power Resources 165
Non-metallic Minerals *165* Metallic Minerals *177*
Power Resources *177*

14 Industries 193
Industrial Policy *193* Industrial Development *196*
Cotton Textile *199* Woollen Textile *203* Art Silk *204*
Jute Industry *204* Sugar Industry *206* Vegetable *Ghee*
and Cooking Oil *208* Chemicals *210* Fertilizer *211*
Cement *212* Iron and Steel Engineering *212*
Cottage and Small Scale Industries *214*

15 Foreign Trade 217
Exports *220* Imports *221* Direction of Trade *224*

16 Transportation 228
Railways *228* Roads *229* Air Transport *231*
Shipping *233* Sea Ports *233*

Index 235

List of Photographs

Photograph   *facing page*

1	The Khyber Pass	2
2	Moen-jo-Daro	2
3	Collecting firewood	3
4	Ploughing a field	3
5	Lake Saif-ul-Maluk	18
6	The Ravi River	18
7	The Arabian Sea	19
8	The Thar Desert	19
9	Waterlogging near Faisalabad	66
10	Air pollution	66
11	Industrial pollution	67
12	A garbage dump	67
13	A tea shop	82
14	A market place	82
15	An artisan	82
16	Karachi	83
17	A fishing village	83
18	Warsak Dam	130
19	Mangla Dam	130
20	*Karez* for irrigation	131
21	A man-made lake	131
22	Rice threshing in Sindh	146
23	Livestock	146
24	Terraced cultivation	147
25	Sugarcane plantations	147
26	Carpet weaving	210
27	Women cleaning shrimps	210
28	National Refinery	211
29	A fertilizer factory	211
30	An unmetalled road	226
31	Camels	226
32	Autorickshaws	227
33	Buses on a mountain road	227

List of Figures

Figure   *page*

1   Administrative Divisions   *frontispiece*
2   Physiography   21
3   Temperature Regions   32
4   Temperature: Hottest Month   34
5   Temperature: Coolest Month   36
6   Rainfall: Annual   38
7   Rainfall Regime   40
8   Rainfall: Monsoon, Western Depression, Thunderstorms
        (April-June) and Thunderstorms (October-November)   41
9   Climatic Regions   43
10 Soils   55
11 Density of Rural Population, 1981   86
12 Forests   108
13 Moisture Regions   114
14 Rainy Days   115
15 Canals   122
16 Salinity Control and Reclamation Zones   125
17 Wheat Regions   140
18 Rice Regions   146
19 Maize Regions   148
20 Sugarcane Regions   152
21 Tobacco Regions   155
22 Cotton Regions   157
23 Selected Non-metallic Minerals   167
24 Limestone, Marble and China Clay   171
25 Selected Metallic Minerals   175
26 Coal, Petroleum and Natural Gas   180
27 Thermal and Hydel Plants   187
28 Cotton Textile   201
29 Woollen, Art Silk and Jute Textile   205
30 Sugar Industry   207
31 Vegetable *Ghee,* Chemical, Cement and Fertilizer   209
32 Iron and Steel, and Engineering   213
33 Small and Cottage Industries   215

List of Tables

Table   *page*

4.1 Mean Monthly Temperature and Precipitation of
     Jacobabad and Sibi   33
4.2 Mean Monthly Temperature and Precipitation
     of Multan and Nokkundi   44
4.3 Mean Monthly Temperature and Precipitation of
     Karachi and Jiwani   46
4.4 Mean Monthly Temperature and Precipitation of
     Lahore and Peshawar   47
4.5 Mean Monthly Temperature and Precipitation of
     Quetta and Zhob   48
4.6 Mean Monthly Temperature and Precipitation of
     Sialkot and Kakul   49
4.7 Mean Monthly Temperature and Precipitation
     of Murree   50
7.1 Population Growth, 1901-1981   76
7.2 Total, Rural and Urban Population and Rural and
     Urban Population as Percentage of Total Population,
     1901 to 1981.   77
7.3 Number and Percentage of Cities by Size and their
     Percentage in Urban Population, 1901 to 1981   78
7.4 Urban Population as per cent of Total Population and
     Intercensal Growth of Total, Rural and
     Urban Population, 1901 to 1981   80
7.5 Cities of 100,000 or larger arranged in descending
     order by size, 1951-1981   83
8.1 Percentage of Population in Major Age Groups and
     Dependency Ratio of Pakistan and Selected Countries in
     Selected Years   90
8.2 Number of Labour Force, Percentage of
     Total Population in Labour Force and
     Dependents per Labourer in Pakistan   91
8.3 Sectoral Share of Labour Force in Percentage,
     1951-86   92

Table		page
8.4	Percentage of Households by Language Spoken, 1981	94
9.1	Fish Catch, 1947-85	102
9.2	Fishermen engaged in Marine and Inland Fishing, 1960, 1970 and 1980	103
10.1	Forest Area of Pakistan, 1983-84	106
10.2	Area of Forest by Types and Range Lands, 1983-84	107
10.3	Forest Products, Average Annual Production in Selected Periods	110
11.1	Some Parameters of Agriculture in Pakistan in Selected Years	113
11.2	Percentage Share of Area Irrigated by Different Sources and Total Irrigated Area in Selected Years	117
11.3	Consumption, Production and Import of Fertilizer in Selected Years	128
11.4	Consumption of Fertilizer per Cultivated Hectare in Selected Years	129
11.5	Number, Area and Average Size of Farms Classified by Tenure 1960, 1972 and 1980	132
11.6	Number, Area and Average Size of Private Farms by Size Groups, 1960, 1972 and 1980	133
12.1	Agricultural Land Use, 1947-48, 1969-70, 1979-80 and 1984-85 (Percentage of the total area)	139
12.2	Province-wise Area and Production of Wheat, 1970-75, 1976-80 and 1981-85	141
12.3	Province-wise Percentage of Wheat Area under Irrigation for 1971-75, 1976-80 and 1981-85	142
12.4	Province-wise Yield of Wheat in kg per hectare for 1971-75, 1976-80 and 1981-85	143
12.5	Province-wise Area and Production of Rice for 1971-75, 1976-80 and 1981-85	145
12.6	Area, Production and Yield per hectare of Maize, for 1971-75, 1976-80 and 1981-85	147
12.7	Area, Production and Yield per hectare of *Jowar* and *Bajra* for 1971-75, 1976-80 and 1981-85	149
12.8	Area, Production and Yield per hectare of Sugarcane, 1947-1985	153
12.9	Province-wise Area, Production and Yield per hectare of Sugarcane for 1971-75, 1976-80 and 1981-85	154

Table		page
12.10	Area, Production and Yield per hectare of Tobacco in Selected Years	156
12.11	Variety-wise Area of Cotton, 1947-85	156
12.12	Variety-wise Production of Cotton, 1947-85	158
12.13	Cattle, 1972-73, 1979-80 and 1984-85	160
12.14	Estimated Milk Production 1974-75, 1979-80 and 1984-85	161
12.15	Buffaloes, 1974-75, 1979-80 and 1984-85	162
12.16	Estimated Meat Production, 1974-75, 1979-80 and 1984-85	162
12.17	Sheep and Goats, 1972-73, 1979-80 and 1984-85	163
13.1	Reserves of Principal Minerals	166
13.2	Production of Principal Non-metallic Minerals in Selected Years	168
13.3	Production of Limestone, Marble and Clays in Selected Years	172
13.4	Energy Supply	178
13.5	Field-wise Location, Year of Discovery and Production of Crude Oil, 1980-81 and 1984-85	181
13.6	Domestic Production and Total Consumption of Petroleum and Domestic Production as Percentage of Total Consumption in Selected Years	182
13.7	Field-wise Production of Gas in Selected Years	184
13.8	Generation of Electricity in Selected Years	185
13.9	Number of Villages Electrified	191
13.10	Sectoral Consumption of Electricity in Selected Years	192
14.1	Cotton Looms and Spindles in Selected Years	199
14.2	Number of Factories and Production of Sugar and Vegetable *Ghee* in Selected Years	206
14.3	Production of Soda Ash, Sulphuric Acid and Caustic Soda in Selected Years	210
14.4	Consumption, Production and Import of Fertilizer in Selected Years	211
14.5	Number of Factories and Production of Cement in Selected Years	212
15.1	Export, Import and Trade Balance 1947-48 (million rupees)	218
15.2	Economic Classifications of Exports of Pakistan 1969-70 to 1987-88 (percentage share)	220

Table *page*

15.3 Ten Leading Exports of Pakistan and their Percentage
Share in Total Exports in Selected Years 220

15.4 Economic Classification of Imports in Pakistan
1969-70 to 1987-88 (percentage share) 222

15.5 Ten Leading Imports of Pakistan and their
Percentage Share in Selected Years 223

15.6 Direction of Exports from Pakistan in Selected
Years (percentage of total export) 224

15.7 Direction of Imports into Pakistan in Selected
Years (percentage of total exports) 225

16.1 Pakistan Railways: Route Kilometres, Passengers,
and Freight Carried in Selected Years 229

16.2 Road Kilometres in Pakistan 230

16.3 Cargo Handled at Karachi Port in Selected
Years (thousand tons) 233

Preface

Pakistan has remained the abode of man since the Paleolithic times. Since that time the natural environment has not changed much, but the economy, the mode of transportation, the energy sources and the life pattern have been transformed. This transformation has been gradual and has taken place through changes in technology, and the social and cultural set-up. For the past 5,000 years the world has seen in Pakistan the emergence of a very advanced river valley civilization in the shape of Moen-jo-daro–Harrappa culture. Pakistan has continued to make progress along with other parts of the world. However since the Industrial Revolution the Western Countries began to take more rapid strides, and Pakistan along with other Third World countries lagged behind. Pakistan with low technology, a weak social organization, unstable political conditions, a large and rapidly growing population and limited financial resources has failed to exploit the natural environment fully. Efforts are being made to develop economic, health, education and social welfare sectors but a breakthrough has not been achieved. This book attempts to relate the achievements made so far and also the disappointments.

Pakistan possesses a diversity of topography, climate, soil and plant cover. Human population differs in number, level of education and technology from one region to another. Therefore spatial diversity in crop distribution, industrial and transportational pattern has emerged. This spatial diversity has been analysed.

Pakistan is facing many environmental challenges like rugged topography, arid climate, floods and earthquakes. Attempts are being made to meet them. In the process some new problems have cropped up. Irrigation to combat aridity has caused salinity and waterlogging in large areas of cultivated land. Population spiral has put a strain on resources. Food deficiency exists. Heavy import of petroleum has to be made. Recently large cities have emerged which have brought in their wake problems of water supply, sewerage, solid waste disposal, air and water pollution. These problems have been pointed out and described.

This book is particularly addressed to college and university students of Pakistan Studies, Geography, Economics and Commerce. General readers and those preparing for competitive examinations will also be benefited.

I express my sincere thanks to Mr. M. Rafique Dhanani, Assistant Professor of Geography, Sindh University, and Mr. Safiruddin, Lecturer in Geography, S.M. Arts College, Karachi, who helped me in the preparation of this book in many ways. I am also thankful to Mr. Murtaza Khan who has done the cartographic work, and Mr. Ghulam Abbas and Mr. Tariq Najmuddin for typing the manuscript. I am indebted to my wife, Mrs. Khurshida Khanam who has always been a source of inspiration.

Fazle Karim Khan

Part I

The Creation of Pakistan

The Khyber Pass, the historic gateway to Pakistan

Moen-jo-Daro, The Mound of the Dead, dating from 3500 BC

Scenes from time immemorial

Collecting firewood

Ploughing a field the traditional way

Chapter 1

Introduction

Pakistan is an old land but a new state. It is a traditional society trying to acquire modern technology. It is a poor country and has to support a large population which is growing at a fast rate. Burdened with heavy foreign debt it suffers from an unfavourable balance of trade. It is under these difficult conditions that Pakistan is trying to achieve an economic break-through while the economy continues to be delicately poised.

Pakistan came into existence in 1947 after throwing off the British yoke, as an avowed Islamic state. Efforts towards economic development have borne some fruit but the comforts of life have not yet reached the masses. A heavy population (84.3 million in 1981) multiplying at an explosive rate (3.1 per cent annually between 1972 and 1981) eats away most of the economic growth.

Nature has endowed Pakistan with sufficient resources. Although a large part of the country experiences arid conditions this is compensated by large streams which irrigate the parched lands. A considerable rugged area is offset by vast fertile plains and the country though poor in metallic minerals is rich in non-metallic minerals. Pakistan has modest resources of coal and oil and it possesses rich fields of natural gas. Further, as exploration continues new oil and coal fields are coming up and potential hydro-power abounds. Some large and some small hydel projects have been completed but many more can be developed. It is true that compared to USA and USSR Pakistan possesses small resources but compared to Holland and Belgium Pakistan is in a happier position. Nevertheless economically all these countries are far ahead of Pakistan. Therefore the responsibility for less development rests largely on human failings and not upon paucity of resources.

Forty-four years after gaining independence the literacy rate is still deplorably low (26.2 per cent). Among the educated persons only 5.8 per cent are graduates and 6 per cent have acquired technical education. Occasionally political instability has marred the economic progress. Long spells of martial law and introduction of several constitutions within a small span of national life bring into focus the political crisis within the country. Political uncertainty and changing economic policy make the capital shy. Domestic saving in Pakistan is very low (6 per cent of the GNP) when it is 24 per cent in India and 26 per cent in Sri Lanka. Furthermore several wars with India have corroded the economy.

Planning for the economic development of Pakistan was undertaken soon after gaining independence. In 1951 the Six-year Development Plan was launched. This was replaced by the First Five-year Plan (1955-60), and was followed by successive five-year plans. The first plan did not yield much result. But it provided experience in planning and some infrastructure was developed. The Second Five-year Plan (1960-65) proved fruitful. The per capita income increased by 3.8 per cent annually and the GNP by 6.7 per cent. The Third Five-year Plan (1965-70) ran into trouble because of war with India and subsequent suspension of US aid. Still, substantial growth was registered. The Fourth Five-year Plan (1970-75) was abandoned because of another war with India and the subsequent secession of East Pakistan (now Bangladesh) in 1971. Thereafter came a period of Annual Plans (1971-78). They did not yield much result because of disturbed political conditions, sharp fall in foreign aid and nationalization of many industries. The Fifth Plan (1978-83) and the Sixth Plan (1983-88) helped in some recovery of the economy.

In spite of many bottle-necks the per capita income at constant factor cost of 1959-60 increased from Rs 351 in 1949-50 to Rs 849 in 1986-87, the index of agricultural production from 74 in 1949-50 to 298 in 1985-86 and production index of manufacturing at 1980-81 base from 35 in 1964-65 to 154 in 1985-86. But Pakistan continues to be a poor developing country and suffers from a heavy adverse balance of payments.

Pakistan has experienced a deficit in the balance of payments every year since 1960. The cause of the deficit has always been an unfavourable balance of trade. In 1979-80 the net deficit in the balance of payments under the current account was $ 1,149 million and in 1985-86, $ 1,236 million. This would have been much higher but for the unrequited transfers. A phenomenal increase in home remittances was recorded from $ 100 million in 1969-70 to $ 2,886 million in 1982-83 which was an all-time high. Since then the remittances have decreased. They were $ 2,595 million in 1985-86. The heavy deficit in balance of payments on the current account is largely met by foreign borrowings.

It was in 1950 that Pakistan accepted foreign financial assistance for the first time. The assistance came under the Colombo Plan. Heavy foreign inflow in Pakistan's economy took place with the launching of the First Five-year Plan. Since then the amount of assistance has been increasing and the terms and conditions are getting stiffer. The quantum of grant has decreased and that of loan has increased. The grant was 80 per cent in the First Plan which dropped to 22 per cent in the Fifth and the Sixth Plan.

The outstanding debt on Pakistan increased from $ 5.8 billion in 1975-76 to $ 11.1 billion in 1985-86. This is a colossal amount. The result has been that net transfer after debt service payment is not very large. It was 56 per cent in 1977-78 and 33 per cent in 1985-86. The redeeming feature is that external debt as percentage of GNP decreased from 43 in 1975-76 to 34 in 1985-86, and as percentage of foreign exchange earnings from 318 to 162. But the situation remains very disturbing.

In the pages that follow, the struggle for Pakistan and its creation is described. An assessment of its natural and human resources is made. The economic activities that are employed to utilize these resources are discussed. The achievements made so far are described and the problems faced are analysed.

Administratively Pakistan is divided into four provinces, Balochistan, North West Frontier Province (NWFP), Punjab and Sindh. Besides these there are Federally Administered Tribal Areas, Northern Areas and Islamabad. The provinces are divided into divisions and divisions into districts which in turn are subdivided into *tehsils*. However provinces and districts constitute the basic units of administration (Fig. 1).

Chapter 2

The Emergence of Pakistan

The creation of Pakistan on 14 August 1947 was the culmination of the struggle that started in 1857 to achieve freedom from British domination over the Indo-Pak subcontinent. The British came to the subcontinent in the early seventeenth century as merchants and eventually became its rulers. They took the reign of the government by overthrowing the Muslims who had ruled the subcontinent for 650 years. Before the Muslims the Hindus dominated the political scene. Still earlier the Dravidians and the aboriginal tribes were the masters. Therefore a glimpse into the history of the subcontinent seems necessary in order to understand the creation of Pakistan.

THE ANCIENT TIMES

The history of Indo-Pakistan goes back to the Stone Age. It was an age of hunting and gathering and towards its close rudimentary agriculture had started. This was followed by the Indus Valley Civilization, a period of well developed agriculture, trade and commerce, art and architecture, cities and buildings, religion and rites. It dates back to 3000-3500 BC. Its collapse is still an unsolved mystery. The Dravidian Civilization followed the Indus Valley Civilization and might also have coexisted with it. It flourished over the major part of the subcontinent with well developed agriculture, religion and social institutions. The Dravidians had occupied a large part of the subcontinent by pushing the aboriginal tribes (Santal, Munda, Oraon, Bhil, Gond etc.) into the more difficult environment of hills and mountains.

THE ARYANS

The Aryans invaded the Indo-Pak subcontinent in the middle of the first millennium BC. They came from Central Asia and entered the subcontinent from the north-west. They first settled in Sapta Sindhu or the Seven Rivers from the Kabul to the Jumna. The Aryans continued their advance eastward and conquered a large part of the Ganges Plains and later crossed the Vindhyas and entered the Deccan plateau. The conquered and the vanquished were the Dasyus or Dasas (the dark-coloured snub nosed slaves as the Aryans called them), i.e., the Dravidians and the aboriginal tribes.

The Aryans were pastoralists. They lived mainly on milk and meat. They worshipped natural phenomena like the sun, the moon, fire, wind, rain etc., but they also believed in one ultimate supreme God. The religious beliefs of the Aryans in association with those of the Dravidians led to the development of Hinduism.

It is a religion believing in many gods and a caste system. The caste is determined by birth and not by one's achievements and accomplishments. By no means can a person belonging to one caste cross over to the other. The whole society is divided into four *varna*s (caste groups). The Brahmans (priests) are at the top and are followed by Kshtriyas (warriors/ rulers), the Vaisyas (traders) and the Sudras (cultivators). All other castes are outside the *varna*. They are low castes. Some of them are 'untouchable'. Water and food are polluted by their touch. The different castes do not intermarry and a number of them cannot interdine. People belonging to other religions occupy a position below all the Hindu castes.

Hinduism spread over the major part of the subcontinent but the subcontinent has never remained one political unit. It was during the reign of the Mauryan King Asoka (250 BC) that the largest kingdom under the Hindus was established. It extended as far south as the Penner River. It is doubtful that Asoka remained Hindu throughout his life. The horrors of the war of Kalinga had so much disturbed him that he came under the influence of Buddha and might have actually embraced Buddhism.

The Hindu domination was not continuous. Buddha founded a religion in the sixth century BC. Buddhism was a strong reaction against the caste-ridden Hinduism. Buddhists established independent kingdoms in some parts of the subcontinent but they eventually lost their hold. Buddhism failed to survive against Brahmanism.

During Hindu rule the subcontinent continued to be intermittently invaded by armies marching from the north-west. The Sakas, the Parthians and the Kushans were some of the groups which came to the subcontinent and established empires. Some of them established extensive empires. The Kushans under Kanishka for example(first/second century AD) established an empire extending from Sinkiang to Varanasi (Benaras) with its capital at Purushapura (Peshawar).

THE MUSLIMS

The Muslims entered the subcontinent in AD 642 and conquered Makran under the command of Abdullah-bin-Abdullah during the caliphate of Hazrat Umer. Sindh was annexed in AD 712 by Muhammad-bin-Qasim who advanced as far as Multan. The Muslims then withdrew from Sindh but Makran continued to remain under the Muslim rule for a long time. In the tenth century Ibn Haukal found that Isa-bin-Madan, an Arab, was ruling over Makran. In AD 1001 the Muslims entered the subcontinent from the north-west under the leadership of Mahmood Ghaznavi. They penetrated as far as Mathura and Somnath (Kathiawar) but held only the Punjab up to Thanesar. The continuous rule of the Muslims began with the decisive victory of Muhammad Ghori over the Rajput princes at Thanesar in 1192. This opened the gateway to Delhi. Within a few years the Ganges Plain as far as Nadia (Bengal) was subjugated and the Muslim rule in the subcontinent was firmly established. From that date up to 1857 for 650 years the sovereign power rested with the Muslims. Their empire did not remain equally extensive all the time. It was most extensive during the reign of Aurangzeb (1707) when it had spread as far south as the Cauvery River. During the end of the Muslim rule, the Moghal Emperor, Bahadur Shah Zafar, was a titular head. The real power was wielded by the British. The Muslim supremacy however was deeply established and widely accepted. Even though the Moghal emperor had neither the wealth nor the power he continued to act as the symbol of sovereignty. The *Mansabdars* who were independent rulers of their states continued to seek recognition of their titles from Delhi even in the far-off areas like Bengal and the Deccan Peninsula. As late as 1765 when the British wielded full power in Bengal, the East India Company got its powers of *diwani* (the right of collection of revenue) regularized by a grant from the Emperor. The Muslim rule finally ended with the formal annexation of the subcontinent by the British Crown in 1858.

THE BRITISH

The British entry into the Indo-Pakistan subcontinent took place through the East India Company. It was a trading company founded on 31 December 1600. It established its first factory in the subcontinent at Surat in 1613. Within a century the company was well set with its chief centres at Bombay, Madras and Calcutta. The company became a great political force after its victory at Plassey in 1757 over Nawab Sirajuddaulah of

Bengal. At that time Bengal was a large province which comprised Bengal, Bihar, Orissa and parts of Assam. In 1765 the East India Company was granted *diwani* in Bengal. From 1757 the territorial responsibility of the company increased rapidly. With the success achieved by the East India Company, the British government began to increase its control over the company. In 1784 the political and military policy of the company was handed over to the Board of Control stationed in London. By the middle of the eighteenth century the political control of the British through the East India Company extended over the whole of the subcontinent. In 1857 an attempt was made to overthrow the British yoke. An armed revolution took place which was ruthlessly crushed. Next year in 1858 the subcontinent was annexed by the British Crown and the Moghal Emperor, Bahadur Shah Zafar, was deposed and exiled to Burma.

The British empire in the Indo-Pakistan subcontinent was established on the ruins of the Muslim rule. This at once put the Muslims and the British in opposite camps. The British distrusted the Muslims. The enmity reached its height during and after the armed struggle for freedom in 1857. The doors of governmental favour were shut to the Muslims. Many Muslims already in the employment of the government were dismissed on frivolous grounds. The Muslims also hated everything that was British including the English language and Western education. This more than anything else harmed the Muslims. In 1835 English replaced Persian as the official language. The Muslims failed to adjust to the new situation. The result was that in 1880-81, the Muslims attending English high school numbered 363 as against 36,686 Hindus. In 1878, there were 57 Muslims with graduate degrees while the number of Hindus was 3,155. The power that the Muslims had exercised was gone and the wealth that they possessed was depleting fast. In the new set-up the Hindus were the allies of the British. They made all efforts to gain the favour of the British. In that they easily succeeded. Soon the Hindus began to control government machinery. They also controlled the business. The agricultural lands were slipping away from the Muslims to the Hindus. The Muslims, who not many years ago had been the lords of the land were devoid of power and wealth. Their condition was miserable. They were dazed and they knew not what to do. It was then that Syed Ahmed Khan, a retired judge, pleaded that the Muslims must not remain aloof. They should try to gain the confidence of the British. He also gave a call to learn English and acquire Western education. For this he established the Anglo-Oriental College at Aligarh in 1875 which later developed into the Muslim University. It was from there that the Aligarh Movement, which inspired the Muslim youth of the subcontinent started. Much was said and is still being said against his unconditional support of the British and the acceptance of Western education in an undiluted form. But he gave hope to the Muslims at a time of despair, and a rudder which was badly needed.

In 1885 Indian National Congress was founded by A.W. Hume, a retired British member of the Indian Civil Service, with the blessings of Lord Dufferin, the Governor General of India. The Governor-General wanted the Indian politicians to meet annually and point out to the government ways to improve its administration. Syed Ahmed Khan advised the Muslims not to join the Congress. He thought that the Hindu-dominated Congress would champion the Hindu cause only and would not safeguard the Muslim interest.

In 1905, the large Bengal Presidency was split into two provinces for administrative reasons. One of the two provinces was Eastern Bengal and Assam in which the Muslims were in a majority. This was vehemently opposed by the Hindus. It was made an all-India issue. To press their demand they started the Swadeshi Movement, a movement to boycott British cloth. The British government ultimately yielded to the Hindu agitation and the partition of Bengal was annulled in 1911.

In 1906 a deputation under the leadership of the Aga Khan met the Viceroy, Lord Minto, and demanded a separate electorate for the Muslims on the plea that they had no confidence in a Hindu majority. The Morley-Minto Reforms were introduced in 1910 which gave a separate electorate to the Muslims. The Congress condemned and opposed the separate electorate. From there onwards whenever any constitutional changes were discussed the Congress tried to grab power for the Hindu majority and the Muslims tried to safeguard their future. The Nehru Report, a formula for the constitution of an independent subcontinent, and Jinnah's Fourteen Points, a suggested amendment of the formula clearly demonstrate Hindu aspiration and Muslim fear. Round Table Conferences also failed to produce any agreed solution because the Hindus wanted to be the future rulers of the subcontinent and the Muslims had no confidence in them.

The Congress government formed in 1937 under the 1935 Act amply demonstrated that the Muslim apprehension was justified. Discrimination against Muslims prevailed in all fields of life. Hindu-Muslim riots became a daily affair. Hindu cultural traditions were introduced in educational institutions and everyday life. The Muslims felt that their religion, tradition and culture were in danger.

The dissatisfaction of the Muslims with the Congress rule facilitated the work of Quaid-i-Azam Mohammad Ali Jinnah who was reorganising the Muslim League. The Muslim League was founded in 1906 under the presidentship of the Aga Khan. Since then it had been voicing the cause of the Muslims. In 1936 Mohammad Ali Jinnah became its president. He was a successful barrister and an experienced politician. He worked hard for Hindu-Muslim unity, so much so that he was called the ambassador of Hindu Muslim unity. He was instrumental in bringing about a rapprochement between the Muslim League and the Congress in 1916. He was a man of vision and conviction. In an excited crowd of more than one hundred thousand in 1920 when the resolution for non-cooperation was moved by Gandhi, Jinnah alone had the courage to oppose it and the foresight to see how futile it was. He was the author of Fourteen Points put forth in reply to the Nehru Report which was the proposed political set-up of the subcontinent after the withdrawal of the British. The implementation of the Nehru Report would have put the Hindu majority in the saddle. On assuming the presidentship of the Muslim League in 1936 the Quaid-i-Azam made an all-out effort to make the Muslim League the sole spokesman of the Muslims of the subcontinent. At the same time the Muslim League was also working on a formula for the future political set-up of the subcontinent. On 23 March 1940 at the annual session of the Muslim League held at Lahore, the Pakistan Resolution was passed demanding a separate independent state in the Muslim majority areas as the homeland for a hundred million Muslims of the subcontinent.

Earlier also the partition of India between the Muslims and the Hindus was suggested by others. These proposals did not attract sufficient public attention. In 1930 Dr Mohammad Iqbal in his presidential address at the annual session of the Muslim League strongly advocated the creation of an independent Muslim state in the north-west of the subcontinent and asserted that that was the final destiny of the Muslims. This produced a stir in the political circles and greatly inspired the Muslim youth.

The long negotiations between Hindus and Muslims over the future political set-up of the subcontinent had failed because the approach was made with a wrong premise. In Western democracy where the majority rule prevails no particular group constitutes the majority or the minority for all times. The members are free to change their allegiance from one party to another and therefore the majority party of today becomes the minority party tomorrow. This situation did not exist in the subcontinent, where the two parties were religious groups. Furthermore the Muslims were not a microscopic minority which could be ignored as a parasitic cultural group. They numbered 100 million. They had their distinct culture, glorious history and political aspirations. As such they constituted a nation and demanded a homeland. Incidentally two large regions on the western and eastern sides of the subcontinent had a Muslim majority which could be made the homeland of the Muslims. In 1946 elections were held. The Muslim League swept the polls. That election proved a referendum for the demand for the creation of Pakistan. The British were opposed to the partition of the subcontinent. Therefore they made further attempts to resolve the Hindu-Muslim deadlock through the Cripps Missions and the Cabinet Mission. The Cabinet Mission Plan presented on 16 May 1946 was a realistic and a positive attempt to preserve the unity of the country and also to satisfy the two parties, the Hindus and the Muslims. According to that plan the union of India was to have three subjects: defence, foreign affairs and communication. All other powers would be vested in the three groups into which the subcontinent would be divided. One group would comprise Balochistan, NWFP, Punjab and Sindh, whereas Assam and Bengal would constitute another group and the third group would include the rest of the country. A constituent assembly would then be set up to formulate the constitution. The Muslim League accepted the plan. The Congress also accepted the plan but took the stand that the constitutent assembly would be sovereign and thus could alter the plan in any way that it desired. That was obviously unacceptable to the Muslim League. Thus a sincere and positive attempt to resolve the deadlock failed. Thereafter the British government, the Congress and the Muslim League agreed over the partition of the subcontinent.

On 3 June 1947 the plan for the transfer of power was announced. Under the plan the Punjab, Sindh, NWFP (after a referendum) and Balochistan in the north-western part of the subcontinent and Bengal including Sylhet district of Assam (after a referendum) would constitute a dominion (Pakistan) and the rest of the subcontinent another dominion (Bharat or India). The provinces of Punjab and Bengal were to be divided between Pakistan and Bharat in such a manner that the contiguous Muslim areas would form part of Pakistan and non-Muslim areas part of Bharat. Besides contiguity of the Muslim and non-Muslim majority areas other factors were also to be considered.

In the light of the 3 June plan two boundary commissions, one for Punjab and another for Bengal were constituted in which there were members of both Pakistan and Bharat. An English Lawyer, Sir Cyril Radcliffe, as the chairman of both the commissions had the power to make the award. Since the other members of the commission did not agree, the partition of the Punjab and Bengal was virtually an award made by Radcliffe.

In the Punjab, all the non-Muslim majority areas without any exception were given to Bharat. On the other hand the following Muslim majority areas contiguous to Pakistan were also given to Bharat.

1. Gurdaspur was a Muslim majority district. It had four *tehsils,* Pathankot, Batala, Gurdaspur and Shakargarh. Pathankot Tehsil had a non-Muslim majority whereas the other three *tehsils* had a Muslim majority. Radcliffe awarded three *tehsils,* Gurdaspur, Batala and Pathankot to Bharat. This award provided Bharat access to the state of Jammu and Kashmir which Bharat could not have had if Gurdaspur and Batala had been given to Pakistan.
2. The Muslim majority *tehsils* of Ferozepur and Zira of Ferozepur District were given to Bharat. This gave Bharat control over Ferozepur Water headworks. All the canals taken off from this headwork irrigated Pakistan and no part of East Punjab (Bharat). Only one canal, namely Bikaner canal, irrigated a state which was outside Radcliffe's terms of reference. Pakistan suffered from the decision because Bharat stopped the supply of water to Pakistan as soon as it got an opportunity to do so.
3. The Muslim majority *tehsils* of Jullundar and Nakodar of Jullundar District were awarded to Bharat. These *tehsils* were located in the angle of Beas and Sutlej Rivers.
4. Ajnala of Amritsar District, a Muslim *tehsil*, was given to Bharat.

THE STATES

Outside the administrative set-up of British India there were 562 states ruled by princes. The states comprised roughly a third of the area occupied by the subcontinent and a quarter of its population. The paramountcy of the states lay with the British Crown. The paramount power was responsible for foreign affairs, external aggression and internal security. The states shared with British India railways, currency, post and telegraphs. In internal affairs the rulers of the states were free within the limits set by treaties and agreements, which differed from one state to another. Most of the states were small and exercised limited powers and jurisdiction. But 140 states were fully empowered. Kashmir, Mysore and Hyderabad were three large states. They compared with the provinces in area and population.

By the Indian Independence Act, 1947, all treaties and agreements between the British government and Indian states were to be terminated on 15 August 1947. The states were free to accede either to Pakistan or India or to remain independent. In case of any dispute the majority of the people living in the state was to decide its future. Ten states had Muslim rulers and the majority of their population was Muslim. They were contiguous to Pakistan and they acceded to Pakistan. These states were Bahawalpur, Khairpur, Lasbela, Makran, Kalat, Kharan, Dir, Swat,

Amb and Chitral. The remaining, more than 500 states acceded to Bharat except Junagadh, Manavadar, Hyderabad and Kashmir which became problems.

Junagadh and Manavadar

Junagadh was a state located on the coast in Gujarat peninsula at a distance of about 300 miles from Karachi. It had a population of 700,000 and an area of 3,337 square miles. Manavadar was a small state contiguous to Junagadh. They were Hindu majority states with Muslim rulers. They acceded to Pakistan. Bharat objected to their accession. Pakistan agreed to decide the matter by a plebiscite to be conducted under the joint supervision of Pakistan and Bharat. But Bharat used force and its army marched into Junagadh on 7 November 1947. Earlier Bharat had already occupied Manavadar and two enclaves of Junagadh within Bharat, namely Mingrol and Bahariawad. Bharat conducted a referendum in Junagadh under its supervision to give legal cover to its occupation. Pakistan did not accept the referendum as Pakistan was not associated with it in any form. Thereupon Pakistan lodged a complaint with the Security Council where it is still pending.

Kashmir

Kashmir is a large state located to the north of Pakistan. Its population is overwhelmingly Muslim but its ruler was Hindu. Some important rivers flow from Kashmir into Pakistan. Its road and rail link is with Pakistan. Karachi port is its natural outlet. Its population is closely linked with that of Pakistan by social, religious and blood ties. Bharat was separated from Kashmir by lofty mountains. It was provided an access into Kashmir through Batala and Gurdaspur, both Muslim majority *tehsils* contiguous to Pakistan, and given to Bharat by Radcliffe.

The Hindu ruler of Kashmir was in a fix. Pandit Kak, the Prime Minister, was in favour of joining Pakistan. Kak was dismissed and in his place Dogra General Janak Singh was appointed Prime Minister. He organized a systematic massacre of the Muslims. Thereupon the Muslims started to resist, particularly those of Poonch who were mostly ex-army men. Some tribesmen went there to help their brethren. Kashmir in the meanwhile signed a standstill agreement with Pakistan. Kashmir acceded to Bharat on 27 October 1947 without informing Pakistan. Indian forces entered Kashmir. Azad Kashmir forces backed by Pakistan resisted the accession. India made a complaint to UNO against Pakistan on 1 January

1948. Through the efforts of UNO on 1 January 1949 a cease-fire took place. The UNO passed a resolution on 5 January 1949 calling for a free and impartial plebiscite to be conducted under the auspices of the United Nations. The principles and procedures for the plebiscite were also laid down. The plebiscite has not been held so far. Bharat has refused to accept any arbitration or mediation in the matter. That is how Kashmir continues to be a disputed territory. The UNO has yet to implement its decision.

EAST PAKISTAN

Another unit of Pakistan was located in the eastern part of the subcontinent. It comprised the major part of Bengal and Sylhet District of Assam. It was named East Pakistan. In December 1971, it seceded from Pakistan and it was recognized by Pakistan in 1974. The new Muslim state is called Bangladesh.

Part II
Environment

Lake Saif-ul-Maluk, high up in the mountains

The Ravi River

The Arabian Sea

The Thar Desert – a barren waste

Chapter 3

Physiography

The physical framework of Pakistan has been built by two major geomorphic processes which have produced two distinct physiographic provinces (Fig. 2):

1. The Western Highlands produced by mountain building movement (Himalayan orogeny) occurring in the Tertiary era.
2. The Indus Plains resulting from the deposition of sediments by the Indus River and its tributaries into shallow bays in the Quaternary era.

WESTERN HIGHLANDS

The Western Highlands of Pakistan extend from the Makran Coast in the south to the Pamir Plateau in the north covering most of Balochistan, NWFP, the Northern Areas and part of the Punjab. The Highlands emerged from the Tethys Sea by the Himalayan orogeny which started in the Eocene and continued intermittently up to the Pliocene period. During the Cretaceous period patchy igneous activity took place. Safed Koh and Waziristan Hills in the NWFP and the Chagai Hills and the Ras Koh in Balochistan have stocks, bosses, dykes and sills to speak of the volcanic activity.

The Western Highlands can be divided into the following physiographic divisions:

Mountainous North
Safed Koh and Waziristan Hills
Sulaiman and Kirthar Mountains
Balochistan Plateau
Potwar Plateau and the Salt Ranges.

Mountainous North

The Mountainous North covers the northern parts of Pakistan (Fig. 2). It comprises parallel mountain ranges intervened by narrow and deep river valleys. East of the Indus River, the mountain ranges in general run from east to west and to its west, from north to south. The important mountain ranges are the following:

— The Himalayas
— The Karakoram and other ranges also called the Trans-Himalayas lying north of the Himalayas
— The Hindu Kush and other ranges also called the Trans-Indus lying west of the Indus River.

The Himalayas

The westernmost parts of the Himalayas fall in Pakistan. There are a number of east-west ranges which have been given different names. The Sub-Himalayas or the Siwaliks are the southernmost ranges. They do not rise to great heights like other Himalayan ranges. Their average height is 600-1,200 metres (2,000-4,000 feet). The rocks have been folded and faulted badly and the ranges have been dissected deeply. They cover the hills of Rawalpindi District.

The Lesser Himalayas lie to the north of the Sub-Himalayas and rise to 1,800-4,600 metres (6,000-15,000 feet). They have been folded, faulted and overthrust. They are spread over Rawalpindi, Abbottabad and Mansehra Districts. Some of the hill stations of Pakistan like Murree, Nathia Gali and Ghora Gali are located there. They are represented by the Pir-Panjal in Jammu-Kashmir.

The Great Himalayas are located north of the Lesser Himalayas. They attain snowy heights (more than 4,600 metres/15,000 feet). They dominate Kohistan District. Some of them are capped by glaciers.

The Karakoram or Trans-Himalayas

The Karakoram and associated ranges in the extreme north rise to an average height of 6,100 metres/20,000 feet. Godwin Austen (K-2) the second highest peak in the world (8,610 metres/28,000 feet) is located in the Karakoram. A number of glaciers cover these ranges. Siachen, Hispar, Biafo, Baltoro and Batura are some of the important glaciers. These mountains can be crossed with great difficulty. Even the passes are 5,500 metres/18,000 feet high e.g., the Karakoram Pass.

The Hindu Kush and other Ranges

The Hindu Kush mountains take off from the western side of the Pamir Plateau which is located to the west of the Karakoram. These mountains take a southerly turn and guard the northern and north-western borders of

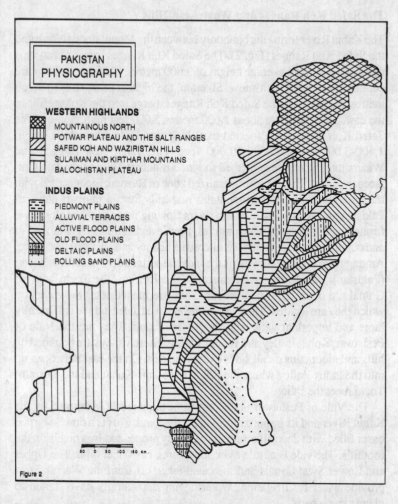

PAKISTAN PHYSIOGRAPHY

WESTERN HIGHLANDS
- MOUNTAINOUS NORTH
- POTWAR PLATEAU AND THE SALT RANGES
- SAFED KOH AND WAZIRISTAN HILLS
- SULAIMAN AND KIRTHAR MOUNTAINS
- BALOCHISTAN PLATEAU

INDUS PLAINS
- PIEDMONT PLAINS
- ALLUVIAL TERRACES
- ACTIVE FLOOD PLAINS
- OLD FLOOD PLAINS
- DELTAIC PLAINS
- ROLLING SAND PLAINS

50 0 50 100 150 Km.

Figure 2

Pakistan. They rise to snowy heights and are covered with a number of glaciers. Some of the peaks rise to great heights like Noshaq (7,369 metres/ 24,376 feet) and Tirich Mir (7,690 metres/25,230 feet).

The Hindu Kush mountains are crossed by a number of difficult passes, like Baroghil Pass (3,798 metres/12,460 feet) in the north and Dorah, Shul, Shera Shing and Shingara Passes in the west. All these passes connect Pakistan with Afghanistan. A number of ranges branch off south of the Hindu Kush and pass through Chitral, Swat and Dir. These ranges are deeply cut by the Chitral, Kunar, Panjkora and Swat rivers. It is in these narrow valleys that most of the people live and practise agriculture.

The Safed Koh Ranges and Waziristan Hills

The Kabul River forms the boundary between the Mountainous North and the Safed Koh Ranges (Fig. 2). The Safed Koh Ranges have an east-west trend and rise to an average height of 3,600 metres/12,000 feet. They are commonly covered with snow. Sikeram, the highest peak, rises to 4,760 metres/15,620 feet. The Safed Koh Ranges merge into the Kohat Hills in the east. These hills are about 1,600 metres/5,000 feet high. South of the Safed Koh Ranges, are located the Waziristan Hills. These hills rise to 1,500-3,000 metres/5,000-10,000 feet. The Safed Koh Ranges and Waziristan Hills were subjected to igneous activity during the late Cretaceous period. The highly mineralized zone of Razmak is connected with the igneous activity. The mountains and hills form a rampart between Pakistan and Afghanistan. Some rivers flowing through the region have formed passes through which armies, people and cultures have moved in and out of South Asia which has altered its history and changed its culture. Among them the Khyber Pass is the most important. It connects Peshawar (Pakistan) with Kabul (Afghanistan). The Kurram, the Tochi and the Gomal are other important passes. They are named after the rivers on which they are located. These rivers have carved at least three sufficiently large and important valleys in that rocky region. They are the Vale of Peshawar, Kohat Valley and Bannu Valley. These valleys are bounded by hills and mountains on all sides except the east. On the east they open up into the Indus Valley where the Kabul River, the Kohat and the Kurram-Tochi meet the Indus.

The Vale of Peshawar is the largest of the three. It is drained by the Kabul River and its important tributary, the Swat. This is a down-warped basin filled with deep alluvium in the valley proper and by gravels on the foothills. The vale is a little over 300 metres/1,000 feet high. The Upper and Lower Swat Canals and the canal taken off from the Warsak Dam provide water for irrigation. Waterlogging and salinity have started to plague some parts.

The Kohat Valley is the smallest and the highest (460 metres/1,500 feet). Drained by the Kohat River its floor is covered with clays, silts, sands and gravels. A number of east-west limestone ridges run across the plain. The valley is spotted with springs. The Tanda Dam on the Kohat River and the *bunds* across the streams supply water for irrigation.

The Bannu Valley is a low (150 metres/500 feet) structural basin. The valley is almost completely bounded by hills and mountains. On the east however the valley opens up into the Indus Plains. The Kurram and the Tochi are the main rivers. A number of hill streams also drain the valley.

The streams have developed braided channels and have filled the valley with deposits ranging from clays to boulders. The dam built on the Kurram River is the main source of irrigation.

The Sulaiman-Kirthar Mountains

Extending from south of the Gomal River the Sulaiman-Kirthar Mountains lie between Balochistan Plateau and the Indus Plains (Fig. 2). These mountains belong to the Himalayan orogeny. The Sulaiman Mountains extend south from the Gomal River. On reaching the Marri-Bugti Hills, they turn northward and extend up to Quetta. Near Quetta they take a syntaxical bend southward and merge into the Nagan Range. Further south they meet the Kirthar Mountains which merge into the Kohistan area of Sindh. The Kohistan area extends eastward up to the Indus River and southward up to the Arabian Sea. The Kirthar Mountains are backed by the Central Brahui Range and the Pab Range. The Sulaiman Mountains rise to an average height of 600 metres/2,000 feet. Their height decreases southward. The Kirthar Mountains descend to a height of 300 metres near the Arabian Sea. Some of the peaks reach considerable heights e.g., Takht-i-Sulaiman (3,487 metres/11,440 feet) and Takatu (3,470 metres/11,390 feet). These ranges are difficult to cross. The most important break is through the Bolan Pass which connects Quetta with Sibi. The mountains are composed of limestone, sandstone and shaly rocks.

The Balochistan Plateau

The Balochistan Plateau which is located west of the Sulaiman-Kirthar Mountains is covered with hills and mountains. There are several basins lying in the areas between these hills and mountains. The plateau occupies an extensive area. It is divided into two parts by the Chaman and Ornach-Nal faults. These faults run from Chaman southward up to the Arabian Sea. The alignment, lithology and morphological characteristics of the mountain ranges lying on the west of the Ornach-Nal faults are different from those lying on their east.

The western part is dominated by a number of subparallel ranges which have a general east-west trend. The hill ranges on the south are lower than those on the north. The important ranges from south to north are the Makran Coast Range (600 metres/2,000 feet), the Central Makran Range (900-1,200 metres/3,000-4,000 feet), the Siahan, Ras Koh and the Chagai. The latter three rise to (1,000-2,000 metres/3,500-6,600 feet). The highest peak, Ras Koh, attains a height of 3,010 metres (9,872 feet). The main rocks involved are shales and limestones. In the eastern part a more complex situation has developed. The mountain ranges have in general a north-south trend. The most spectacular of the mountains is the Toba Kakar Range which runs from close to Chaman in a SW-NE direction. It rises to 1,500 metres (5,000 feet). The central part of the plateau is dominated by the Quetta syntaxis where the mountains take a hairpin turn towards the south and merge into the Kalat Plateau. Further south the Khuzdar Knot represents a complex folded area. South of this the ranges continue to keep a north-south trend. The eastern hills are largely formed of limestone and sandstone.

Khojak Pass near Chaman and Gonshero Pass in the Chagai Hills help in movement between Pakistan and Afghanistan. The Ras Koh, the Chagai Hills and the Muslim Bagh area witnessed igneous activity during the Cretaceous times along with Safed Koh and Waziristan Hills. The Chagai Hills were again subjected to volcanic activity during the Pleistocene times. A number of craters still exist. Koh-i-Sultan (2,333 metres/7,654 feet) is the most spectacular of the craters.

The basins lying between the hills and mountains are either depositional or structural. The rivers flowing through the basins are starved of water most of the time. They have carved narrow channels. In most parts the channels are shallow but in some areas they are deep. The foothills sloping into the valley floor are skirted with alluvial fans and talus cones. They are strewn with boulders and gravels near the hills and slope down gently into sands and silts which are given to orchards. The valley bottom is covered with fine sands, silts and clays where vegetables and grains are produced. Some of the important basins are the Zhob Valley and the Baji Valley in the north, the Quetta Valley and the Mastung Valley in the central part and the Hingol and the Kech in the south. Between the Chagai Hills and the Siahan Range there is a large structural basin occupied by an extensive desert with sand plains and dunes. This is a region of inland drainage with a number of playa lakes locally called *hamun*. The most important playa lake of the region is Hamun-i-Mashkel.

The eastern coast of Balochistan is occupied by the Lasbela Plains. It is a triangular area with its apex in the north and its base in the south along the coast. It is an alluvial plain formed by the Porali River which enters the area from the north. This is a perennial stream which shrinks into a narrow channel during the dry season. The Porali River has a number of tributaries which become active when fed by rains. These streams inundate only part of the area during the rainy season. The eastern part is gravelly. The sand dunes dot many places.

The coastal plains along the Makran Coast are very narrow. At many places the craggy scarps of the hills project into the Arabian Sea. Some areas are covered with extensive sand deposits.

The Potwar Plateau and the Salt Ranges

The Potwar Plateau and the Salt Range region is located to the south of the Mountainous North and lies between the Indus River on the west and the Jhelum River on the east (Fig. 2). Its northern boundary is formed by the Kala Chitta Ranges and the Margalla Hills and the southern boundary by the Salt Ranges. Between the northern and southern ranges is located the Soan Basin.

The Kala Chitta Ranges rise to an average height of 450-900 metres (1,500-3,000 feet) and extend for about 72 km (45 miles). Their western part is composed of sandstone and the eastern side of limestone. The ranges are cut by deep valleys. A few miles north of the eastern extremity of the Kala Chitta Ranges, the Margalla Hills appear and extend eastward into the Kurang River. They attain an average height of 900 metres (3,000 feet) with several peaks rising to over 1,200 metres (4,000 feet). The south facing slope is steep. The main Potwar Plateau extends north of the Salt Range. It is an undulating area 300-600 metres (1,000-2,000 feet) high. Small hills of bare rocks rise steeply above the surface. A few large and high hills are also there. Khairi Murat is the largest and most spectacular. It is about 39 km (24 miles) long running southward from the neighbourhood of Rawalpindi. It rises approximately to 1,000 metres (3,000 feet). The Soan River dominates the topography. The Soan River and its tributaries have developed gullies and ravines to form typical badland topography. They are called *khaderas*. The Soan and other rivers have also produced large tracts of alluvial plains where agriculture is practised.

The Salt Ranges have a steep face towards the south and slope gently into the Potwar Plateau in the north. They extend from near the Jhelum River in the east and run westward along a sinuous path up to Kalabagh where they cross the Indus River and enter Bannu District. The Salt Ranges comprise parallel ranges and rise to an average height of 750-900 metres (2,500-3,000 feet). Sakesar Peak 1,527 metres (5,010 feet) is the highest point in the Salt Ranges. The ranges are badly faulted. Rivers like the Khewra, the Makrachi, the Jarhanwala and the Jamsukh have cut the ranges deeply and have formed gorges. In some areas badland topography has developed. A number of beautiful solution lakes dot the region. The Uchchali, Khabeki and Kallar Kahar are some of the important lakes. The Potwar Plateau and the Salt Ranges are rich in minerals like rock salt, gypsum, limestone, coal and oil. Exploitation of the minerals has started.

THE INDUS PLAINS

The Indus Plains have been formed by the alluvium laid down by the Indus and its tributaries. The Indus is a mighty stream about 2,900 km (1,800 miles) long and has a catchment area of 963,500 sq km (372,000 sq miles). From its source in the Mansarowar Lake upto Sazli, the Indus flows from east to west in a valley several miles deep between lofty mountains like the Karakoram and the Great Himalayas. At Sazli the river takes a southerly turn and its most tortuous and difficult journey starts as it cuts the mountains that lie across it by deep gorges. This twisting and turning journey ends at Kalabagh where the Indus enters the plains. The river which is confined up to Kalabagh in a channel .4 km (a quarter mile) wide on an average spreads out into a 16 km (ten miles) wide channel. The Indus then flows majestically into the Arabian Sea.

The Indus receives a number of tributaries while flowing through the mountains. The most important right hand tributary is the Kabul River which joins the Indus a little south of Tarbela. On entering the plains a number of small tributaries flow into the Indus from the west. The Kurram-Tochi, and the Gomal are the important ones. The left hand tributaries of the Indus are large rivers. They are the Jhelum, the Chenab, the Ravi and the Sutlej. They combine at Punjnad and flow as one stream for about 72 km (45 miles) before joining the Indus. South of it, the Indus makes almost a lone journey to the Arabian Sea without receiving any notable tributary. The average annual discharge of the Indus (92 million acre feet at Attock) is substantially more than the combined discharge of the Jhelum (22 million acre feet at Marala), the Ravi (6.2 million acre feet at Balloki) and the Sutlej (16.6 million acre feet at Sulaimanki). There is a great fluctuation in their seasonal discharge. In all the streams, it reaches a low ebb during the winter season. The Indus and the Jhelum which are fed by the melting glaciers start to swell in March and reach their peak in July when the rainy season comes. The Chenab, the Ravi and the Sutlej begin to rise from May and reach their peak in August. The difference between the minimum (25,000 cusecs) and the maximum about (350,000 cusecs) discharge of the Indus at Attock is more than ten times. The difference between the minimum and the maximum discharge of other rivers is also substantial. The fluctuation necessitates the building of dams so that the stored water can be utilized when the flow is low.

The swelling of the Indus and its tributaries during the summer season causes floods. It is estimated that severe floods come on an average every 7-8 years. They cause damage to land and property. Sometimes the rivers change their courses under the pressure of water. They spread fertile silts in some areas and coarse sands in others. All these processes have built the Indus Plains and have made them agriculturally very important. The Indus Plains slope down from north to south. In the north they rise to about 300 metres (1,000 feet) and drop to about 75 metres (250 feet) near Punjnad. From there they slope gently to the Arabian Sea. A height of 75 metres (250 feet) is covered in 560 km (350 miles). That means on an average the fall is less than one foot per mile. The Indus Plains have a few outcrops of Pre-Cambrian hills located near Sargodha, Chiniot and Sangla. They are together called Kirana Hills. A few hills of Tertiary limestone are also present, e.g., the Khairpur Hills at Sukkur and Ganjo Takar Hills at Hyderabad.

The Indus Plains can be divided into the following physiographic divisions:

Piedmont Plains
Alluvial Terraces
Active Flood Plains
Old Flood Plains
Deltaic Plains
Rolling Sand Plains and Dunes.

Piedmont Plains

Extensive Piedmont Plains have developed between the Indus River and the Sulaiman-Kirthar mountains. They have been built by the alluvial fans developing along the rivers flowing eastward down the mountains. Two smaller areas of alluvial fans have emerged south of the Siwaliks between the Jhelum and Chenab River and between the Chenab and Ravi River (Fig. 2). Most of the rivers rolling down the Sulaiman-Kirthar mountains become active only when rainfall takes place. They flow down the mountain slopes swiftly. On reaching the foothills they lose their speed and drop part of their load within the stream which is split into a number of narrow channels. These narrow channels become so overburdened that they die before they reach the Indus River towards which they flow. The gravels, sands and silts thus deposited form the alluvial fans. Some of the alluvial fans merge into one another. The Piedmont Plains are dominated by the alluvial fans. A high percentage (40 per cent) of the alluvial fans of Pakistan have a low gradient, from 1° to 2°. Another 50 per cent have a gradient between 2° and 4.5°. Only 10 per cent of the alluvial fans have a gradient over 4.5°. A large number (45 per cent) of the alluvial fans are small in size, about 1 to 2.5 miles in radius. The radius of about 45 per cent of them ranges from 2.5 to 4.5 miles. Only 10 per cent have a radius larger than 4.5 miles. The greater part of the Piedmont Plains has good soils and suitable topography for agricultural purposes. The rainfall though scanty is the main source of water. Irrigation facilities are available only in patches. Drought prevents it from turning into a blooming agricultural region.

Alluvial Terraces

Some parts of the interfluves of Upper Indus Valley are occupied by alluvial terraces. The terraces are locally called *bars* and the interfluves, *doabs*. These terraces are depositional and were formed during the Pleistocene times. They are separated from the adjoining flood plains by river-cut bluffs ranging in height from 5 to 15 metres (15 to 50 feet). Sandal Bar in the Chaj or Jech Doab (between the Jhelum and the Chenab), the Nili Bar in the Rechna Doab (between the Ravi and the Chenab) and the Ganji Bar in the Bari Doab (between the Ravi and Sutlej-Beas) are the best known terraces. Another terrace is located south of the Sutlej River in Bahawalpur. The sediments of the terraces are called 'old alluvium' in contradistinction to the 'new alluvium' of the flood plains. The 'old alluvium' is composed of compact calcareous silty clays. Layers of ferruginous material are found in some places. The southernmost parts of the *bars* are dotted with sand dunes. The surface in general is flat with a gentle slope towards the south-west. This has helped in laying canals which have turned the terraces into excellent agricultural lands.

A large part of the Sindh Sagar Doab between the Indus and the Jhelum is most likely occupied by a terrace, but at present most of it is covered with a desert called Thal. It has an undulating surface. Sand dunes called *tibbas* dot the surface here and there. Between the sand dunes narrow flat areas called *pattis* occur. With the extension of the irrigational facilities the region is being turned into an excellent agricultural area.

Active Flood Plains

The active flood plains, locally called *bet*, are narrow strips of land along the Indus River and its main tributaries, the Jhelum, the Chenab, the Ravi and the Sutlej (Fig. 2). They are most extensive along the Indus varying from 24 to 40 km in width. They are least extensive along the Ravi where their width varies from 3 to 5 km. They are absent from the southern part of the Ravi river. The active flood plains are inundated almost every year. The rivers which move freely within the narrow belt of the *bet* have braided channels with many towheads. They are covered with rich alluvium and are important farming areas.

Old Flood Plains

The old flood plains cover extensive areas between the *bet* (active flood plains) and the 'bar uplands' in the Upper Indus Valley and between the *bet* and the desert areas in the Lower Indus Valley (Fig. 2). The old flood plains are a few km above the active flood plains and are normally safe from floods. But they are inundated in years of severe floods which come every 7-8 years and they are consequently covered with alluvium. Meander scars, oxbow lakes, old levees and other features speak of their past history. In Sindh the abandoned channels are called *dhoros*. Small salt lakes, *dhands*, are another remarkable feature of the old flood plains in Sindh. The old flood plains constitute the main agricultural areas of Pakistan.

Deltaic Plains

The Indus River has built a large delta at its mouth (Fig. 2). The apex of the delta has shifted its position southward several times. Once it was close to Hyderabad. At present it is south of Thatta. The area bounded by the Kalri and the Pinyari, the two distributaries of the Indus River, is taken as the Indus Delta. The Indus Delta is still growing. The advance is primarily towards the south-west. Between 1896 and 1954 the delta extended seaward five miles off Khar Creek. The delta is scarred with old and present channels of the Indus and its distributaries. At the coast barrier bars have developed. Inland there are extensive mud flats sliced by tidal channels. The inland limit of the mud flats is marked by a cliff. Inland from the cliff agriculture is gaining importance.

Rolling Sand Plains and Dunes

An extensive area in the south-west of Pakistan is covered with rolling sand plains and dunes (Fig. 2). It is an area separated from the Indus Valley by the dry channels of the Ghaggar River in the Punjab, which is called East Nara or Dhoro Purna River in Sindh. This extensive desert is called Cholistan or Rohi in Bahawalpur, Pat in northern Sindh and Tharparkar or Thar in southern Sindh. It is not drained by any perennial stream. Therefore wind action is dominant in the formation of topography. A vast expanse of sand plains with innumerable sand dunes dominates the scene. In the south latitudinal dunes dominate while in the north transverse dunes abound. Agriculturally it is a poor area. With the extension of irrigational facilities some areas have been reclaimed. In patches *barani* (rain-fed) farming is practised.

Chapter 4

Climate

The major part of Pakistan is dominated by dry climate. A small area in the north experiences humid subtropical climate. In the extreme north because of great heights Highland climate prevails. The controlling factors are the following:

1. The subtropical location of Pakistan from approximately 23 1/2°N to 37°N latitudes. This tends to keep the temperature high, particularly in summer.
2. The oceanic influence of the Arabian Sea keeps down the temperature contrast between summer and winter at the coasts.
3. The continental effect accentuates the differences in temperature between summer and winter in the interior of the country.
4. The higher altitudes in the west and north keep down the temperature throughout the year. In the extreme north because of great heights, the mountain tops record freezing temperature all the year round. The hills and mountains also attract more rain than the plains do.
5. The monsoon winds which come in July and continue to blow up to September bring rainfall. Pakistan receives only the tail-end of the monsoons, therefore the monsoon season is neither as prolonged nor as wet as that in India.
6. The Western Depressions originating from the Mediterranean region and entering Pakistan from the west bring rainfall in winter. These cyclones make a long land journey before coming to Pakistan and are thus robbed of most of their moisture by the time they reach Pakistan.
7. Thunderstorms cause some amount of rainfall particularly in the north.
8. A temperature inversion layer at a low elevation of approximately 1,500 metres (5,000 feet) in the southern part of Pakistan during the summer season does not allow the moisture-laden air to rise and condensation to take place.

TEMPERATURE

The temperature conditions of a place are better appreciated when expressed in some descriptive terms. This has been attempted by several climatologists. The one suited to Pakistan is given below:

Hot:	32°C or more	(90°F or more)
Warm:	21°C to 32°C	(70°F to 89°F)
Mild:	10°C to 21°C	(50°F to 69°F)
Cool:	0°C to 10°C	(32°F to 49°F)
Cold:	Below 0°C	(Below 32°F)

Pakistan can be divided into the following temperature regions (Fig. 3):

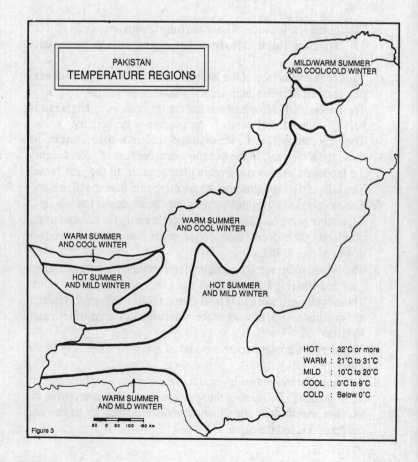

PAKISTAN
TEMPERATURE REGIONS

MILD/WARM SUMMER
AND COOL/COLD WINTER

WARM SUMMER
AND COOL WINTER

WARM SUMMER
AND COOL WINTER

HOT SUMMER
AND MILD WINTER

HOT SUMMER
AND MILD WINTER

WARM SUMMER
AND MILD WINTER

HOT	: 32°C or more
WARM	: 21°C to 31°C
MILD	: 10°C to 20°C
COOL	: 0°C to 9°C
COLD	: Below 0°C

50   0   50   100   150 Km

Figure 3

1. Hot summer and mild winter: The temperature of the hottest month 32°C or more, and winter temperature between 10°C and 21°C.
2. Warm summer and mild winter: Summer temperature between 21°C and 32°C, and winter temperature between 10°C and 21°C.
3. Warm summer and cool winter: Summer between 21°C and 32°C and the coolest month temperature between 0°C and 10°C.
4. Mild summer and cool/cold winter: Summer temperature between 10°C and 21°C and the coolest month (January) temperature less than 0°C in some areas and between 0°C and 10°C in other areas.

Hot Summer and Mild Winter

Hot summer (mean temperature of the hottest month 32°C/90°F or more) and mild winter (mean monthly winter temperature between 10°C and 21°C) is experienced over a large area which extends from the Indus Plains to southern and western Balochistan (Fig. 3). In this region summer is hot. In the hottest month the temperature rises above 32°C. Sibi is the hottest station. Jacobabad which has long been regarded as the hottest place in Pakistan is in reality not as hot as Sibi. In the hottest month (June) the mean temperature at Sibi is 38.1°C and at Jacobabad 36.8°C (Table 4.1). Month

Table 4.1: Mean Monthly Temperature and Precipitation of Jacobabad and Sibi

Month	Jacobabad		Sibi	
	T°C	Prec. (mm)	T°C	Prec. (mm)
January	14.7	7.1	13.8	16.8
February	18.3	8.6	17.1	17.5
March	23.9	7.6	23.1	17.8
April	29.9	2.3	29.5	6.3
May	35.0	3.6	35.3	3.6
June	36.8	6.1	38.1	6.9
July	35.3	26.9	36.5	37.8
August	33.6	21.8	35.2	20.3
September	32.3	0.8	33.3	4.6
October	28.1	0.3	27.8	0.5
November	22.0	0.5	21.3	4.8
December	16.6	2.8	15.7	5.8
Annual	27.2	88.4	27.2	142.7

by month in summer, Sibi records higher temperature than Jacobabad. Both the stations are close to each other. The area surrounding Sibi-Jacobabad becomes a hot oven in summer. Outside this region also very hot conditions prevail where the temperature in the hottest month (June) remains above 35˚C/95˚F. That area extends from Sibi on the west to the Pakistan-India border on the east, and from a little north of Multan in the north to a little south of Nawabshah in the south.

The summer heat cannot be fully appreciated without examining the mean maximum temperature. The highest maximum temperature in the Indus Plains is recorded in June. Sibi with the highest temperature 45˚C, Turbat 44.8˚C, Reti 44.7˚C, Jacobabad 44.3˚C and Fort Abbas 43.3˚C are the only stations where the maximum temperature rises above 43˚C/

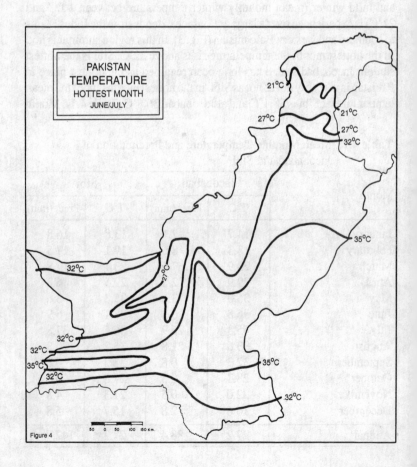

PAKISTAN
TEMPERATURE
HOTTEST MONTH
JUNE/JULY

Figure 4

110°F. All other stations record lower temperature but nowhere is it less than 38.9°C (Badin).

The extreme temperatures recorded further reveal unbearable summer heat. Jacobabad recorded a temperature of 52.8°C (127°F) on 4 July 1955. The majority of stations in the region have recorded temperatures over 49°C (120°F). Summer is not only hot but also long. It is particularly long in the south where it extends from March to November. In the central part of the Indus Plains and southern Balochistan the summer begins in March and continues up to October. The remaining four months, November to February, are winter months. In the northern Indus Plains and in western Balochistan summer comes in April and continues up to October. Winter is of five months, duration from November to March. The winter is mild. The temperature all over the region varies from 10°C to 21°C. January is the coolest month. South of Multan the temperature remains above 13°C and to its north below 13°C because of latitudinal difference. The mean minimum temperature of the coolest month (January) at no station reaches freezing point. The lowest recorded is 1°C (34°F) at Dalbandin and 2.5°C (35°F) at Risalpur. That does not mean that the region is free from frost. Though the mean monthly temperature has never dropped to freezing point, freezing temperatures have been recorded at all the stations within the region on individual days. Even stations like Hyderabad, Lasbela and Turbat located far in the south and not very far from the sea have experienced temperatures below 0°C (Hyderabad –1°C on 31 January 1935, Lasbela – 5°C on 17 January 1935 and Turbat –.5°C on 2 February 1950). However in the south this does not occur every year and the cold is not severe. On the other hand in north Punjab and the adjoining parts of the NWFP, and in western Balochistan frost occurs for a few days in winter every year.

Warm Summer and Mild Winter

Warm summer (21°C to 32°C) and mild winter (10°C to 21°C) prevail over a narrow coastal strip of Pakistan (Fig. 3). The oceanic influence is so marked that though located nearer to the equator than any other part of Pakistan, the mean monthly temperature always remains below 32°C/90°F. Another notable effect of the sea is the uniformity of temperature all over the region. In June, the hottest month, the temperature varies from 31°C to 32°C at the various stations and in January, the coolest month, the temperature ranges from 18°C to 19°C.

Summer in the coastal region is mild and long. It comes in March and continues up to November. During these nine months the mean monthly temperature remains above 21°C/70°F. The maximum temperature remains lower than that in the Indus Plains as a consequence of the oceanic influence. The highest temperatures recorded are also not as high as those in the Indus Plains. At no station on the coast has the temperature ever risen to 49°C/120°F. The highest temperature recorded at Karachi was 48°C/118°F on 9 May 1938.

The coastal region experiences a mild winter which extends from December to February. January is the coolest month when the temperature varies from 18°C to 19°C. The mean minimum temperature remains above 10°C. Freezing temperatures have been recorded at Karachi and Pasni but never at Ormara and Jiwani. During the winter season there are cold spells caused by cold katabatic winds blowing down the Balochistan Plateau.

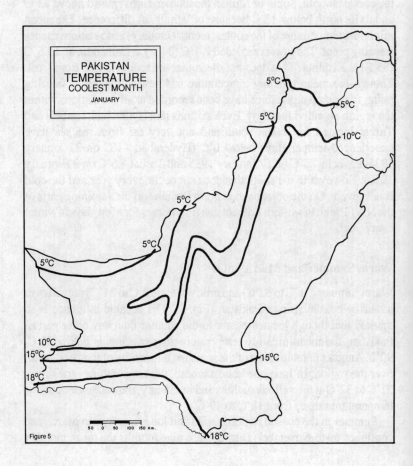

Figure 5

These winds are popularly called 'Quetta Waves' in Karachi and *goorich* in southern Balochistan.

Warm Summer and Cool Winter

Warm summer (21°C to 32°C) and cool winter (0°C to 10°C) is experienced in the major parts of the Western Highlands of Pakistan (Fig. 3). Summer is comparatively short, ranging for five months, from May to September in most parts. At the stations located at an elevation of less than 1,100 metres/3,500 feet, summer comes in April and continues up to October (seven months), whereas at stations above 1,600 metres/5,000 feet the summer is short, from May to August/September. June or July is the hottest month when the mean temperature rises to 27°C/80°F or more but at no station does it rise to 32°C/90°F. The mean maximum temperature does exceed 32°C but at most stations it is below 38°C/100°F. The absolute highest temperature ever recorded exceeded 38°C at all stations except Kalat where it was 37.5°C. But at no station did it reach 49°C/120°F.

Winter in the Western Highlands of Pakistan is long and cool. In most parts it lasts for nearly seven months from October to April. During the coldest month January, the mean monthly temperature drops below 10°C but it does not reach 0°C. Kalat recorded the lowest mean January temperature 3°C/37°F. The mean January temperature does not clearly reveal the cold experienced in the region. At all stations the temperature drops below freezing point during cold spells which last for several days. Such cold spells are quite frequent. Even when the cold spell is not there, on many nights the mercury drops below freezing point. Consequently snowfall takes place. Cold winds which accompany the cold spells intensify the biting cold. The lowest temperature recorded also presents a grim picture. At all stations it has gone below –7°C (Kalat –14°C, Quetta –16°C, Parachinar –16°C and Muslim Bagh –13°C).

Mild Summer and Cool/Cold Winter

Mild summer (10°C-21°C) and cool/cold winter (below 10°C) prevail over the northern mountains of Pakistan at an elevation of 2,000 metres or more. This is a region where lofty mountains exist. Narrow valleys wind through mountain ranges. From valley bottoms to mountain peaks the rise in altitude is sharp. The temperature drops rapidly as elevation increases. The valley bottoms may record a temperature of 20°C but the mountain tops overlooking the valleys may be clad with snow. In general at an altitude of about 4,500 metres, and above, the temperature remains below freezing point throughout the year. Between 2,000 and 4,500 metres, the mean January temperature (coolest month) varies from 0°C to 5°C. The night temperature in January usually drops below freezing point. In summer the mean monthly temperature rises above 10°C but remains below 21°C. The day temperature may rise to 30°C but the fall at night is sharp. So the daily range of temperature is high (more than 25°C). The shade temperature remains much lower than the sun temperature. The difference may be 25°C.

RAINFALL

The major part of Pakistan experiences dry climate. Humid conditions prevail over a small area in the north. The whole of Sindh, most of

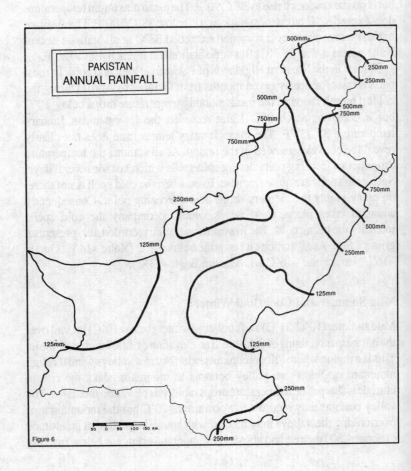

Figure 6

Balochistan, the major part of the Punjab south of Sahiwal and the central part of the Northern Areas receive less than 250 mm/10 inches of rainfall in a year (Fig. 6). Three large areas, (1) Northern Sindh and Southern Punjab, (2) North-western Balochistan and (3) the central part of the Northern Areas have to contend with an annual rainfall of less than 125 mm. North of Sahiwal the rainfall steadily increases and aridity starts to diminish. However the true humid conditions appear after the rainfall increases to 750 mm/30 inches on the plains and 625 mm/25 inches on the highlands.

There are two sources of rainfall in Pakistan, the Monsoons and the Western Depressions. The monsoon rainfall takes place from July to September. The Western Depressions bring rainfall primarily from December to March. In the intervening periods, October-November and April-June a small quantity of rainfall comes from thunderstorms.

The Monsoon Rainfall

Pakistan receives the tail-end of the monsoon winds which enter Pakistan after crossing India. They usually reach Pakistan in early July and continue to blow up to September. Most of the rainfall which takes place in Pakistan from July to September is from the monsoons.

Since the monsoons come into Pakistan from the east, the eastern parts receive more rainfall from the monsoons (Fig. 8). The main monsoon winds enter northern Punjab while the secondaries get into southern Punjab and Sindh. Therefore, the northern areas receive more rainfall. The hills and mountains in the north record more than 20 inches (500 mm) of rainfall and the amount decreases sharply as one gets into the plains (Fig. 8). From Sargodha southward the rainfall drops to less than 250 mm and a short distance south of Sahiwal it drops below 125 mm. The highest rainfall during the monsoon season is received by Murree (850 mm/34 inches) and the lowest by Nokkundi (1.25 mm/.05 inches).

Rainfall from the Western Depressions

The Western Depressions enter Pakistan from the west after passing through Iran and Afghanistan. Most of their moisture is robbed on their long land journey. Therefore, they bring a small amount of rainfall to Pakistan (Fig. 8). In spite of this, the western parts of the Western Highlands receive more rainfall from the Western Depressions than from other sources (Fig. 7).

The onslaught of the Western Depressions begins in December and continues in full strength up to March. Thereafter they become weak and their visits become less frequent. However, the rainfall received from December to March is taken as that from the Western Depressions. Since this period coincides with the winter season, some precipitation at higher elevations is in the form of snowfall.

It is in the northern highlands that the highest amount of rainfall (250 mm) takes place because of the Western Depressions (Fig. 8). Northern Punjab, the hilly areas of the NWFP and northern Balochistan receive 125-250 mm of rainfall. Sindh then is the driest area where in most parts the rainfall is less than 25 mm (one inch).

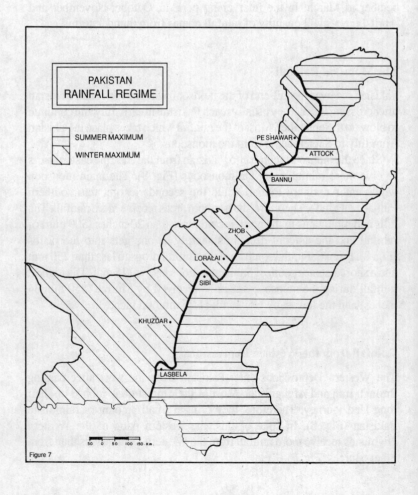

Figure 7

Rainfall from Thunderstorms

There are two periods of thunderstorms in Pakistan: (1) April-June (2) October-November. These periods are the driest parts of the year, particularly October-November. During these periods thunderstorms caused by convection bring sporadic and localized rainfall. From April to June a few areas in the extreme north, e.g., Chitral, Murree Hills and Safed Koh, register more than 125 mm/5 inches of rainfall. In the rest of Pakistan, the

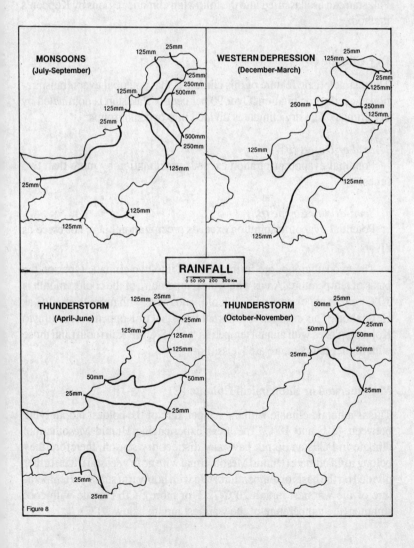

Figure 8

rainfall is less than 50 mm and over major parts of Sindh and Balochistan it is less than 25 mm. October-November is the driest period in Pakistan (Fig. 8). The wettest areas are then a few patches of northern mountains where the rainfall is more than 50 mm. In other areas the rainfall is less than 25 mm.

CLIMATIC REGIONS

Pakistan can be classified into the following climatic regions by Koppen's method:

Dry Climate (B)

The characteristic feature of this climate is that potential evapotranspiration exceeds precipitation. Over 90 per cent of Pakistan is dominated by dry climate. The dry climate is divided into two subgroups:

Arid or Desert (BW)
Potential evapotranspiration exceeds precipitation by more than two times.

Semi-arid or Steppe (BS)
Potential evapotranspiration exceeds precipitation but is not twice as great.

The two subgroups are further divided into two climatic types on the basis of temperature. Areas where the temperature of the coolest month is 10°C or less are classed as Kalt (cold) and those with more than 10°C as Heiss (hot). This criterion is different from that of Koppen. According to Koppen, places with annual temperature of 18°C are Kalt (cold) and those with higher temperature are Heiss (hot).

Mesothermal or Subtropical Climate (C)

This is a humid climate with the temperature of the coldest month lying between –3°C and 18°C. The areas experiencing Humid Mesothermal climate in Pakistan do not have any distinct dry season, therefore they belong to Cf climate (Humid Mesothermal with no dry season). It is further divided on the basis of temperature: Cfa with hot/warm summer (temperature of the warmest month 20°C/72°F or more); Cfb climate with cool summer (the temperature of the warmest month below 20°C).

Highland Climate (H)

The northern areas of Pakistan are dominated by very high mountains. The climate changes there by altitude rather than by latitude. Therefore it is classified as Highland Climate.

Thus the following climatic types are experienced in Pakistan:

Dry Climate (B):

Arid (BW)
1. Arid with hot summer and mild winter (BWh).
2. Arid with warm summer and mild winter (BWh').
3. Arid with warm summer and cool winter (BWk).

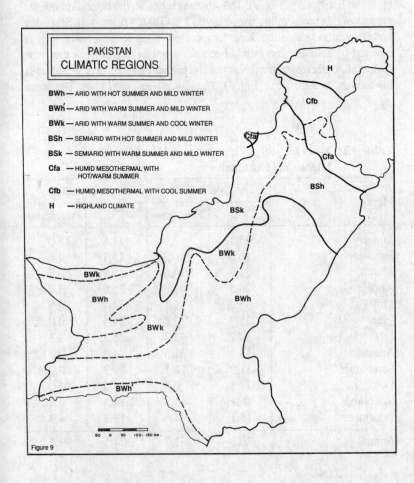

Figure 9

Semi-arid (BS)
4. Semi-arid with hot summer and mild winter (BSh).
5. Semi-arid with warm summer and cool winter (BSk).

Humid Mesothermal or Subtropical (C).
6. Humid Mesothermal with hot/warm summer (Cfa).
7. Humid Mesothermal with cool summer (Cfb).

Highland Climate (H)

1. *Arid with Hot Summer and Mild Winter (BWh)*
Arid with hot summer and mild winter prevails over a large area comprising most of the Indus Plains extending westward into Balochistan up to the Iran border (Fig. 9). The summer is hot. In the hottest month the mean monthly temperature rises above 32°C (Table 4.1 and 4.2). Sibi is the hottest station where the June temperature rises to 38°C. The region covered by Sibi and Jacobabad becomes a hot oven and from there the temperature decreases northward in the higher latitudes and southwards towards the coastal areas (Fig. 4). The day is particularly hot. The mean

Table 4.2: Mean Monthly Temperature and Precipitation of Multan and Nokkundi

Month	Multan		Nokkundi	
	T°C	Prec. (mm)	T°C	Prec. (mm)
January	13.1	7.9	11.5	15.0
February	16.6	10.2	15.1	7.6
March	21.7	14.0	19.9	6.3
April	28.5	6.6	25.9	3.6
May	33.7	6.1	31.4	0.5
June	35.9	12.4	34.5	0.0
July	34.7	45.7	35.7	1.3
August	33.4	31.5	34.2	0.0
September	31.9	20.1	29.9	0.0
October	27.5	0.8	24.5	0.0
November	20.7	1.8	18.3	0.8
December	15.1	4.6	13.3	4.3
Annual	26.1	161.7	24.5	39.4

maximum temperature in the hottest month rises to over 38°C at all stations and at some stations it crosses 43.3°C. Some of the extreme temperatures recorded (Jacobabad 52.8°C and Sibi 51.7°C) reveal the extremely hot conditions prevailing in that region. The summer is not only hot but also long. In the south it extends for nine months (March-November). In central Punjab and western Balochistan, it is seven months long (April-October).

The winter is mild. The winter temperature hovers between 10°C and 21°C (Table 4.2). The mean monthly temperature at no station drops to freezing point though freezing temperatures have been recorded on specially cold days. The winter is of three months' duration in the south (December-February) and of five months (November-March) in central Punjab and western Balochistan.

Aridity is the basic characteristic of the region. The potential evapo-transpiration exceeds rainfall by more than two times. The annual rainfall in most areas is less than 250 mm (10 inches). Only in central Punjab it is 250-375 mm (10-15 inches). At Multan it is 162 mm and at Nokkundi 39 mm. Four summer months at Nokkundi are rainless (Table 4.2). The rainfall is concentrated in two seasons: July-September and December-March. The Indus Plains receive the maximum rainfall in summer from the monsoons, and the Balochistan Plateau in winter from the Western Depressions. The rainfall is inadequate everywhere for agriculture. Farming essentially depends upon irrigation. Rain-fed farming is practised only in years of good rainfall. In some areas dry farming is practised.

2. *Arid with Warm Summer and Mild Winter (BWh')*

Arid with warm summer and mild winter is experienced in Pakistan in a narrow coastal strip (Fig. 9). The oceanic influence keeps the temperature lower than that in the interior in summer and higher in winter. The temperature in the hottest month(June) remains between 21°C and 32°C unlike the interior where it rises above 32°C (Table 4.2 and 4.3). The temperature in the coolest month (January) varies from 18°C to 19°C whereas in the interior, it drops below 15.5°C (60°F). The uniformity of temperature is a unique characteristic of the coastal region. Occasionally, katabatic winds moving down the Balochistan Plateau bring brief cold spells, otherwise the winter is pleasant. But it is very short (December-February). Aridity prevails all over the coastal region of Pakistan. The annual rainfall is less than 250 mm (10 inches). The rainfall is slightly higher in the east than in the west. The rainfall at Karachi is 221 mm, at Ormara 146 mm and at Pasni 130 mm. On the east the monsoons are the main source of rainfall and on the west, the Western Depressions.

3. *Arid with Warm Summer and Cool Winter (BWk)*

Arid climate with warm summer and cool winter prevails over the central and north-western plateau of Balochistan (Fig. 9). In that region the mean monthly temperature in summer crosses 32°C but rarely exceeds 38°C. July is the hottest month. The summer season in most areas begins in May and continues up to September. The winter is of seven months' duration (October-April). The mean monthly temperature in the coolest month (January) remains between 0°C and 10°C. For some days in the year, the temperature drops below freezing point. The nights are very chilly. The severity of the winter cold is felt more than that of the summer heat. The educational institutions observe winter vacation.

Aridity is severe in this region. The annual rainfall is less than 250 mm. In spite of relatively lower temperature the potential evapotranspiration is greater than precipitation by more than two times. The winter precipitation exceeds summer rainfall.

4. *Semi-arid (Steppe) with Hot Summer and Mild Winter (BSh)*

The semi-arid climate with hot summer and mild winter is experienced

Table 4.3: Mean Monthly Temperature and Precipitation of Karachi and Jiwani

Month	Karachi		Jiwani	
	T°C	Prec. (mm)	T°C	Prec. (mm)
January	17.7	7.6	18.9	67.6
February	20.1	12.7	20.4	18.0
March	24.5	4.6	23.3	10.4
April	28.2	2.3	26.7	8.6
May	30.5	1.3	29.7	0.8
June	31.4	8.9	30.9	0.0
July	30.0	101.1	29.7	8.6
August	28.6	47.5	28.5	1.8
September	26.6	23.4	27.9	0.3
October	27.6	3.3	26.9	0.3
November	23.9	3.0	23.9	9.9
December	19.5	5.6	20.3	22.6
Annual	25.7	221.3	25.6	148.9

over a small area of northern Punjab extending into the adjoining areas of the NWFP (Fig. 9). The characteristic feature is that the potential evapotranspiration exceeds precipitation but is less than two times as great. The annual temperature remains above 18°C (64.4°F) and the coolest month temperature above 10°C. The climate is thus classified as BSh.

The summer is hot with mean monthly temperature climbing to over 32°C. In June, the hottest month, Lahore records 33.9°C and Peshawar 32.9°C (Table 4.4). The mean maximum temperature of the hottest month exceeds 38°C. It is 41.16°C at Lahore and 40.2°C at Peshawar. The scorching heat forces much of the outdoor work to be suspended during the hottest part of the day. The summer is seven months long (April-October). In winter the temperature drops below 21°C but even in the coolest month the mean monthly temperature does not drop below 10°C. At Lahore, the January temperature is 12.2°C and at Peshawar 10.7°C. Frost is rare but not unknown. The annual rainfall ranges between 325 and 755 mm. The rainfall is less than potential evapotranspiration. Except for a narrow strip on the west, the region receives more rainfall in summer but in winter also there is considerable rainfall.

Table 4.4: Mean Monthly Temperature and Precipitation of Lahore and Peshawar

Month	Lahore		Peshawar	
	T°C	Prec. (mm)	T°C	Prec. (mm)
January	12.2	31.2	10.7	38.6
February	15.2	23.1	13.1	41.1
March	20.4	24.4	17.4	64.8
April	26.6	15.7	22.9	41.9
May	31.9	8.1	29.1	14.5
June	33.9	38.9	32.9	6.6
July	32.1	121.7	32.6	33.8
August	31.2	122.9	31.0	40.6
September	30.0	80.0	28.9	14.2
October	25.5	9.9	23.7	9.9
November	18.7	3.6	17.4	9.9
December	13.8	10.7	12.5	15.2
Annual	24.2	490.2	22.7	331.1

5. *Semi-arid (Steppe) with Warm Summer and Cool Winter (BSk)*

The northern part of the Balochistan Plateau and the adjoining high-lands of the NWFP experience semi-arid climate with warm summer and cool winter (Fig. 9). The summer is warm with temperature ranging from 21°C to 32°C. July is the hottest month when the temperature at Quetta is 26.7°C and at Zhob 29.5°C (Table 4.5). Mean maximum July temperature exceeds 32°C but does not rise above 38°C.

The winter is cool. The mean monthly temperature of the coolest month (January) drops below 10°C but not below 0°C. At Quetta the January temperature is 3.5°C and at Zhob 6.5°C. In winter on many days the temperature goes down to freezing point. Frost is common. The low temperature is induced by high elevation. The precipitation in that area is low, ranging from 250 to 275 mm. The rainfall at Quetta is 244 and at Zhob 382 mm. The rainfall is less than potential evapotranspiration. It is a semi-arid region. Maximum precipitation comes in winter from the Western Depressions. A considerable part of winter precipitation is as snowfall.

6. *Humid Mesothermal with Hot/Warm Summer (Cfa)*

Humid mesothermal climate with hot/warm summer prevails over a

Table 4.5: Mean Monthly Temperature and Precipitation of Quetta and Zhob

Month	Quetta		Zhob	
	T°C	Prec. (mm)	T°C	Prec. (mm)
January	3.5	52.3	6.5	36.6
February	6.3	52.6	9.9	25.9
March	10.6	42.7	14.4	63.2
April	15.5	18.3	19.4	37.3
May	20.4	10.2	24.1	32.5
June	24.1	4.1	29.5	9.1
July	26.7	21.1	29.5	64.5
August	25.3	8.9	29.3	51.1
September	20.3	0.3	26.3	7.4
October	14.1	3.3	19.6	5.1
November	8.9	4.8	13.1	19.6
December	5.3	25.1	8.7	29.5
Annual	15.1	243.7	19.2	381.8

small area of northern Pakistan (Fig. 9). The temperature in the warmest month rises to 32°C on the eastern side where the elevations are lower. On the western side (NWFP), the temperature of the warmest month remains between 21°C to 32°C. The temperature of the hottest month (June) at Sialkot is 33.9°C and at Kakul 27.7°C (Table 4.6). The temperature of the coolest month drops below 18°C but nowhere does it drop below 0°C (32°F). In the east, it remains above 10°C (50°F) but in the west it drops below 10°C.

The rainfall in the northern part of Pakistan is more than that in the rest of the country. It is more than potential evapotranspiration. Annual precipitation is over 625 mm (25 inches). In the eastern part, summer is rainier and in the western part, winter is more rainy. At Sialkot the annual rainfall is 883 mm, and 1,203 mm at Kakul (Table 4.6).

7. *Humid Mesothermal with Cool Summer (Cfb)*

Humid mesothermal climate with cool summer is experienced over a small highland extending north from Murree (Fig. 9). The temperature of the warmest month at Murree is 21.1°C (Table 4.7). In the coolest month the temperature on many winter days falls below freezing point.

Table 4.6: Mean Monthly Temperature and Precipitation of Sialkot and Kakul

Month	Sialkot		Kakul	
	T°C	Prec. (mm)	T°C	Prec. (mm)
January	12.0	46.5	7.4	80
February	14.9	42.2	10.3	68.1
March	19.9	40.9	13.7	124.5
April	26.4	20.3	19.7	91.4
May	32.1	13.2	23.3	62.2
June	33.9	56.1	27.7	33.0
July	31.1	269.0	25.9	276.9
August	29.7	248.4	24.6	237.2
September	29.3	97.0	23.6	91.2
October	24.9	21.3	19.3	51.1
November	18.3	7.9	14.3	32.3
December	13.4	20.3	10.5	55.4
Annual	23.9	883.1	18.3	1,203.3

Murree is the wettest station of Pakistan. It receives an annual precipitation of 1,640 mm with more than 50 per cent coming from the monsoons. Snowfall is common in winter.

Highland Climate (H)

The northern part of Pakistan is dominated by high mountain ranges intertwined by narrow river valleys. The valley bottoms are 2,000 metres high while the surrounding mountains range from 4,500 to 6,000 metres. Therefore the climate changes vertically. The valleys may be enjoying mild summer and cool winter while the mountain tops experience arctic climate (mean monthly temperatures below freezing point throughout the year).

The mean January (coolest month) temperature ranges from 0°C at the snow-line (4,500 metres) to 5°C at the valley bottoms (2,000 metres). Usually in January at night the temperature drops below 0°C. In June (the hottest month) the mean monthly temperature rises above 10°C but does not exceed 21°C. The daily range of temperature remains high (25°C). The difference between shade and sun temperature is also high (25°C). The insolation is intense.

Table 4.7: Mean Monthly Temperature and Precipitation of Murree

Month	T°C	Prec. (mm)
January	2.9	120.1
February	4.4	111.8
March	8.1	154.9
April	13.5	102.4
May	18.4	61.5
June	21.1	106.7
July	19.7	362.2
August	18.7	358.1
September	17.5	134.4
October	14.2	53.3
November	10.1	20.6
December	5.8	53.8
Annual	12.9	1,639.8

The precipitation is low. It is 250-500 mm in the southern, western and northern parts. It decreases to less than 125 mm in the central and eastern parts. The whole region lies in the rain shadow of the Lesser Himalayas and Hindu Kush Mountains. The central part falls behind still higher mountains, the Great Himalayas. Low precipitation is also caused by high elevation. Above 3,000 metres the moisture-holding capacity of the air is greatly reduced because of low temperature. Most of the rain comes from the monsoons in the east and from the Western Depressions in the west.

Chapter 5

Soils

Soils give support to plants and act as an agent supplying wholly or in part, nutrients, water, air and heat.

FACTORS OF SOIL FORMATION IN PAKISTAN

The factors which control the soils of a region are (1) climate (temperature and precipitation in particular), (2) vegetation and living organisms, (3) parent material, (4) topography and (5) time.

Climate

Aridity prevailing over the major part of Pakistan is the main climatic characteristic that affects its soils. This has resulted in paucity of soil water and scantiness of vegetation cover. Soil alkalinity and salinity have been encouraged. The soils are rich in basic but poor in nitrogenous matter. Similar conditions with slightly less intensity are experienced in the subhumid regions. Humid areas are relatively smaller in extent. In the extreme north, there are areas with a perpetual cover of snow where development of soil has not taken place.

Vegetation and Living Organisms

Vegetation cover over most of Pakistan is scarce. This has resulted in scantiness of organic matter in the soils. Humus formation is limited and pH in general is high.

Soil organisms play an important role in homogenization which is a very important process of soil formation in Pakistan. Loose stratified materials send out roots extensively throughout the upper soils and to some extent in the subsoil. Most of the plants are annuals. After their death some of the roots are eaten by micro-organisms and animals (rodents, white ants etc.). Some roots are decomposed and become part of the soil forming humus. The soil animals and micro-organisms mix the soil and disturb the stratification. Thus porous stable soil with well-distributed organic matter is developed. Homogenization does not take place in soils which are either too wet or too dry or are alkaline or saline.

Parent Material

The soils of Pakistan are derived from two types of parent materials:

1. Alluvium, loess and wind-reworked sands. They are of mixed mineralogy.
2. Residual material obtained from weathering of underlying rocks. Most of the rocks are calcareous (limestone or calcareous shale). In some localized areas like Swat volcanic rocks such as granites have produced noncalcareous soil material. Very small quantities of salts are released from most rocks and soils are therefore nonsaline. Saline playa lakes which are of small areal extent are exceptions.

Topography

Topographically Pakistan is divided into two broad divisions: The Western Highlands and the Indus Plains. Because of topographic differences these two regions have developed different soils.

In the Western Highlands, the rocks are strongly folded and faulted. Tilted steep slopes, accentuated by deep stream erosion are common. Exposed bare rocks without any soil cover are seen here and there. Where soils have developed they have formed into thin veneer. Scree and colluvium are common. On gentler slopes and in mountain valleys thick residual soils have developed.

In the Indus Plains the slopes in general are gentle but are sufficient to grade the soils on textural basis. The relatively higher areas are covered with sands and the lower basins and channel infills with loamy clays. Silts and loams occupy the intermediate levels. Topography also affects the soil water. Convex slopes are well drained whereas concave areas suffer from poor drainage. In areas of low rainfall and limited flooding, the depressions are likely to have alkaline soils whereas the higher areas have nonsaline soils. The reverse is true in areas of higher rainfall or deep flooding.

Time

Soil formation is a complex phenomenon and therefore takes considerable time. The conversion of the bedrocks into regolith is a time-consuming process. The blending together of the minerals and the organic matter in the soils by the action of micro-organisms involves a long period of time. Homogenization which is a common process of soil formation in the Indus Plains requires about 20 years for the upper one foot of the soils and about 100 years for the next lower foot.

SOIL CLASSIFICATION

The soils of Pakistan have acquired distinct characteristics from the parent material and by their mode of formation. The river-laid sediments have developed into alluvial soils. The topographic differences within the region covered with alluvial soils have produced textural, chemical and other differences. Therefore it is possible to subdivide the alluvial soils. The desert sands have turned into distinct soils. The hills, mountains and plateaus have produced residual soils with patches of alluvial, loess and other soils. Accordingly the soils of Pakistan can be classified as given below (Fig. 10).

Alluvial Soils of the Flood Plains
Alluvial Soils of the Bar Uplands
Soils of the Piedmont Plains
Desert Soils
Soils of the Potwar Plateau
Soils of the Western Hills and Mountains.

Alluvial Soils of the Flood Plains

Within the flood plains of Pakistan, flood conditions differ from one region to another. Areas close to rivers are flooded every year. Areas at some distance from the rivers are inundated in years of severe floods, while the coastal areas are subjected to tidal flooding. This has affected the soil texture, the soil water, the soil pH and other soil characteristics. Accordingly different areas have developed different types of soil (Fig. 10).

Loamy and some sandy soils
Loamy and clayey soils
Mainly loamy saline estuarine soils
Soils of the tidal flats.

Loamy and some Sandy Soils

The active flood plains are covered with loamy and some sandy soils. They occupy the narrow strips along the Indus River and its tributaries, the Jhelum, the Chenab, the Ravi and the Sutlej. They are most extensive along the Indus River where they are 25 to 40 km wide. The towheads between the braided channels of the stream are also covered with these soils. They are flooded almost every year during the rainy season (July-August). They are thoroughly flooded and are free from salinity. They are renewed with fresh deposits of alluvium whenever the flood comes. Loams dominate the area. Sandy soils occur on the towheads and in other areas in small patches.

Loamy and Clayey Soils

The old flood plains are covered with loamy and clayey soils. The old flood plains lie between the active flood plains (*bet*) and the Bar Uplands

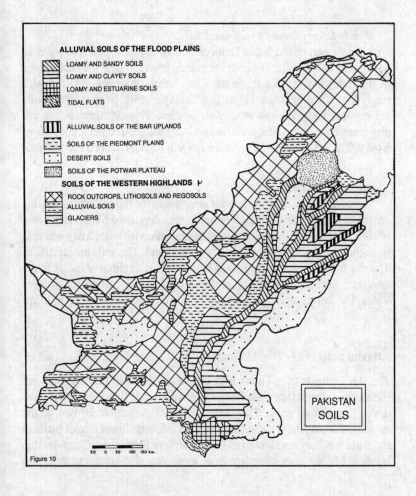

ALLUVIAL SOILS OF THE FLOOD PLAINS

LOAMY AND SANDY SOILS
LOAMY AND CLAYEY SOILS
LOAMY AND ESTUARINE SOILS
TIDAL FLATS

ALLUVIAL SOILS OF THE BAR UPLANDS
SOILS OF THE PIEDMONT PLAINS
DESERT SOILS
SOILS OF THE POTWAR PLATEAU

SOILS OF THE WESTERN HIGHLANDS

ROCK OUTCROPS, LITHOSOLS AND REGOSOLS
ALLUVIAL SOILS
GLACIERS

PAKISTAN SOILS

50 0 50 100 150 Km.

Figure 10

in the northern Indus Plains and between the active flood plains and the desert region in the southern Indus Plains. The old flood plains were subjected to flood in the recent past. At present they remain free from flood in most years. Only in years of heavy rainfall are they locally flooded. Therefore the soils have experienced considerable stability and are appreciably homogenized. Saline and alkaline patches are observed here and there, particularly close to the desert areas. In such patches the pH ranges from 8.0 to 8.4 and in exceptional cases up to 9.0. Loam is the predominant soil with patches of clayey soils on the back slopes and in the meander scars and the channel infills. The levees and meander bars are covered with sandy loams. The colour ranges from brown in humid and well-drained areas to greyish brown in dry areas.

Mainly Loamy Saline Estuarine Soils

A major part of the Indus Delta excluding the tidal plains is covered with loamy saline soils. The soils are graded from levees to the back slopes of the Indus and its distributaries. The meander bars are covered with sandy loams and the channel infills with clayey soils. In general the soils are porous. They are low in organic content. Homogenization has not progressed much. In most parts, the soils are saline. The pH values range from 8.0 to 8.5. Over large areas Solanchak soils have been recognized.

Soils of the Tidal Flats

The tidal flats occupy the coastal areas along the Indus Delta. The soils are mainly clays derived from the sediments deposited by the Indus and reworked by the tides. In low-lying areas the tides visit twice a day whereas in slightly higher areas they come twice a month. The soils are stratified. The sea water has turned the soils highly saline. Sodium chloride is the main salt. There are some tidal lakes which are occasionally filled with sea water. The sea water evaporates after some time and a crust of salt is left behind.

Alluvial Soils of the Bar Uplands

The Bar Uplands (the Kirans Bar, the Sandal Bar and the Nili Bar) are Pleistocene alluvial terraces. They are well above the flood plains and have developed mature soils. They are classed as Noncalcic Brown in the subhumid areas where the soils have been leached almost free of lime. In the arid areas they are classed as Brown Soils or Sierozems. Considerable leaching of lime has taken place from Sierozems also but not as thorough as that from the Noncalcic Brown. In both the soils a layer rich in lime occurs at about three feet from the surface. Texturally the soils are silt loams and clay loams. The soils are quite fertile and are extensively cultivated with the help of irrigation.

Soils of the Piemont Plains

The Piedmont Plains cover an extensive area between the Sulaiman-Kirthar mountains and the Indus River. Two relatively smaller areas occur in the northern part of the Punjab along the Pir Panjal mountains. The foothills of these mountains are occupied by stony fans and aprons which are formed of loose material washed down from the mountains by occasional heavy rainfall. The stream beds are filled with gravels and coarse sands. Some fine material is arrested between the gravels and stones. These predominantly stony soils are strongly calcareous and are of little agricultural importance. Gently sloping plains lie beyond the foothills. They are formed by alluvium laid down by sheet floods and shallow intermittent streams with shifting channels. They are covered mainly with sandy loams and silts and they are strongly calcareous. In some areas dunes have developed by wind action. The soils are quite fertile and produce good crops after rains and on application of irrigation.

Desert Soils

There are three large areas of desert soils in Pakistan: Thar-Cholistan, Thal, and Kharan (Fig. 10). These soils are generally classed as regosols. The Thar-Cholistan is the most extensive. It is about 720 km long and 80 km wide. It is located in the eastern part of Pakistan. In the south it is covered primarily by latitudinal dunes and in the north by transverse dunes. The sands involved are yellowish to pale brown in colour. They are calcareous and rich in minerals. The dunes are occupied by loamy sands and the interdunal valleys by soils of finer texture (sandy loams). They are very weakly-developed soils. The Thal area lying between the Indus and the Jhelum rivers is a river terrace covered with a comparatively thin layer of grey sands. Dunes oriented in various directions cover the region. Calcareous loamy sands form the ridges and sandy loams cover the interdunal areas. When the calcium carbonate is leached from them, they are classed as Sierozem. Old river channels are filled with silt and clays. The Kharan Desert occupies a large area of western Balochistan and is covered with sands. With the virtual absence of vegetation, soil formation is minimal.

Soils of the Potwar Plateau

The Potwar Plateau is covered with three types of soils: (1) Loess, (2) Alluvial, (3) Residual.

All the soils are extensively eroded, deeply dissected and badly gullied. The wind-deposited loess are brown in colour and moderately alkaline in reaction. They are very fertile. Unfortunately they do not occupy large areas and are badly eroded.

The alluvial soils cover the narrow river valleys and the alluvial terraces. The soils of the river valleys are fine sands and loams whereas those of terraces are clay loams and loamy clays. They are fertile soils and are suitable for farming.

The residual soils of the Potwar Plateau have been derived primarily from the decomposition of shale and sandstone. They have formed into brown clayey soils. Part of calcium carbonate has been eluviated from the surface to a foot below. They are poor soils and are suitable for pasture.

Soils of the Western Highlands

The Western Highlands are dominated by steep rock outcrops bare of soils. Some parts of the extreme north are covered with glaciers. Therefore over large areas soils are absent. Wherever soils are found lithosols and regosols cover the hills and mountains and alluvial soils fill the river valleys and basins.

Lithosols and Regosols

Limestone, shale and sandstone are the main rocks involved in the formation of the Western Highlands. Volcanic rocks cover the area in patches. Limestone yields very little soil. Shales, sandstone and volcanic rocks have produced a thin veneer of soils. Most of the soils formed on the slopes are removed by wind, water and gravity. Thin stony soils lie over the bedrock and are classed as lithosols. Over the flatter areas, regosols dominate. They are also thin soils but unlike lithosols they are usually not stony. In the northern subhumid region podzolization on a limited scale has started. Agriculturally lithosols and regosols are of very little importance.

Alluvial Soil

The wide basins bounded by hills and mountains are covered with alluvial soils. So are the narrow river valleys which wind through and run between hills and mountains. The foothills are covered with talus cones and alluvial fans generally composed of gravels, pebbles and coarse sands.

Beyond the foothills, the valley floors are covered with silt and loam. They are fertile soils of great agricultural value in the rocky waste of the Western Highlands. The most extensive and important areas of alluvial soils in Balochistan are the Lasbela Plains drained by the Porali River, the valleys of Dasht, Mastung, Quetta, Pishin and Zhob. In NWFP the valley of Kabul River, Kurrum, and Swat are important.

SOIL EROSION

Soil erosion is a menace which destroys the soils. It is unfortunate that the problem of soil erosion has not roused much public and government attention.

Water and wind are the two main agents of erosion in Pakistan which are aided by landslides and soil creep. Soil erosion has been further accelerated by reckless cutting of the forests, overgrazing and poor management of the farm lands. It must be noted that wind and water erosion both work together particularly in the desert and semi-desert areas.

Water Erosion

Rain and rivers are the two main agents of water erosion. With every rain a film of soil is washed away. This is sheet erosion. The damage increases as the intensity of rainfall increases. In Pakistan cloudbursts are common which accelerate soil erosion. Within a few years five to six inches of top soil, rich in nutrients and organic matter is removed. After some time the water flowing down the slope forms narrow and shallow channels. Thus the rill erosion starts. In course of time these channels widen and deepen and turn into gullies. If this is not checked in time, badland topography develops with a closely spaced series of deep and wide gullies. Gully erosion is most extensively typified in the Potwar Plateau. It is estimated that more than two million acres of cultivated land have been lost in the upland districts. In Jhelum District alone 50,000 acres of productive land were eroded in 40 years between two settlements. Gully erosion is taking place in the Piedmont Plains along the Pir-Panjal Mountains and the Sulaiman-Kirthar Mountains.

In the smaller intermontane valleys like Quetta-Pishin and Nari-Bolan damage by gully erosion is reported. The river erodes the bank and the bed. Its erosive power increases manifold during the time of flood. In the hills its role becomes menacing because of the steepness of the slopes. Land slides and soil creep help in the work of erosion. The rivers of Pakistan while flowing through the hills and mountains usually have narrow and deep valleys. Therefore most of the eroded material is washed down into the plains. The Indus River at Kalabagh (where it enters the plains) carries 2,900 tons of sediments per square mile, and the Jhelum at Mangla 5,968 tons per square mile. These sediments are laid down in the plains. It is estimated that the Indus deposits 25,000 acre feet of sediments per year, the Jhelum 7,000 acre feet and the Chenab, 8,000 acre feet. Thus the agricultural lands of the plains are enriched every year by good soils brought down from the uplands.

The rivers flowing over the plains also erode the banks and the beds but most of the eroded material is redeposited in some other part of the plains. Therefore the erosion over the plains cannot be counted as a total loss. But still millions of tons of good soils are drained into the Arabian Sea by the Indus and other rivers.

Wind Erosion

Wind erosion becomes more potent in regions where vegetation cover is minimal. Therefore the desert and semi-desert areas are more affected. The wind picks up the fine soil particles and leaves behind the infertile coarse sands. As this process continues the coarse sands form into dunes and the land is completely taken off from the plough. Gorrie (1948) estimated that the desert of Sindh was advancing north-westward by half a mile annually. With the extension of irrigation in some of these areas, this estimate may not hold good today. The Thar desert of Sindh, the Cholistan of Bahawalpur, the Thal of Sindh Sagar Doab, and the Kharan Desert of Balochistan are most affected by wind erosion. The introduction of canal irrigation in parts of Cholistan and Thal has reduced the danger of wind erosion. Still wind erosion continues to be a major threat to agriculture in desert and semi-desert areas of Pakistan.

Chapter 6

Environmental Challenge

The earth is the home of man. He lives on the earth and gets sustenance from it. Early man lived on wild fruits and raw meat of birds and wild animals. He quenched his thirst from the first brook that he came across. He roamed about naked and slept in the open. His life was not much different from that of other animals. Today he can grow crops, domesticate animals, build factories and fly in the air. He is busy conquering space. Man, who could only use his muscles in the beginning has now discovered the secrets of nuclear energy. He has harnessed the tides and is exploiting solar energy. He eats better food and lives in greater comfort. His achievement is a consequence of high technical competence gained in exploiting the physical environment.

Human progress has not been all blessing. In his zest to make greater and yet greater use of natural resources, man has polluted the water and the air. He has been responsible for acid rain, smog and acid fog. He has damaged the ozone layer and may impair the ecosystem beyond the point of repair and thus put into jeopardy his very existence. Man has unfolded the secrets of nuclear energy. But once unleashed he does not know how to control this giant which may destroy humanity. The fact is that he still does not even know how to safely dispose of nuclear waste. In recent years human population has increased at such a fast rate that there is a fear that we will run out of resources.

All countries do not have an equal share in technology and resources. Pakistan is a country with low technology and modest resources. Technology does not alone determine how best the resources can be exploited. Political stability and peace, social justice and harmony, well-defined economic goals and hard work are some of the other prerequisites for maximum development. Political stability and peace in Pakistan have been marred by several wars with India and internal strife. Social harmony of the required level has not been achieved because of the lack of social justice. Well-defined economic goals do not exist. Sometimes we follow the goal of nationalization and soon after we turn to privatization. We profess Islam but in general we show little respect for Islamic values. The nation is hard-working but most of the labour is wasted in aimless efforts. It is in this context that the man-environment relationship in Pakistan should be examined.

The physical environment of Pakistan has been a blessing in many forms but it also poses challenges in a number of ways. Extensive plains have proved a boon but lofty and rugged mountains have created many problems. Temperature-wise most parts of Pakistan enjoy an year-long growing season but the problem of aridity has got to be solved. Large areas are covered with alluvial soils which are sufficiently fertile but are deficient in organic matter. Plant cover in Pakistan is sparse and forests usually occupy less accessible areas.

Efforts are being made to face the environmental challenge and solve the problems. In the wake of steps taken for the solution of the problems, new problems have cropped up. Canal irrigation adopted to combat aridity has caused salinity and waterlogging in large cultivated areas. Tubewells installed to bring more land under the plough in northern Balochistan have resulted in the depletion and even death of some of the *karezes*. Insecticides and pesticides used on crops have imparted a toxic effect to the soils. Smoke emitted from factory chimneys and automobiles and other vehicles has polluted the air in industrial areas and large cities. Industrial refuse particularly chemicals drained from the factories into rivers and coastal water have polluted the water in Karachi and other industrial centres.

The environmental problems in Pakistan have emanated from three sources:

Nature	— Topographic and climatic constraints, floods, desertification and earthquakes
Man-nature interaction	— Population growth and resources, salinity and waterlogging, soil erosion and soil toxicity
Man	— Urban growth, air pollution, water pollution, solid wastes.

TOPOGRAPHIC CONSTRAINTS

Topography influences human life in various ways. Its effect on farming and transportation is most pronounced. The level topography of the Indus Plains puts minimal constraint on the development of agriculture and the network of transportation. But in the Western Highlands ruggedness of topography makes development of farming and transportation difficult. Man has to take a number of measures to circumvent this constraint.

In the Complex Mountainous North which is most rugged, agriculture is confined to the narrow river valleys like the Swat. When the river valleys failed to support the growing population, terrace farming on hill slopes was adopted. In the areas to the south of the Complex Mountainous North, farming is confined to alluvial fans and basins lying between mountains. A vast expanse of barren lands in the Western Highlands stands out as a challenge to human ingenuity.

No transportational network exists in the Western Highlands. The Complex Mountainous North which is dominated by lofty mountains with steep slopes and which is very sparsely populated has witnessed meagre development of transportation. There are no railways but in this difficult terrain fairly populated river valleys have been served with dangerous serpentine roads which have to cross difficult passes and are under constant threat of blockade by landslides. An engineering feat was performed when a road (Silk Route) was built in the snowy heights to connect Pakistan and China through Khunjerab Pass. To the south of the Complex Mountainous North, topography becomes less rugged and mountains are not that high. Railways appear on the scene but they are mostly feeder or strategic routes. At many places they cross mountains through tunnels like the railroute between Sibi and Quetta, and Quetta and Chaman. Comparatively there are many more roads. For modern technology topography does not present unscalable obstacles for road development and roads can be built if economic necessity exists.

CLIMATIC CONSTRAINTS

Most areas of the Indus Plain and many of the river basins and alluvial fans of the Western Highlands are arable. But only 60 per cent of the arable land is cultivated. Rainfall deficiency is the main constraint. About 90 per cent of the total area of Pakistan is either arid or semi-arid. To combat this environmental challenge irrigation on a large scale is practised. The Indus Plains are interlaced with an intricate network of canals, the parallel of which exists nowhere in the world. Tubewells, Persian wheels, *karezes* and *kaurjos* are other irrigation systems in Pakistan. No less than 72 per cent of the cultivated land of the country is irrigated.

A resting period for farming in the winter season is induced in those parts of Pakistan where the temperature drops below freezing point (usually at an elevation of 2,000 metres or more). In such areas crops can be grown only in the summer season. The rest of Pakistan enjoys an year-long growing season. In such areas marked variation in temperature between summer and winter seasons takes place. Consequently the same crops cannot be grown in both seasons. Pakistani farmers through centuries of experience have learnt to adjust to seasonal temperature differences by growing *rabi* crops like wheat, grams and barley in winter and *kharif* crops like rice, cotton and maize in summer.

FLOODS

Floods are yet another hazard in Pakistan. During the summer season the snow accumulated on the mountains located in the north of Pakistan melts. This coincides with the main rainy season. Therefore the Indus and its tributaries swell and almost every year they overflow their banks. The flood in most years is not serious. The flood water spreads fertile silt over the lands along the banks which gain in fertility. However every 7-8 years severe floods come. They cause damage to the crops and houses and sometimes livestock and human lives are also lost. In some vulnerable areas roads and railways are also damaged and traffic is temporarily suspended. Serious floods occurred in 1973, 1974 and 1978. It is estimated that in 1973, floods inundated 3.6 million hectares, killed 1,600 persons and demolished 3 million huts and houses.

To check floods, over 5,000 km of embankments have been built along river banks. At selected places second defence embankments have been constructed to contain the excess water. Marginal embankments have been built to ensure that the river does not change its course and that it continues to flow under the railway and road bridges, and through the barrages. Emergency exits have been constructed at some bridges and dams, yet the floods come. It is not possible to confine the water in the channels. Probably it is also not desirable. To minimize the damage done by the floods, a monitoring system has been developed and flood warning is widely publicized through radio, television and newspapers. That is all that can be done at the present level of technology.

DESERTIFICATION

The major part of Pakistan is dry. The arid lands have existed as deserts for a long time. Some semi-arid lands also turned into desert when the scanty plant cover was destroyed by overgrazing or was cleared by human beings. Plant cover once removed from dry lands does not easily reappear because of harsh climatic conditions. In addition the deserts were marching towards the marginal lands and encroaching on them by sand blasts and moving sand dunes. Man has been fighting against aridity since a long time in Pakistan and has succeeded in reclaiming extensive desert areas. Through *karezes* (in Balochistan), *kaurjos* (diversion canals in Makran, Balochistan) and wells, he is able to create man-made oases within desert wastes. With inundation canals taken out from the Indus and its tributaries he succeeded in reclaiming considerable desert lands of the *bet* (the flood plains). With the introduction of perennial irrigation in 1859 a great onslaught on deserts was started. The deserts began to recede. At the time Pakistan was created a large desert (Thal) existed in the heart of Punjab. Reclamation of the Thal was started with the help of canals taken off from Jinnah and Chashma Barrage. A large part of the Thal Desert has now turned into gardens. With the introduction of tubewells in Balochistan barren deserts are now dotted with green fields and orchards. Still, two large parts of Pakistan are occupied by deserts. Thar-Cholistan Desert occupies the eastern part of Pakistan and Kharan Desert spreads over the western part of Balochistan. They are likely to remain a big challenge for a long time.

EARTHQUAKES

No part of Pakistan can be said to be completely safe from earthquakes. However some areas are more vulnerable than others. The Western Highlands are more susceptible to seismic activity than the Indus Plains. Within the Western Highlands Quetta Zone extending southward up to Kalat is the most active area in Pakistan. The reason is that the areas of faults (cracks)and young fold mountains particularly where they take a sharp bend are weak parts of the earth. They are more subject to earthquakes than others. Quetta Zone is one of such regions. It is there that the Sulaiman Mountains take a sharp syntaxical bend. The Quetta Fault is located there and the Chaman Fault is close by. In a period of two months, October and November 1978, as many as 62 earthquakes were recorded. A major earthquake occurred on 30 May 1935 when about 30,000 persons lost their lives and almost the entire Quetta City was in ruins.

Two seismic zones of high intensity are located in the Complex Mountainous North. One of them is located in the Karakoram Region which is associated with the Karakoram Fault. Another is located to its south in Abbottabad, Mansehra, Kohistan and Swat Districts. It is associated with faults occurring in Indus-Kohistan Seismic Zone and Hazara Lower Seismic Zone and with the Western Himalayas syntaxis. Many earthquakes have taken place in this region. However on 28 December 1974, a severe earthquake rocked the area. It has been called Pattan Earthquake and it created havoc in Pattan, Dubair, Palas and other villages.

More than 5,000 people were killed and many more injured. The number of houses destroyed was more than 5,000 and at least the same number were damaged. The Karakoram Road was badly damaged over a distance of 80 km.

Earthquakes are a natural hazard beyond human control. In Pakistan monitoring of earthquakes has considerably improved but forewarning is not yet possible. Nothing much has been done to assure safety from earthquake damage except that in 1936 Quetta Building Code was framed, and the structural design of important projects like Tarbela Dam and Mangla Dam was formulated after geological investigation and assessment of seismicity of the site.

POPULATION GROWTH AND RESOURCES

Pakistan possesses a large population, modest resources and low technology. Resources are not fully developed; the standard of living is low and Pakistan is counted as a poor country. The population is growing at an explosive rate. The population doubled in 50 years from 1901 to 1951 and it doubled again in 21 years from 1951 to 1972. From 1972 to 1981 the population increased by 28.3 per cent. The population in 1981 was 84.3 million. This will increase to 150 million by AD 2000 if the present growth rate continues. This large population has to be fed, housed and clothed and it will depend on how best we make use of our environment, climate, land, water, and minerals.

With increasing population, per capita share in the land is decreasing in Pakistan. In spite of the fact that the total cultivated area has increased by one-third from 1951 to 1981, the per capita cultivated area has decreased by two times. Per capita cultivated area dropped from .48 hectare (1.2 acres) in 1951 to .42 hectare (1.04 acres) in 1961, .39 hectare (.96 acre) in 1972 and .24 hectare (.59 acres) in 1981. It is from this small parcel of land that food and cash crops have to be obtained.

At the time Pakistan was created the country was self-sufficient in wheat, the staple food. Because of an increase in population, a deficiency in wheat was registered in 1952-53. This deficiency continued until 1980 and heavy import of wheat had to be made. During this period efforts were made to increase wheat production by bringing more land under wheat and by increasing its per unit yield. In 1981 self-sufficiency in wheat was achieved. Thereafter in good years no import is made but in bad years import becomes necessary. Even this state will not continue. Population is increasing and we are soon going to face a heavy deficit. Heavy imports were made in 1985, 1986 and 1989. Improvement in the wheat position has

Waterlogging in the Punjab near Faisalabad

Air pollution caused by congested traffic

One of many factories causing air and water pollution

Solid waste accumulating on a garbage dump

not fully improved the food position. Heavy imports of edible oil and pulses have to be made. This is a matter of concern for Pakistan which claims to be an agricultural country.

Pakistan is deficient in mineral resources, particularly metallic minerals which in general are located in inaccessible and thinly populated areas. Their exploitation poses technological and economic problems. Pakistan is not well equipped to solve either of them.

Pakistan is deficient in energy in spite of the fact that the per capita consumption of energy in Pakistan is low, about 10 times less than the world average. Load shedding of electricity is common, causing reduced industrial production, hindrances in tubewell irrigation and inconvenience to common consumers. About 38 per cent of the villages are not yet electrified. In cities many households have no electricity.

Pakistan is deficient in petroleum. Up to 1983-84, domestic production met 11 per cent of the local demand. A breakthrough was achieved in 1984-85 when 19 per cent of the home requirement was met by local supplies. By 1987-88, the local production equalled 37 per cent of the total consumption of oil in the country. Gas requirements are met from domestic sources and new gas fields have recently been discovered. This clearly demonstrates that oil and gas exploration in Pakistan has not been thoroughly done. Lack of technology, trained personnel and financial resources are the main handicaps.

The installed capacity of hydroelectricity in Pakistan in 2,548 MW whereas economically utilizable potential is 20,000 MW. It is obvious that nature has been quite benevolent in this respect. Faulty planning and financial difficulties are the major constraints.

Coal produced in Pakistan is of inferior quality (lignite and sub-bituminous). It is of low heating value. The bulk is used in brick kilns. It cannot be claimed that all the coal reserves have been explored. In 1981 a large new field was discovered (Sonda-Thatta coal field). Thus it can be concluded that nature has been quite generous in providing Pakistan with energy resources. It is human failing not to make the best use of the resources.

SALINITY AND WATERLOGGING

The agricultural lands in Pakistan particularly in Punjab and Sindh are faced with acute problems of salinity and waterlogging. This is the outcome of perennial canal irrigation which was introduced to combat aridity (for details see Chapter 11). With perennial canals it became possible to water the crops whenever the need was felt. As a consequence of seepage of water from the unlined canals and the percolation of water from the irrigated fields, the water table began to rise. When the water table rose to five feet below the surface the saline water reached the surface by capillary action. With a further rise of the water table, waterlogging took place. It is estimated that 26 per cent of the irrigated area of Pakistan is affected by salinity, of which 8 per cent is severely affected. Sindh is the worst affected province where 48 per cent of the soil is saline, of which 18 per cent is strongly saline.

As a remedial measure it has been decided to bring down the salinity below the danger level and to flush away the salt from the soils. For this the country has been divided into a number of Salinity Control and Reclamation Project Zones (SCARP). The reclamation work has been started phase-wise. The water table is lowered by pumping water out by tubewells. This plan proved a success but brought in its wake other problems. Ground water in some areas, particularly Sindh is saline. It cannot be used for irrigation, therefore it cannot be drained into the canals. The safest way of disposal is to drain the water into the sea. This involves new engineering problems and added cost. In addition to this tubewells installed began to wear out in a few years. They needed repair and in some cases installation of new tubewells was required. Furthermore installation of thousands of tubewells resulted in a heavy pressure on electricity which is already in short supply. Long spells of load shedding also create problems. Above all the whole plan involves a heavy expenditure. But the work on SCARP is continuing as no better alternative is known.

URBAN GROWTH AND ENVIRONMENTAL PROBLEMS

Some of the environmental problems are exclusively the creation of man. Such problems are found in the most pronounced form in urban areas. Pakistan has registered unprecedented urban growth during recent years. The urban population was 9.8 per cent in 1901. That increased to 17.8 per cent in 1951 and to 28.3 per cent in 1981. Some of the cities have grown to gigantic size (over 500,000) like Karachi, Lahore, Faisalabad, Rawalpindi, Hyderabad, Multan, Gujranwala and Peshawar. The collection of a large population has created problems of housing, sewage disposal and water supply. The disposal of an enormous quantity of solid wastes every day poses another problem. The municipality is unable to transport and dispose off the entire solid waste of the cities. Rag pickers and stray animals do part of the job. Some waste is disposed of by burning. A substantial part is left to rot and pollute the air. The use of automobiles, motor cycles, and rickshaws has given rise to noise problems. Air and water pollution are not only a nuisance but have turned into health hazards also.

AIR POLLUTION

Air pollution is caused by vehicles and stationary sources. The vehicles like automobiles, trucks, rickshaws, aircraft and others run by internal-combustion engines are responsible for carbon monoxide, hydrocarbons, nitrogen oxides, and lead pollution. Stationary sources of air pollution are industrial plants, power-generating stations, construction projects and solid wastes. These sources add pollutants like sulpur dioxide, nitrogen oxides and particulates (dust, ash, soot, metals and various chemicals). The main concern about the air pollution is that it adversely affects human health. It causes eye, nose and throat irritation and lung infection manifested by bronchitis, asthma, tuberculosis and even cancer.

In general, urban places and industrial centres are reported to have more air pollution. In Pakistan this is particularly true of large cities which also have many industrial establishments. Karachi, Hyderabad, Lahore, Faisalabad, Gujranwala, Sialkot, Rawalpindi, and Peshawar may be mentioned.

Karachi possesses the greatest number of the industrial units of Pakistan and 33 per cent of all the registered vehicles. The number of vehicles increases every year by about 20 per cent. The result is that air pollution is on the increase. The smoke level has increased by about five times from 1969 to 1983. M.A. Jinnah Road and Saddar are the most affected parts of the city where vehicular traffic is the heaviest. Traffic congestion and traffic signals causing slow movement of vehicles and the tunnel effect produced by multi-storeyed buildings on both sides are other important factors. It is worth noting that fast moving vehicles cause less pollution than slow moving vehicles. Pollution is more in winter than in summer as higher wind velocity in summer dissipates the smoke.

Surveys carried out in Karachi show that in areas of heavy vehicular traffic the air contains carbon monoxide, smoke and particulate matter beyond permissible limits. The tree leaves along M.A. Jinnah Road are no longer green. Quaid-e-Azam's Mausoleum, Mereweather Tower etc. have been affected.

WATER POLLUTION

In cities, sewage and industrial discharge are the main sources of water pollution. Problems become more severe in large and more industrialized cities. The common practice is to let the waste water drain into rivers or canals. In Nowshera the Kabul River receives the water discharged from industries, sewage and homes. The Leiah Nullah is the recipient in Rawalpindi, the Ravi in Lahore, a canal in Faisalabad and the Lyari and the Malir in Karachi. In Karachi the dirty water of the rivers goes into the sea. The coastal water is thus polluted. The water of the Lyari goes into the Manora Channel which is enclosed from three sides. Thus its water does not mix freely with the vast expanse of the Arabian Sea and its pollution increases and persists. Furthermore the ships which anchor in Karachi harbour discharge oil and other refuse in the sea water. The consequence is that the coastal water of Karachi is extremely dirty and highly polluted.

Some idea of the extent of pollution in the effluents of the Lyari can be appreciated from the fact that the chloride content is 1,000-1,300 ppm, sulphate, 850-1,200 ppm, phosphate, 35-50 ppm and total dissolved solids (TDS) 2,000 ppm. An analysis of the coastal water at Karachi indicates that the water at Karachi harbour has a higher quantity of total dissolved solids (TDS), chloride, bicarbonate, calcium, magnesium, sodium and potassium. The five hundred major industries and many more smaller units located at Sindh Industrial Trading Estate (SITE) are the main contributors to the pollution of the Lyari and coastal water. The sewage plays a secondary role. The direct effect of the contaminated water has been that the salt produced in the salt works located on the Mauripur Road is no longer fit for human consumption. Health hazards to the residents of the Lyari area and the workers of the dockyards can only be assessed if a continual watch on their health is kept. No assessment of the ill effects on the air by polluted water has been made. But its effect must be considerable. Other urban centres of Pakistan particularly the large cities and the industrial centres are faced with similar problems on a smaller scale. The solution lies in the treatment of industrial waste and domestic sewage. But so far virtually no treatment of the industrial refuse is done and only partial treatment of the domestic sewage is done. It is a pity that ships treat the coastal water of Pakistan as the dumping yard for their refuse. In the ports of the developed countries they are not allowed to do this.

Safe and clean drinking water is a basic necessity. In many rural areas drinking water is not available in adequate quantity. Sometimes the water has to be fetched from long distances. Dry conditions prevail over a large part of Pakistan. In many parts there are no streams. Rain water collected in ditches and small lakes is used for drinking and domestic purposes. People wash their clothes, take a bath and draw water for drinking from the same ditch. After some days it becomes filthy, polluted and unfit for human use. Yet some people have no option but to use it. The use of contaminated water is one of the major causes of disease in the rural areas.

In cities, water supply in general is the responsibility of the municipalities and corporations. Many cities suffer from inadequate supply of water. To cope with this problem water is supplied to different parts according to a fixed schedule. People do not get water throughout the day, instead they receive water only for specified hours. The cities are growing at a fast rate and the water need is also increasing. To meet the increasing demand new sources of water are being tapped. Hab Dam was recently built to meet the expanding water need of Karachi city. Yet the scarcity continues.

The general practice in Pakistan is to treat the drinking water with chlorine. The ill effects of chlorine on the lungs is now well known. More serious than that are the leaks and cracks in the underground water pipes through which dirty water, sewage and germs mix with drinking water and cause intestinal diseases and impair the proper function of the liver. The residents of the old parts of Karachi are the worst sufferers.

REMOTE SENSING APPLICATIONS

In recent years, remote sensing data collected via various satellites by SUPARCO (Space and Upper Atmosphere Research Commission) has helped in environmental studies relating to geomorphic analysis and mapping of tidal land forms, changes in river courses, and flood inundation studies; natural vegetation mapping and classification of waterlogging and salinity; identification of land surface features, changes in soil cover and geological analysis; population surveying potential, urban landuse studies and transportation networks. Atmospheric pollution studies are also being carried out.

Part III

The People

Chapter 7

Population: Growth and Distribution

The economy of a country and its population are very intimately related. To run the economic machinery persons of different age, sex, qualification and experience are required. Therefore an analysis of population size, age structure, sex composition and the quality of population is necessary. The stage of economy of a country is brought out by its occupational structure and rural-urban composition of population. An estimation of the number of persons to be fed, clothed, housed and employed in the future is done by population projection. Therefore, an analysis of the population of Pakistan is essential in order to understand its economy.

Pakistan has a population of 84.3 million (1981) with a density of 105 persons per sq km (272 persons per square mile). The majority of Pakistanis (71.7 per cent) live in villages. The urban population is about 28.3 per cent. The population is growing at a very fast rate. It increased by 28.3 per cent from 1972 to 1981.

THE GROWTH OF POPULATION

The population of Pakistan is growing at a very rapid rate. From 16.6 million in 1901, it increased to 84.3 million in 1981, a five-fold increase in 80 years (Table 7.1). A closer examination reveals that in 50 years from 1901 to 1951, the population was doubled and it doubled again in 21 years from 1951 to 1972. From 1972 to 1981, the population increased by another 28.3 per cent. If the growth rate of 1972-1981 continues, the population of Pakistan will be 149.4 million by AD 2000.

The population growth of any country is the outcome of natural increase (birth minus death) and net migration (immigration minus emigration). In Pakistan the most potent component of population growth is natural increase. Net migration has played a minor role.

The data on birth and death is fragmentary and unreliable. Vital registration is incomplete. Surveys conducted on national basis *(Pakistan Growth Survey*, 1962, *Pakistan Growth Estimate*, 1968-71 and 1976-79, *World Fertility Survey*, 1975 and *Pakistan Demographic Survey*, 1984) are helpful but not accurate. However, a general agreement exists among demographers about the trend of births and deaths in Pakistan. Both birth and death rates have exhibited a declining trend. Births have dropped at a slower rate and deaths at a sharper rate. Crude birth rate dropped from 49 in 1931 to 45 in 1941 and 41 in 1978. According to some estimates it has dropped to 38. About 40 per thousand may be considered a good approximation of the present day crude birth rate. During the same period the death rate decreased from 36 in 1931 to 31 in 1941 and 10 in 1978 where it seems to be stuck. Thus the gap between births and deaths is increasing in favour of birth. Consequently the natural increase is rising. It was 1.3 in 1931, 1.4 in 1941 and 3.1 in 1981. The death rate decreased primarily because of improvement in medical facilities which considerably controlled the epidemics, tuberculosis, malaria and other diseases. A further drop in the death rate through medicines alone is difficult. Some cut is possible by improvement in diet and better hygienic life. But there is a great scope for reducing birth. If fertility is controlled the natural increase will start to slide down. It is then that population growth will also decrease. The growth rate during 1972-1981 according to the census was 3.06. *Pakistan Demographic Survey*, 1984 puts the growth rate at 3.1. The National Institute of Population Studies estimates the growth rates for the 1981-86 period as

Table 7.1: Pakistan—Population Growth, 1901-81

Census year	Population (in thousands)	Intercensal Growth (per cent)	Annual Growth Rate (per cent)	Growth Rating
1901	16,576	—	—	—
1911	19,382	16.9	1.6	Very Rapid
1921	21,109	8.9	0.8	Moderate
1931	23,542	11.5	1.1	Rapid
1941	28,282	20.1	1.9	Very Rapid
1951	33,740	19.4	1.8	Very Rapid
1961	42,880	27.0	2.4	Explosive
1972	65,309	52.3	3.7	Explosive
1981	84,254	28.3	3.1	Explosive

Source: *Population censuses of Pakistan.*

2.85. If these growth rates continue according to the census the population will reach 149.4 million by AD 2000, according to Pakistan Demographic Survey 150.5 million and according to National Institute of Population Studies 143.7 million. This is the population that Pakistan must plan to feed, clothe and house by the turn of the century.

URBANIZATION

Urbanization in Pakistan has progressed appreciably. In 1901 only 9.8 per cent of the total population lived in urban places. After that a steady increase took place. In 1951 urban dwellers were 17.8 per cent and in 1981, 28.3 per cent. It is estimated that by AD 2000 the percentage will be 37.8. The increase in urban population is substantial but in the world context Pakistan is a country with a low level of urbanization. In 1900, 14 per cent of the world's population lived in urban places, 30 per cent in 1950 and 41 per cent in 1980. Comparatively Pakistan is far behind and the gap between Pakistan's urban population and that of the world has increased rather than decreased. In 1901 Pakistan's urban population was 4 per cent less than that of the world's average. The difference became 12 per cent in 1951 and 16 in 1981. This clearly brings out the fact that the pace of urbanization in Pakistan is slower than the world taken as a whole. One may erroneously

Table 7.2: Pakistan—Total, Rural and Urban Population and Rural and Urban Population as Percentage of Total Population, 1901-81

Census year	Total (in thousands)	Rural (in thousands)	Urban (in thousands)	Percentage of Total Population	
				Rural	Urban
1901	16,576	14,957	1,619	90.2	9.8
1911	19,382	17,693	1,689	91.3	8.7
1921	21,109	19,051	2,058	90.2	9.8
1931	23,542	20,773	2,769	88.2	11.8
1941	28,282	24,267	4,015	85.8	14.2
1951	33,740	27,721	6,019	82.2	17.8
1961	42,880	33,226	9,654	77.5	22.5
1972	65,309	47,976	17,333	73.5	26.5
1981	84,254	60,412	23,842	71.7	28.3

Source: *Population Census of Pakistan*, 1961, 1972 and 1981.

conclude that the high rate of urbanization in the Western countries has pulled up the average percentage of the urban population of the world and thus Pakistan is unable to keep pace. The fact is that the urban growth of the Western World has greatly slowed down. It is the developing countries where urbanization is taking place at a rapid rate. Pakistan however registered higher urban growth than the other South Asian countries (India, Bangladesh, Sri Lanka and Nepal).

Urban growth takes a logistic curve. In the initial stage the curve is flattish. The urbanization is slow up to a period when urban population reaches 25-30 per cent. After that the Acceleration Stage starts and continues until urban population reaches 60-70 per cent. Beyond that urbanization slows down and the Terminal Stage is reached. In the Initial Stage the emphasis is on agrarian economy. In the Acceleraton Stage the emphasis is on manufacturing, trade, transport and services, and a decided, concentration of population takes place. Pakistan, with 28 per cent urban population is at the threshold of the Acceleration Stage. During the next decade rapid urbanization is likely to take place. By AD 2000, 37.8 per cent of the population is expected to live in urban places. Even then the level of urbanization in Pakistan will be less than the world's average which will be 50 per cent. It will also be less than that of the developing countries where 45 per cent of the population will be urban dwellers.

The urbanization process in Pakistan can be better understood, if distribution of urban population among urban places of different sizes is analysed. The percentage share of small, intermediate and large cities in

Table 7.3: Pakistan—Number and Percentage of Cities by Size and their Percentage in Urban Population, 1981

City Size	Number of Cities	Percentage of Total Number of Cities	Percentage of Urban Population
1,000,000 and larger	3	0.7	38.9
500,000-999,999	5	1.2	14.5
100,000-499,999	21	5.1	12.0
50,000-99,999	35	8.5	9.7
25,000-49,999	73	17.7	10.3
10,000-24,999	171	41.4	11.5
Smaller than 10,000	105	25.4	3.1
Total	413	100	100

Source of raw data: *Population Census of Pakistan*, 1981.

the urban population differs. The small towns (population less than 25,000) accounted for 22 per cent of the urban population in 1951. Their share decreased to 15 per cent in 1981 (Table 7.3). Towns in the next higher category (25,000-50,000) had a smaller share, 14 per cent in 1951 which decreased to 10 per cent in 1981. Towns in the next higher category (50,000-99,000) had a still smaller share in 1951 (7 per cent), which increased to 10 per cent in 1981. Large cities with a population of 100,000 and more have the lion's share of the urban population. In 1951, their number was only 10 out of 238 but they accounted for 55 per cent of the urban population. Thereafter their share increased in every census and in 1981 it stood at 65 per cent when they numbered 29 out of 413.

A revealing picture emerges when the large cities are divided into groups by size. The first group may be taken to be the cities with a population of 100,000 to 500,000. Their number was 7 in 1951. That increased to 21 in 1981. But their share in urban population decreased from 24 per cent in 1951 to 12 per cent in 1981. In the second category belong cities with a population of 500,000 to one million. Their number was one in 1951 and 5 in 1981. Their share has remained stationary at 14-15 per cent during this period. It is the large cities with a population of more than one million which have shown the greatest dynamism. This is the only category the share of which in the urban population has increased. Their number was one in 1951 and 3 in 1981. They accounted for 18 per cent of the urban population in 1951 and 39 per cent in 1981. These 3 cities are Karachi, Lahore and Faisalabad. Karachi became a one-million city in 1951, Lahore in 1961 and Faisalabad in 1981. The share of Faisalabad in 1981 was 5 per cent, that of Lahore 12 and that of Karachi 22 per cent. In other words more than one-third of the urban population of Pakistan lives in Lahore and Karachi taken together and more than one-fifth lives in Karachi alone.

Stages of Urbanization

The urban population of Pakistan increased at a rate lower than that of rural population during 1901-11 (Table 7.4). According to Gibbs this is a characteristic of countries in stage 1 of urbanization. In stage 2, urban population increases at a rate faster than that of the rural population indicating that there is a net migration from rural to urban areas. Pakistan entered stage 2 in 1911-21, through which it is still passing. Pakistan has not entered stage 3 when the rural population registers a decrease.

According to Reissmann Pakistan is in Stage 1 of urbanization. Reissmann has put four measures of urbanization:

1. Urban growth measured by the percentage of population in cities of over 100,000.
2. Industrialization measured by national product derived from manufacturing.
3. Emergence of middle class measured by per capita income.
4. Rise of nationalism measured by the percentage of literacy among the population over the age of fifteen.

On the basis of each one of the above criteria, the countries of the world are ranked and divided into quartiles. Pakistan, along with India, Egypt and Turkey belongs to the first quartile and thus is placed in stage 1 of urbanization.

Cities by Size

It is a common observation that there are only a few large towns in a country, a fair number of intermediate towns and a comparatively large number of small towns. Pakistan is no exception (Table 7.3).

This distribution can be explained by the nature of goods and services that the towns offer. Most of the towns are central places. Services like trade, education, health, administration etc. which need central location are concentrated in towns. The people living in the surrounding areas take

Table 7.4: Pakistan—Urban Population as per cent of Total Population and Intercensal Growth of Rural, Urban and Total Population 1901-81

Census year	Urban Population	Intercensal Population Growth		
		Urban	Rural	Total
1901	9.8	—	—	—
1911	8.7	4.3	18.9	16.9
1921	9.8	21.9	7.7	8.9
1931	11.8	34.6	9.0	11.5
1941	14.2	45.0	16.8	20.1
1951	17.8	49.9	14.4	19.4
1961	22.5	60.4	19.7	26.9
1972	26.5	79.5	44.4	52.3
1981	28.3	36.7	25.2	28.3

Source of raw data: *Population Census of Pakistan*, 1951, 1961, 1972 and 1981.

advantage of these services. But all the services cannot be located in every centre. Some services need a small supporting population while some need a large population. Thus there is an hierarchical order of urban centres. However the central place of a higher order carries the services of the lower order also. Within this general framework of city size distribution, three patterns have been recognized:

Distribution in hierarchical order
Rank-size rule
Primate distribution.

Distribution in hierarchical order has been put forth by Christaller. In classical central place theory Christaller claims that in a homogenous plain with population evenly distributed and equal facilities of transport and movement available to all points, there will be a fixed number of central places in each hierarchical group. There will be only one city of the highest order and the number will increase in a predetermined ratio as the hierarchical order decreases. The assumptions of Christaller are such that they are not met anywhere in the world. The same holds true for Pakistan also. In Pakistan the number of cities does increase as the hierarchical order decreases but they do not follow the rigid ratio as stipulated by Christaller.

Rank-size rule is usually attributed to Zipf though others had pointed it out before him. This rule states that there is a relationship between the size of a town and its rank. If the towns of a country are ranked in a descending order by population, the largest city (rank one) will be twice as large as the second largest city, three times as the third largest city, four times as large as the fourth largest city. Thus if the rank of a city is known, its population can be found out by dividing the population of the largest city of the country by the rank of the city in question. Pakistan does not conform to rank-size rule. In 1981, the third largest city (Faisalabad) was five times smaller than the largest (Karachi), the ninth (Sialkot) was seventeen times smaller and the twelfth (Islamabad) was 25 times smaller. The story was similar in previous censuses also.

The primate distribution presented by Mark-Jefferson asserts that the largest one or two cities of a country dominate the other cities very decisively. The gap between the primate city and other cities is much more than envisaged by the rank-size rule. There is also a marked gap between the intermediate size cities.

In Pakistan, Karachi and Lahore dominate the urban scene. They together accounted for more than one-third of the urban population of

Pakistan throughout the period from 1951 to 1981. The intermediate size towns (25,000-99,999) are small in number. Their percentage share in the total number of towns was 26 in 1981, whereas that of small towns was 67 (Table 7.3). In earlier censuses their percentage was even lower. It was 17 in 1972 and 13 in 1961. Pakistan thus presents the picture of a country with primate distribution with two dominant cities, Karachi and Lahore. The gap between the two primate cities is also increasing. In 1951, Karachi was 1.25 times larger than Lahore; in 1961, 1.47 times; in 1972, 1.6 times and in 1981, 1.7 times. Primacy is the rule in general of the countries with a short history of urbanization and with a simpler economic and political set-up. As time passes the economic system and political set-up become more and more complex, and the primate distribution gives place to rank-size rule.

Karachi was the only one-million city in 1951. Lahore joined the group in 1961 and Faisalabad in 1981. Faisalabad was the fifth largest city in 1951. It acquired the fourth position in 1961 after displacing Rawalpindi and the third position in 1972 after displacing Hyderabad (Table 7.5). Faisalabad owes its rapid growth largely to industrial development. Rawalpindi was relegated from the fourth position in 1951 to the sixth in 1961. But with the establishment of the federal capital (Islamabad) close by, Rawalpindi is growing at a fast rate and once again holds the fourth position since 1972. It is competing very closely with Faisalabad for third position and there is a strong possibility that it will be a one-million city by 1991. Among other cities Islamabad, the federal capital, recorded phenomenal growth between 1972 and 1981, increasing from 77,000 to 201,000. Hyderabad slipped from the third position in 1951 to the fifth position in 1972, where it seems to be entrenched for the time being. Sialkot lost ground sharply between 1951 and 1961. But with the revival of the sports industry its position seems to have stabilized. A remarkable feature of 1972-81 intercensal period is that there was no change in the rank of the ten largest cities (Table 7.5).

DISTRIBUTION OF URBAN PLACES

One of the main functions of the urban places is to serve the surrounding areas. Therefore in a region of uniform population distribution and with a network of easy transportation spread all over the region, one may expect uniform distribution of towns. The towns of the lower order will be spaced closely and the distances between towns will increase as their hierarchical order increases. In Pakistan the population is very unevenly distributed. The Western Highlands are sparsely populated. Population concentration

Preparing tea in a
Chai Khana, Peshawar

A busy market place – buying and selling foodstuff

An artisan engraving
brass artifacts

Karachi, the largest city of Pakistan

One of many fishing villages along the Arabian Sea coast

is most marked in the canal irrigated areas of the Indus Plains particularly in the Punjab Plains. Accordingly there are only a few towns in the Western Highlands. South of Peshawar up to the Arabian Sea, Quetta is the only large city. Balochistan presents a good example of truncated hierarchy, with lines of transportation disturbed by rugged terrain and the population

Table 7.5: Pakistan—Cities of 100,000 or Larger Arranged in Descending Order by Size, 1951-81.

1951	1961	1972	1981
Karachi	Karachi	Karachi	Karachi
Lahore	Lahore	Lahore	Lahore
Hyderabad	Hyderabad	Faisalabad	Faisalabad
Rawalpindi	Faisalabad	Hyderabad	Rawalpindi
Faisalabad	Multan	Rawalpindi	Hyderabad
Sialkot	Rawalpindi	Multan	Multan
Peshawar	Peshawar	Gujranwala	Gujranwala
Gujranwala	Gujranwala	Peshawar	Peshawar
Multan	Sialkot	Sialkot	Sialkot
	Sargodha	Sargodha	Sargodha
	Quetta	Sukkur	Quetta
	Sukkur	Quetta	Islamabad
		Jhang	Jhang
		Bahawalpur	Sukkur
		Sahiwal	Bahawalpur
		Mardan	Kasur
		Wah Cantt	Gujrat
		Kasur	Okara
		Gujrat	Mardan
			Shekhupura
			Mirpurkhas
			Larkana
			Wah Cantt
			Attock
			Rahimyar Khan
			Jhelum
			Chiniot
			Dera Ghazi Khan
			Nawabshah

Source: *Population Census of Pakistan*, various years.

concentrated in watered valleys. The spacing of towns does not fit into any geometric pattern. In the Indus Plains where the population is more evenly spread and the network of roads and railways has made movement easier, some pattern in spacing of cities does emerge. The lowest order towns (smaller than 10,000) are more closely spaced. The average distance between any two of them was 27 km in 1972. The average distance increases as the city size increases. Thus the average distance between towns with a population of 10,000 to 25,000 was 29 km/17.9 miles, those with a population of 25,000 to 50,000, 34.4 km/21.4 miles, those with a population of 50,000 to 100,000, 66.6 km/41.4 miles and those with a population of more than 100,000, 81.9 km/50.8 miles. In 1951 the distance among all categories of cities was greater. The decrease in the distance from 1951 to 1972 was induced by an increase in population and in the number of urban places which resulted in closer spacing of towns. From 1972 to 1981, the number of towns remained almost the same and therefore no appreciable change in the spacing of cities took place.

DISTRIBUTION OF RURAL POPULATION

The distribution of rural population brings out the man-land relationship effectively in an agricultural country like Pakistan. The pressure on land in Pakistan has been continuously increasing. In 1901, the density of rural population was 19 persons per sq km (49 persons per sq mile) which increased to 35 in 1951 and to 75 in 1981. In other words the rural density doubled in 50 years from 1901 to 1951 and after 1951 it took 30 years only to double again.

Rural population in Pakistan is very unevenly distributed. In some areas the population density drops below three persons per sq km (Chagai and Kharan districts), in some areas it rises above 350 persons per sq km (Sialkot, Kasur, Mardan and Peshawar districts). The uneven distribution of population is largely the outcome of the differential capability of land to support population. The differential capability has been induced by diversity of topography, soils, rainfall and irrigational facilities.

Pakistan has a marked diversity of topography. There are lofty mountains, rugged hills, extensive plateaus and vast plains. The mountains and the hills with scanty soil cover and considerable slope do not attract a large population. It is in the river valleys which cut through the mountains and hills, and which are underlain with sufficiently thick soils that population is concentrated. Normally the plateaus with thin soil cover have moderate population and the plains with deep soils have dense population. But the limiting factor in Pakistan is the availability of water. Semi-arid and arid conditions prevail over most parts of Pakistan. Therefore the population distribution closely follows the water distribution, the rain and irrigation water. The availability of water largely determines the availability of cultivated areas. The cultivated area in its turn attracts population. In-migration is higher in better farming areas, which increases the population density. Pakistan may be divided into the following population density regions:

1. Thinly Populated Region   :   10 persons or less per sq km/25 persons per sq mile.
2. Moderately Populated Region   :   11-50 persons per sq km/16-125 persons per sq mile.
3. Thickly Populated Region   :   51-100 persons per sq km/126-250 persons per sq mile.
4. Very Thickly Populated Region: 101-200 persons per sq km/250-500 persons per sq mile.
5. Most Thickly Populated Region: More than 200 persons per sq km/500 persons per sq mile.

Thinly Populated Region (10 persons or less per sq km)

The southern and western part of Balochistan except Turbat District is thinly populated (Fig. 11). It is an area comprising hills, mountains and plateaus. The coastal plains are narrow and are interrupted by the projection of hills here and there. The rainfall is very scanty. The average annual rainfall is less than 250 mm. In north-western Balochistan it is less than 125 mm. Therefore desert conditions prevail. Rain-fed agriculture is not very dependable. Dry farming is practised in some areas. Neither the streams nor the terrain are fit for canal irrigation. However some of the streams are dammed and irrigation on a small scale is practised. A limited area is irrigated by *karez*. Therefore a small percentage of land is cultivated (2.5 per cent) and a low percentage of cultivated land is irrigated (25 per cent). Consequently the density of population is very low.

Moderately Populated Region (11-50 persons per sq km)

There are three moderately populated regions in Pakistan: Western, Eastern and Northern (Fig. 11). The Western region covers a narrow belt of Sindh Kohistan. From there it extends northward into the Sibi Plains. Further north it widens to include northern Balochistan and South Waziristan. The major part of the western regions is rugged and covered

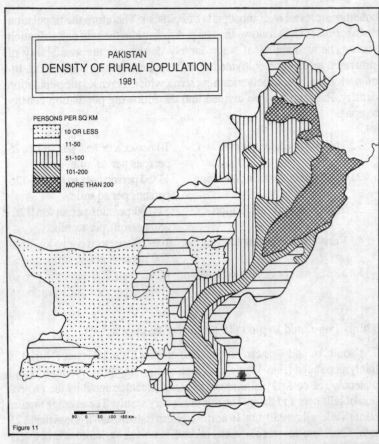

Figure 11

with hills and mountains. The narrow river valleys offer some opportunity for agriculture. The Sibi Plains topographically are quite suitable for farming but the rainfall is very low as in other parts of the western region. Irrigational facilities are limited, therefore the potential to support population is low. The western region is connected with the eastern region by the Indus Delta.

The eastern region is an extensive area covering the deserts of Thar and Cholistan. Soils are sandy and saline. They respond well when water is available, but the rainfall in the region is low (less than 250 mm in most parts). Perennial streams are almost non-existent.Consequently the cultivated area is not extensive and the population is comparatively low.

The northern moderately populated region is an isolated area covering Chitral District. It is a rugged region located at a very high altitude. Winter is very severe and long. Agriculture is possible on a very limited scale. The out-migration is heavy and population density is moderate.

Thickly Populated Region (51-100 persons per sq km)

The thickly populated region covers a large compact area comprising the Piedmont Alluvial Plains, a major part of Sindh Sagar Doab, part of the Potwar Plateau, Kohat District, Kurram Agency and adjoining tribal areas (Fig. 11). Kohistan and Swat districts form an isolated thickly populated region. Agriculture in these regions is limited by aridity in the south and ruggedness of topography and poor soils in the north. In the south the soil of the Piedmont Plains, though in parts stony is excellent for agriculture. But the paucity of water is a great handicap and rain-fed agriculture is practised. The Indus River flows east of the Piedmont Alluvial Plains. The canals taken out from the dams and barrages built on the Indus (Tarbela Dam, Chashma Barrage, Taunsa Barrage) and the Kurramgarhi Barrage on the Kurram River have helped in the development of agriculture. This is a region where extension of agriculture is taking place and the population is increasing. Already it has turned into a thickly populated region.

Very Thickly Populated Region (101-200 persons per sq km)

The very thickly populated region (Fig. 11) comprises the Indus Valley in Sindh, the Punjab, the major part of Chaj Doab except Gujrat District and the western part of the Potwar Plateau (Jhelum District). North-eastward from the Punjnad the region extends along the southern valley of the Sutlej into Rahimyar Khan, Bahawalpur and Bahawalnagar Districts. The Bannu Valley and Dir District are isolated parts of the region. Most of the very thickly populated region is plain, covered with rich alluvial soils and drained by mighty streams like the Indus, the Jhelum, the Chenab and the Sutlej. It is covered with extensive canal systems taken out from a number of barrages and dams like Kotri, Sukkur, Guddu, Punjnad, Trimmu, and Mangla. It is one of the most fertile and agriculturally important regions of Pakistan. This region has received a very large number of in-migrants who have contributed to its thick population.

Most Thickly Populated Region (more than 200 persons per sq km)

There are two areas which are most thickly populated (Fig. 11). The major area extends from Multan District northward into Sialkot District, covering Rechna and Bari Doab. It is the agricultural heart of Pakistan. It is irrigated by the Upper and Lower Chenab Canals and also by the Upper and Lower Bari Doab canals. The percentage of cultivated land rises to 80 and that of irrigated land to 85. This is also the area where rural in-migration is the highest. Another very thickly populated region extends from Rawalpindi District on the east to Malakand on the west, including Mansehra, Abbottabad, Peshawar and Mardan Districts. Part of this region is drained by the Kabul River from which canals have been taken out. The irrigational facilities and rich alluvial soils have turned it into an important agricultural area. In other areas the Tarbela Dam and Rawal Dam have helped in the development of agriculture. The rain-fed agriculture is also important in this region. Consequently the concentration of population is heavy.

Chapter 8

Population Composition

Population composition or population structure refers to various aspects of population like age, sex, marital status, language, education, religion, race, economic activities and others. These characteristics throw light on important social, political and economic patterns of a population. Some aspects of population composition of Pakistan are discussed in this chapter.

AGE COMPOSITION

Age composition has considerable economic and demographic significance. It reveals the number of active labour force (adults), the future labour force (children) and the retired labour force (aged) in a population. The adults are also the main earners and the children and the aged in general are dependents. Thus the following three basic age groups are of importance:

Children	0-14	years
Adults	15-64	years
Aged	65	years and over

The adults are the most productive, both economically and biologically. They constitute the bulk of the labour force. They support the young and the aged. Therefore a high percentage of adults in a population is a healthy sign. The percentage of adults in Pakistan is not very high and is steadily decreasing (Table 8.1). It was 52.9 per cent in 1951 which dropped to 52.8 per cent in 1961, to 52.0 per cent in 1972 and then to 51.2 per cent in 1981. The percentage of adults in Pakistan is similar to that of other developing countries. In India it was 54.7 per cent in 1971. In contrast the developed countries have a much higher percentage of adults. It was 61.8 per cent in USA in 1970, 63 per cent in UK in 1971 and 69.1 per cent in Japan in 1970 (Table 8.1). The dependency ratio (percentage of children and aged to adults) in the developing countries, therefore, is much higher than that in the developed countries. In Pakistan, the dependency ratio is slowly increasing. It was 89 in 1951 which increased to 89.4 in 1961, to 92.3 in 1972 and 95.3 in 1981. India, in 1971 had a dependency ratio of 82.8. But the developed countries have a much lower dependency ratio, USA 61.8 (1970), UK 58.7 (1971) and Japan 44.7 (1970).

Pakistan, like many other developing countries possesses a high percentage of children. From 1951 to 1981 the young population has never been less than 42.5 per cent. In India it was 42.0 per cent in 1971. In contrast the percentage of children in USA was 28.3 in 1970 and in Japan and UK, 24 per cent in 1970. This reveals that the labour market in Pakistan will remain very competitive in future also. An effort to create new jobs may ease the situation. The high percentage of children also means that the birth rate is likely to remain high and population growth may continue to take place at an explosive rate.

The percentage of the aged in Pakistan is low like that of the other developing countries. It was 4.3 per cent in 1981. In India it was still lower, 3.3 per cent in 1971. Comparatively, USA (9.9), Japan (6.9) and UK (13.1) had a higher percentage of the aged. In Pakistan the percentage of the aged population fluctuated from 3.9 to 4.7 per cent from 1951 to 1981. This explains the higher death rate and shorter length of life as compared to the developed countries.

Table 8.1: Percentage of Population in Major Age Groups and Dependency Ratio of Pakistan and Selected Countries in Selected Years

Countries	Percentage of Total Population				
	Year	Children	Adults	Aged	Dependency Ratio
Pakistan	1951	43.2	52.9	3.9	89.0
Pakistan	1961	42.5	52.8	4.7	89.4
Pakistan	1972	43.0	52.0	4.2	92.3
Pakistan	1981	44.5	51.2	4.3	95.3
India	1971	42.0	54.7	3.3	82.8
Japan	1970	24.0	69.1	6.9	44.7
UK	1971	23.9	63.0	13.1	58.7
USA	1970	28.3	61.8	9.9	61.8

Source of raw data: *Census of Pakistan* 1951, 1961, 1972 and 1981, *UN Demographicr Year Book*, 1973.

LABOUR FORCE

The age structure determines the labour force available for employment but the number actually employed depends upon the number of job opportunities and the qualification and experience of the job seekers.

Labour Force Participation

The labour force in Pakistan is steadily increasing. It increased from 5.7 million in 1901, to 9.8 million in 1951, to 24.5 million in 1981 and to 28.9 million in 1985-86 (Table 8.2). But the percentage of total population in the labour force has not increased. It dropped from 34.8 per cent in 1901 to 30.7 per cent in 1951, to 29.5 per cent in 1981, and then to 28.7 per cent in 1985-86. This is much lower than the world's average which is 42 per cent. The developed countries have 44.8 per cent of their population in the labour force whereas the developing countries have 40.7 per cent. The fall in the labour force participation ratio in Pakistan has resulted in the increase of dependents per labourer. The number of dependents per labourer was 1.88 in 1901, which increased to 2.26 in 1951 and 2.84 in 1981 (Table 8.2). In 1985-86 it was 2.48. One important reason for low labour force participation rate in Pakistan is the extremely poor representation of

Table 8.2: Number of Labour Force, Percentage of Total Population in Labour Force and Dependents per Labourer in Pakistan

Year	Labour Force (in millions)	Percentage of total population in Labour Force	Dependents per Labourer
1901	5.7	34.8	1.88
1911	6.1	34.1	1.93
1921	6.1	33.3	2.00
1931	6.8	31.8	2.14
1951	9.8	30.7	2.26
1961	12.8	32.4	2.09
1973	17.2	28.4	2.52
1981	24.5	29.5	2.84
1985-86	28.9	28.7	2.48

Source: Farooq, *Labour Force Participation Rates in Pakistan*, 1961, *Pakistan Development Review*, Vol. III, No. 1 Spring, 1968, *Government of Pakistan Housing Economic and Demographic Survey*, 1973, Part I, Table 17, *Government of Pakistan Economic Survey*, 1980-81, p.3 and *Economic Survey*, 1986-87, p. 15.

females in the labour force. It was 2.2 per cent in 1981 and 6 per cent in 1985-86.

Sectoral Employment

The primary sector (agriculture, forestry, fishing and mining) absorbs the majority of the labour force in Pakistan (Table 8.3). Its percentage share has however, decreased from 65.3 in 1951, to 50.6 in 1984-85. It increased to 54 per cent in 1985-86. This increase is not easy to explain. Forestry, fishing and mining are minor employers. Agriculture accounts for the bulk of the labour force in the primary sector.

The share of the manufacturing sector in the labour force increased from 11.6 per cent in 1951 to 20.2 per cent in 1961, but dropped continuously thereafter and was 13.8 per cent in 1984-85. This signifies relatively poor performance of the manufacturing sector. The employment in the tertiary sector (trade, transport, construction, office work etc.) is increasing rapidly and reached 35.6 per cent in 1984-85 but dropped to 33 per cent in 1985-86. In the developed countries the tertiary sector employs the majority of the labour force and the primary sector the least.

Overseas Employment

Emigration of Pakistani workers particularly to the Middle East is a notable feature of the 1970s. In 1971, 3,534 workers went abroad through the Bureau of Emigration and the Overseas Employment Corporation. That increased to 140,145 in 1977. Since then it has decreased slightly. In 1980, 133,197 workers were sent abroad.

Table 8.3: Sectoral Share in the Labour Force in Percentage, 1951-86

Year	Primary (Agriculture, Forestry, Fishing and Mining)	Secondary (Manufacturing)	Tertiary (Transport, Trade etc)
1951	65.3	11.6	23.1
1961	59.3	20.2	20.5
1970-71	57.6	15.3	27.1
1980-81	52.7	14.1	33.2
1984-85	50.6	13.8	35.6
1985-86	54.0	13.1	32.9

Source: *Economic Survey of Pakistan*, 1986-87, Table 1.9

It is estimated that in 1980, about 1.4 million Pakistanis were working outside Pakistan. The employment abroad has somewhat eased the problem of unemployment within Pakistan. But in the 1980s a large part of the labour force working abroad came back because of recession in the Middle East.

Unemployment

Unemployment is of two types, open and disguised. The disguised unemployment includes under-employment and periodical unemployment. Unemployment as a whole is difficult to measure but the measurement of under-employment is almost an impossible task. The census of 1951 and 1961, and the labour force survey of 1974-75 estimate the open unemployment in Pakistan to be 2 per cent. The census of 1981 and the labour force survey of 1985-86 puts the unemployment rate at 3-4 per cent. Serious doubts have been expressed about these estimates because even in the developed countries the percentage of unemployment is much higher. The Housing Economic and Demographic Survey, 1973 puts the unemployment rate at 13.0 per cent. The unemployment according to that survey is higher in the urban centres (17.7 per cent) than in the rural areas (11.5 per cent). This estimate sounds more realistic.

LANGUAGES

Most of the languages spoken in Pakistan belong to the Aryan sub-family of the Indo-European family. Brahvi is the only exception and it belongs to the Dravidian family The giant Indo-European family includes diverse languages like English, German, French, Persian, Hindi and Bengali. Aryan is one of its sub-families. Three branches of this sub-family are represented in Pakistan namely Iranian, Dardic and Indo-Aryan.

Iranian Branch

In the very early days of their wanderings some Aryans living in Iran developed the Iranian branch of Aryan languages. Of them Persian, Pashto and Balochi are well known. The latter two are well represented in Pakistan.

Balochi
Balochi has its roots in the languages of Iran particularly Middle Persian or Pehlavi. It has freely absorbed words from modern Persian and

Arabic. In Pakistan over 3 per cent of the families claim Balochi as their mother tongue. Their main concentration is in Balochistan particularly south of Quetta, while others live in the adjoining parts of Sindh and Punjab. About 56 per cent of the Balochi-speaking families live in Balochistan which constitutes 36 per cent of the total families of the province (Table 8.4). Sindh accounts for 32 per cent of the Balochi-speaking families which is about 4.5 per cent of the total families living in Sindh. About 0.6 per cent of Punjabi families are Balochi speaking.

Pashto
Pashto is another language of the Iranian branch of the Indo-Aryan sub-family of languages. In Pakistan Pashto is the main language of the NWFP, northern Balochistan and the tribal areas. There are Pashto-speaking pockets in Attock and Mianwali Districts of the Punjab. About 13 per cent of Pakistani families are Pashto speaking. About 68 per cent of the families living in NWFP speak Pashto, 25 per cent of those in Balochistan and nearly 100 per cent of those in the tribal areas. A little over 3 per cent of the Sindhi families are Pashto speaking and less than 1 per cent of those of the Punjab.

Dardic Branch

Dardic languages were developed by the groups of Aryans who entered Chitral and then moved eastward into Northern Areas and Kashmir. The

Table 8.4: Percentage of Households by Language Spoken in Pakistan, 1981

Languages	Pakistan	Balochistan	NWFP	Punjab	Sindh
Urdu	7.6	1.4	0.8	4.3	22.6
Punjabi	48.2	2.2	1.1	78.7	7.7
Pushto	13.2	25.1	68.3	0.7	3.0
Sindhi	11.8	8.3	0.1	0.1	52.4
Balochi	3.0	36.3	—	0.6	4.5
Brahvi	1.2	20.7	—	0.1	1.1
Hindko	2.4	0.1	18.1	0.4	0.4
Siraiki	9.8	3.1	4.0	14.9	2.3
Others	2.8	2.8	7.6	0.7	6.0

Source: *Handbook of Population Census Data*, Population Census Organisation, Government of Pakistan, 1985, Table 10.

Aryan languages were mixed with the local dialects and as a consequence the Dardic languages were developed. Khowar in Chitral, Shina in Gilgit and Hunza, Kashmiri in Kashmir and Kohistani in Kohistan District are some of the important Dardic languages.

Indo-Aryan Branch

The Aryans in very large numbers entered the Indus Valley and then moved east into the Ganges Valley and later to South India. They were responsible for the development of a number of Prakrits spoken in different parts of the Indo-Pakistan subcontinent. Around AD 1000 the Prakrit stage came to a close and their place was taken by modern Indo-Aryan languages which took their birth from various Apabrahmsa (local Prakrits). The important Indo-Aryan languages represented in Pakistan are Hindko, Siraiki, Punjabi, Sindhi, Urdu and Gujrati.

Hindko and Siraiki

Hindko and Siraiki belong to Lahnda (west) group of languages. The speakers of this group live mostly in Punjab and Abbottabad and Mansehra Districts of NWFP. They are closely related to Punjabi but differ in grammar and vocabulary. Lahnda is divided into two sub-groups, one lies to the north of the Salt Range and the other to its south. In the north Pothwari and Hindko are spoken. Hindko is more important than Pothwari. About 2.4 per cent of the families in Pakistan are Hindko speaking. Their main concentration is in Abbottabad and Mansehra District of NWFP where they are in the majority. In this province 18 per cent families are Hindko speaking. Pothwari is spoken in Rawalpindi District and parts of Jhelum and Gujrat.

Siraiki is the main Lahnda language south of the Salt Range. Siraiki speakers are mainly concentrated in Multan Divison. Siraiki has considerable affinity with the Sindhi language. About 10 per cent of the families in Pakistan claim Siraiki as their mother tongue. In the Punjab they constitute 15 per cent of the population, 3 per cent in Balochistan and 2 per cent in Sindh. Over 88 per cent of the Siraiki speakers live in the Punjab. Thali, spoken in Sindh Sagar Doab and Dera Ismail Khan District is also a Lahnda language.

Punjabi

Punjabi and its various dialects are derived from Takka Apabrahmsa and Upangara Apabrahmsa. It has an affinity with Urdu and Lahnda languages. The Punjabi-speaking population is spread in all the provinces of Pakistan. About 48 per cent of the households in Pakistan are Punjabi speakers. But their main concentration is in the Punjab where 79 per cent of the families are Punjabi-speaking. In Sindh 8 per cent of the families are Punjabi-speaking, in Balochistan 2 per cent and in NWFP 1 per cent.

Sindhi

Sindhi language has developed from Vrachada Apabrahmsa. It has several dialects, of which Vicholi is the most important. It is the dialect of central Sindh and of Sindhi literature. Lar is the dialect of Lower Sindh. Lasi, a transitional dialect, between Lari and Vicholi is spoken in Lasbela District of Balochistan. Another dialect is Thari, spoken in the eastern desert of Sindh. In Pakistan 12 per cent of the population is Sindhi-speaking. Their main concentration is in Sindh, where 52 per cent of the families are Sindhi-speaking and where 96 per cent of the Sindhi speaking families live. A substantial number of Sindhi speakers live in Balochistan, accounting for 8 per cent of the total families of the province.

Urdu

Urdu is the national language and lingua franca of Pakistan. It has developed from a number of Prakrits spoken in Punjab, UP, Bihar and adjoining areas. Urdu is written in Persian script with much of its vocabulary derived from Persian and Arabic. Urdu is closely related to Punjabi. Before the creation of Pakistan it was widely spoken by the urban population of areas now forming Pakistan. It was the language of the elite and educated Muslims. After the creation of Pakistan, Urdu became its national language. The migrants from northern and central India, Hyderabad and Bombay are Urdu speaking. Today Urdu is spoken all over Pakistan. Only in remote villages is it not well-understood.

Gujarati

Gujarati is the language of the migrants from Gujarat, Cutch and adjoining areas of India. It has a well developed literature and is written in a modified form of Devnagri script. Most of the Gujarati-speaking families in Pakistan are settled in Sindh.

Dravidian Language Family

Brahvi is the only Dravidian language spoken in Pakistan. It is closely related with Telugu and other Dravidian languages spoken in southern India. It has absorbed vocabulary freely from Balochi, Sindhi and Persian. A little over 1 per cent families in Pakistan speak Brahvi. They are mostly concentrated in east central Balochistan. About 21 per cent households in Balochistan are Brahvi-speaking and about 1 per cent of those in Sindh.

LITERACY

Literacy in Pakistan is one of the lowest in the world. It has however, increased steadily from 13.2 per cent in 1952 to 18.4 per cent in 1961, 21.7 per cent in 1972 and 26.2 per cent in 1981. Marked differences exist between rural and urban, and male and female literacy. Still more significant are regional differences.

The literacy ratio of urban population is 47.1 whereas that of rural is 17.3. The difference in social patterns and in the availability of educational facilities are some of the factors responsible for this gap. The difference between male and female literacy is also considerable. Whereas 35 per cent of the males are literate, only 16 per cent of the females belong to this category. In the context of rural-urban set-up the difference becomes very pronounced. The literacy among urban males is 55.3 per cent and among rural females 7.3. The heavy rural population (72 per cent) has pulled down the literacy ratio of Pakistan.

The regional difference in literacy in Pakistan is considerable. In general, literacy decreases as the accessibility and level of urbanization decrease. Districts with a large urban population have a high literacy ratio. Therefore the Western Highlands which are least accessible and least urbanized have a very low literacy ratio. In all the districts of Balochistan except Quetta the literacy is not more than 10 per cent. The same is the position of Kohistan and Swat of NWFP. In all other districts of NWFP except Abbottabad the literacy ratio, though higher, is below the national average. In this category Peshawar is also included. In most parts of the Punjab and Sindh also the literacy ratio though not so low as that in the Western Highlands is below the national average. The exceptions are Karachi, Hyderabad and Sukkur in Sindh, Faisalabad, Lahore, Gujrat, Jhelum and Rawalpindi in the Punjab, and Islamabad where the literacy rate is above the national average. Quetta in Balochistan and Abbottabad in NWFP also belong to this group. All these districts have large urban centres.

RELIGION

Pakistan was created as a homeland for the Muslims living in British India. Therefore soon after the creation of Pakistan a heavy migration of

Muslims from India and of non-Muslims from Pakistan took place. It is estimated that about seven million persons migrated from India to Pakistan and about the same number left Pakistan for India. It was between East Punjab (Bharat) and West Punjab (Pakistan) that the migration of the religious groups was almost complete. From other parts of Bharat the migration of the Muslims was fractional.

Pakistan was carved out of those parts of British India where the Muslims were in a majority. The immigration of the Muslims and emigration of the non-Muslims further increased the percentage of the Muslims in Pakistan. The percentage of the Muslims in the territories constituting Pakistan was 79 per cent in 1941 and that increased to 97 per cent in 1951. In 1981 the percentage of the Muslims in the total population was 96.7. Provincewise the percentage of the Muslims in Sindh was 92.3, Punjab 97.5, Balochistan 98.3, NWFP 99.5 and FATA (Federally Administered Tribal Areas), 99.6.

In 1981, non-Muslims constituted 3.3 per cent of the total population of Pakistan. Among the non-Muslims the Christians and the Hindus were more numerous. The Christians numbered a little over 1.3 million (about 1.6 per cent) and the Hindus, a little less than 1.3 million (1.5 per cent). Other religious groups (Ahmadis, Parsis, Buddhists, Sikhs and others) constituted about 0.2 per cent.

The majority of the Christians live in Punjab (about 1.1 million) where their percentage is 2.2. The majority of them occupy a compact area in the north-eastern part of the province spread over Lahore (5.4 per cent), Shekhupura (5.2 per cent), Gujranwala (4.4 per cent) and Sialkot (4.4 per cent). Most of the Hindus live in Sindh (1.221 million out of 1.276 million) where they form 6.4 per cent of the total population. The overwhelming majority occupies a compact area of eastern Sindh comprising Tharparkar (37.2 per cent), Sanghar (16.5 per cent), Badin (16.3 per cent) and Hyderabad (8.9 per cent)

Part IV

The Economy

Chapter 9

Fishing

Fishing is a minor sector of Pakistan's economy. Its contribution to the country's GNP is about 0.7 per cent. Forestry is the only sector the contribution of which to the GNP is less than that of fishing. But fish and fish products constitute one of the major exports. They contribute about 3 per cent by value to the total export of Pakistan. Fishing provides employment to about 200,000 fishermen. It is the traditional occupation of a large number of them and they do not like to change their profession.

The total nominal catch of fish in Pakistan has increased from 40,000 tons in 1947 to 379,000 tons in 1984-85. Nominal catch (live weight equivalent to landings) comprises commercial, industrial and subsistence catch. Subsistence catch is fish caught and consumed by fishermen on board the vessel and their families at home and also caught and consumed by anglers for their personal pleasure. The subsistence catch is estimated to be 10 per cent of the total catch. With small fluctuation, the increase in production has been steady (Table 9.1). There are two sources of fish in Pakistan, marine and inland.

THE MARINE FISHERIES

The marine fisheries are much more important than the inland fisheries. Generally the share of marine fisheries is 85 per cent in the total catch of the country.

Marine fishing is carried on along the coastal waters of Pakistan. The coast is divided into two parts: the Sindh coast and the Balochistan coast. The Sindh coast is more important for fish catch. It accounts for 68 per cent of the total marine catch though it comprises less than 30 per cent of Pakistan's coast. The Balochistan coast which covers 70 per cent of the country's coast accounts for only 32 per cent of the marine catch. The Sindh coast has the advantage of a wider continental shelf (about 130 km wide as against 30-50 km of Balochistan). It has the additional advantage of receiving the water of the Indus River which brings a sufficient quantity of fish food. The Balochistan coast also receives a number of streams like the Hab and the Dasht but they are relatively small streams and bring smaller quantities of fish food. Fishing is done throughout the year. The peak period is November-January for fish and October-November for shrimp. June-July is the breeding time which is the leanest period for catch. June-July has been officially declared as closed period otherwise it was adversely affecting the fishing industry. Of the total marine catch 90 per cent is fish and 10 per cent is shrimp.

INLAND FISHERIES

The inland fisheries produce about 15 per cent of Pakistan s total fish catch. The rivers, the dams, the ponds, the *dhands* and *dhoros* are the sources of fish. The province of Sindh accounts for 70 per cent of the inland fish catch. Next comes Punjab with 27 per cent. NWFP contributes 1 per cent and Mangla Dam reservoir, 2 per cent. Balochistan has virtually no inland fishing.

FISHING CRAFTS

The main device employed to increase the catch of fish has been improvement in fishing crafts both in efficiency and number. In 1947, the sail boats were the only vessels used. After a few years, the trawler was introduced. There were only two in 1955, which increased to 86 in 1960. In 1970 there were 443 trawlers, in 1980, 1,296 and in 1983, 1,431. The trawler has been primarily helpful in increasing the production of shrimps. The number of gill-netters has been increasing steadily from 52 in 1955 to 160 in 1960,

Table 9.1: Fish Catch in Pakistan, 1947-85 (thousand metric tons)

| Year | Marine | | | Inland | Grand Total |
	Sindh Coast	Balochistan Coast	Total		
1947	23.9	9.0	32.9	7.0	39.9
1950	26.4	10.9	37.3	10.4	47.7
1960	45.8	16.3	62.1	18.5	80.6
1970	102.4	37.4	139.8	18.7	158.5
1980	175.3	57.7	233.0	46.3	279.3
1985	—	—	308.0	70.6	378.6

Source: *Fisheries Statistics,* 1980, Directorate of Marine Fisheries, Government of Pakistan, Karachi, p. 15 and *Economic Survey of Pakistan,* 1986-87. Statistics Table 3.1

707 in 1970, 909 in 1980 and 1,125 in 1983. Since 1975 sail boats are being fixed with motors and their number is on the increase from 230 in 1975 to 1,333 in 1980 and 3,792 in 1983. The gill-netters and mechanized-cum-sail boats have made it possible to move far from the coast to the deep waters. They now go as far as 50 km from the coast for fishing while the sail boats can go as far as 3-5 km (2-3 miles) offshore. But the largest number of fishing crafts are the traditional sail boats. Their number is also on the increase. They were 2,355 in 1955; 3,061 in 1960; 5,343 in 1970 and 5,859 in 1980. Their number has started to decrease since 1981. In 1983 it was 3,242. The inland fishing is done only by sail boats. Their number increased from 1,400 in 1955 to 1,700 in 1960; 4,933 in 1970; 7,246 in 1980 and 8,300 in 1983.

FISHERMEN

The total number of fishermen i.e., active fishermen on board the fishing vessels and labourers and technicians engaged in shore installations was 191,456 in 1980 (Table 9.2). Of them 39 per cent were engaged in marine fisheries and 61 per cent in inland fisheries. Of the total fishermen about 60 per cent were full-time, 23 per cent part-time and 17 per cent occasional workers.

The number of fishermen has been steadily increasing. It increased from 100,215 in 1960 to 191,456 in 1980. The number of inland fishermen is increasing more rapidly. Up to 1973 the number of marine fishermen exceeded that of inland. Since 1974 the inland fishermen are in majority. The province of the Punjab accounts for the largest number of inland fishermen (72 per cent). Sindh comes next with 23 per cent and is followed by NWFP with 5 per cent. There is virtually no inland fishing in Balochistan.

Table 9.2: Fishermen Engaged in Marine and Inland Fishing in Pakistan, 1960, 1970, 1980.

| Year | Marine | | Total | Inland | Grand Total |
	Sindh Coast	Balochistan Coast			
1960	44,430	15,785	60,215	40,000	100,215
1970	61,000	28,600	89,600	73,180	162,780
1980	54,896	19,625	74,521	116,935	191,456

Source: *Fisheries Statistics,* 1980, Directorate of Marine Fisheries, Government of Pakistan, Karachi.

It is of interest to note that though the number of inland fishermen is increasing rapidly, the production of fish from inland sources has not registered any appreciable increase. Further inland fishing accounts for only 15 per cent of the total fish catch of Pakistan but employs more fishermen than in marine fishing. This is paradoxical.

LOCAL CONSUMPTION AND EXPORT OF FISH

The per capita consumption of fish in Pakistan, 1.6 kg is very low. Comparatively per capita consumption of fish in Europe is 20 kg and in Japan, 64 kg. In Pakistan fish consumption is particularly low in Punjab and NWFP, where it is less than .25 kg. It rises to 5 kg in Sindh and 15 kg in Balochistan. In Pakistan about 70 per cent of fish caught is consumed locally. Of this, subsistence consumption is about 9 per cent. The entire catch of inland fish is sold in the local market. Pakistan exports about 30 per cent of the total catch of fish. The entire export comes from marine catch. Pakistan exports fish and fish products to more than 39 countries. Japan is the main market. Its share in terms of value of fish exported from Pakistan is about 50 per cent. Shrimp is the main item imported by Japan. USA, West Germany, UK and France are other important importers. Fish and fish products account for about 3 per cent of the total export of Pakistan by value.

Chapter 10

Forests

Pakistan is poor in forest resources. The sectoral share of forests in the GNP is lowest, 0.1 per cent. About 3.8 per cent of the total area of Pakistan (excluding Northern Areas) is under forest (Table 10.1). For a balanced economy 20-25 per cent of the total area of a country should be under forests. Province-wise NWFP has the highest percentage (15.6) under forest, followed by Sindh (4.2), Punjab (2.7) and Balochistan (2.1). The present position is much better than that in 1947-48. At present the forest area (30,170 sq km) is twice as large as that in 1947-48 (13,800 sq km). The increase in forest area has been achieved by afforestation and regeneration. During the five year period (1975-79) on an average annually 106 sq km were afforested and 202 sq km were regenerated. During 1980-84, annually 226 sq km were afforested and 230 sq km were regenerated. The low percentage of forest area in Pakistan is the result of aridity prevailing over most areas and the reckless cutting of the forests in the past.

FOREST TYPES AND DISTRIBUTION

The major ecological determinants of the forest types of Pakistan are the following:

 i) Arid and semi-arid conditions prevailing over most parts of the Indus Plains and the Balochistan Plateau.
 ii) Humid conditions over northern hills and mountains.
 iii) Diversity of topography ranging from low plains to lofty mountains rising to snowy heights.

In arid and semi-arid areas most parts are bare of vegetation. In some areas spotty scrub forests have developed. In better watered areas like river banks and deltas, riverain and mangrove forests have emerged. In humid hills and mountains forest types change with altitude. The dry subtropical forests dominate up to a height of 1,000 metres (3,000 feet) and coniferous from 1,000 to 4,000 metres. Above the tree-line dwarf alpine forests occur up to the snow-line.

The following forest types are recognized in Pakistan (Fig. 12).
1. Alpine forests from 4,000 metres up to the snow-line.
2. Coniferous forests from 1,000 to 4,000 metres.
3. Subtropical dry forests below 1,000 metres.
4. Tropical Thorn or *rakh.*
5. Riverain or *bela* forests.
6. Mangroves.
7. Irrigated Plantations.

Alpine Forests

Above the tree-line (4,000 metres) the alpine forests occur in the districts of Chitral, Dir, Swat, Kohistan and Northern Areas. The long severe winter with many days of freezing temperatures and short cool growing season does not permit full growth of trees. Dwarfed and stunted growth of silver fir, juniper and birch takes place in sheltered nooks. Often the trees are prostrate. As the mountains rise to the height of the tree-line they become craggy and steep and their areal extent is limited. In such a severe climate and difficult topography the Alpine forests occur over a small area. They are not of much economic importance.

Coniferous Forests

The coniferous forests occur from 1,000 to 4,000 metres. The Northern Areas, Swat, Dir, Malakand, Kohistan, Mansehra and Abbottabad districts of NWFP and Rawalpindi District of the Punjab are the main areas covered with coniferous forests (Fig. 12). The largest area of the coniferous

Table 10.1: Forest Area of Pakistan under the Control of Forest Department, 1983-1984 (thousand hectares)

Provinces	Forest Area	Forest Area as per cent of total area
Balochistan	716	2.1
NWFP	1,164	15.6
Punjab	548	2.7
Sindh	589	4.2
Pakistan	3,017	3.8

Source: *Agricultural Statistics of Pakistan,* 1984, Table 122.

forests is in the NWFP followed by Northern Areas (Table 10.2). Fir (*Abies* spp.) and spruce (*Picea morinda*) occupy the highest altitudes, deodar (*Cedrus deodara*) and kail (*Pinus excelsa*), the intermediate heights, and chir (*Pinus roxburghii*), the lower areas. A significant number of broad leaf deciduous trees are oaks (*Quercus*), maple (*Acer*), willow (*Salix*), birch (*Betula*), horse chestnut (*Acer indica*), poplar (*Populas*), walnut (*Juglans*) and juniper (*Juniperus*). These forests are the source of timber in Pakistan. The timber is put to industrial uses and for making furniture and boxes.

The coniferous forests also occur in Balochistan hills covering an area of 116,000 hectares at an elevation of 1,500-3,000 metres in Quetta and Kalat divisions. Chilghoza (*Pinus gerardiana*) and Pencil Juniper (*Juniperus macropoda*) are the two most common species but they are of limited economic importance.

Subtropical Dry Forests

The hills and foothills of Gujrat, Jhelum, Rawalpindi and Attock districts of the Punjab, Mansehra, Abbottabad, Mardan, Peshawar and Kohat districts of NWFP up to a height of 1,000 metres are covered with dry evergreen forests with some dry deciduous patches. In Balochistan

Table 10.2: Area under Forests by Types and Range Lands in Pakistan under the Control of Forest Department, 1983-84 (thousand hectares)

Category	NWFP	Punjab	Sindh	Balochistan	Northern Areas	Total
Coniferous	1,022	68	—	116	285	1,491
Scrub	115	283	6	595	658	1,657
Riverain *(bela)*	0.3	56	232	2	—	290.3
Irrigated Plantations	0.3	127	70	1	2	200.3
Linear Plantations	2	14	—	0.4	—	16.4
Mangroves	—	—	281	2	—	283
Mazri Lands	24	—	—	—	—	24
Range Lands	150	2,857	489	372	2,104	5,972
Total	1,313.6	3,405	1,078	1,088.4	3,049	9,934

Source: *Agricultural Statistics of Pakistan*, 1984, Table 123.

they are confined to the Sulaiman mountains and other hilly areas where they are represented by scattered patches of dry mixed scrub. Reckless cutting and fire have turned it essentially into an open forest with occasional dense patches. The open areas are covered with grasses and are used for grazing. The dominant trees are phula (*Acacia modesta*) and kao (*Olea cuspidata*). Chestnut, juniper, walnut and oak are some of the deciduous trees which occur. Kao and occasionally chir occur at higher elevations. The most common use of the trees is for firewood, though some timber is also obtained.

Tropical Thorn Forests

The tropical thorn forests are dominated by xerophytic scrub called *rakh* in the Punjab. They are most widespread in the Punjab plains. They

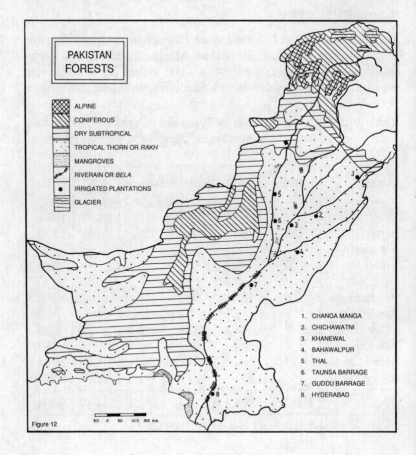

PAKISTAN FORESTS

ALPINE
CONIFEROUS
DRY SUBTROPICAL
TROPICAL THORN OR *RAKH*
MANGROVES
RIVERAIN OR *BELA*
IRRIGATED PLANTATIONS
GLACIER

1. CHANGA MANGA
2. CHICHAWATNI
3. KHANEWAL
4. BAHAWALPUR
5. THAL
6. TAUNSA BARRAGE
7. GUDDU BARRAGE
8. HYDERABAD

50 0 50 100 150 Km.

Figure 12

occupy small areas in Sindh and scattered patches in southern and western Balochistan. They are open low forests dominated by thorny hardwood trees. The scrubs in general are 6-10 metres high. The common species found are *Acacia* spp., *Prosopis spicigera, Tamarix* spp., *Capparis* spp., *Salvadora oleades, Dodoenia viscosa* etc. They are primarily used as firewood.

The Riverain or *Bela* Forests

Narrow belts along the banks of the Indus and its large tributaries are occupied by the riverain forests locally called the *bela* forests. They are more commonly found in Sindh. They cover the active flood plains which are inundated almost annually. Babul (*Acacia arabica*) and shisham (*Dalbergia sissoo*) are the most common species found. In waterlogged areas willow and *Butea forondosa* occur. *Prosopis spicigera, Tamarix* spp. and *Populus euphratica* are other species found in the riverain forests. Shisham is an important source of wood for making furniture. Babul and other species provide firewood and are put to miscellaneous uses like making agricultural implements, house posts etc.

Mangrove Forests

The Indus delta and the adjoining areas and the Hab delta are covered with mangrove forests (Fig. 12). Lack of fresh water has resulted in the stunted growth of trees and in the occurrence of a limited number of species. *Avicennia officanilis* is the main species. *Ceriops* and *Rhizophoras* are next in importance. In better watered areas, the trees rise 6-8 metres but normally their height is 3 metres. The main economic importance of the mangroves is that they supply firewood.

Irrigated Forests

The development of irrigated man-made forests is a unique characteristic of Pakistan. It was in 1866 that the first irrigated forest was established at Changa Manga, 90 km south-west of Lahore. The purpose was to supply firewood to the steam-engines of the railways. But in 1888 Dandot coal field was discovered and the firewood for the railway engines was no longer required. However there was considerable demand for firewood in Lahore, Gujranwala, Amritsar and Gujrat and for constructional timber in Karachi, Quetta and other cities. The irrigated forests of Changa Manga became economically so valuable that more forests were developed. By the time Pakistan was created in 1947, there were ten such forests covering an area of 76,902 hectares. Except for the one at Sukkur Barrage, all were located in the Punjab. After the creation of Pakistan this process has continued.

Extension of irrigated forests since then has taken place at Thal, Kotri, Taunsa and Guddu. By 1983-84 there were 200,000 hectares of irrigated forests in Pakistan. The main problem in further extension and maintenance of these forests is that from November to March the water available for irrigation is inadequate. This adversely affects the healthy growth of trees.

Besides planting compact forests, linear plantations along rivers, canals, roads and railways have also been started. By 1983-84, 16,000 hectares were covered with linear plantations. The most common trees planted in irrigated forests are shisham (*Dalbergia sissoo*), babul, *Eucalyptus* spp. and *Prosopis* spp. These forests have become an important source of timber and firewood in Pakistan.

FOREST PRODUCTS

Timber and firewood are the two major forest products of Pakistan. Timber is used for furniture, house construction, railway sleepers, industries and other purposes. With growth in population and rise in standard of living, the consumption of timber is increasing. But the production of timber in Pakistan is slowly decreasing (Table 10.3). The timber produced in Pakistan is insufficient for local consumption. In 1975-76 about 300,000 tons of wood and wood manufactures besides paper and pulp worth more than 90 million rupees were imported. That increased to over

Table 10.3: Forest Products of Pakistan Average Annual Production in Selected Periods

Year	Timber (thousand cubic metres)	Firewood (thousand cubic metres)	Resin (tons)	*Mazri* (tons)	Ephedra (tons)
1966-70	324	487	—	—	—
1971-75	274	459	6441*	17191*	1445*
1976-80	200	467	4370	18075	1155
1981-84	214	469	5554	34000	905

*Data: 1973-75
Source: *Agricultural Statistics of Pakistan*, 1983, Table 131 and *Agricultural Statistics of Pakistan*, 1984, Table 127.

624,000 tons in 1979-80, worth over 163 million rupees and then to 228,000 tons, worth 120 million rupees in 1983-84. This shows that in spite of Pakistan's efforts at afforestation, regeneration and plantation, the gap between the need and the production of forest products is increasing. The irrigated forests, the coniferous and the *bela* (riverain) are the main source of local supply of timber. Annually 214,000 cubic metres of timber were extracted from the forests of Pakistan during 1981-84. The forests of Pakistan supplied about 469,000 cubic metres of firewood annually during 1981-84. Firewood is extracted from all the forests of Pakistan.

Among the minor forest products, resin, ephedra and *mazri* (nannorrhops) are the most important ones. Resin is put to industrial uses in making varnish etc. It is extracted from chir. NWFP and the Punjab are the two provinces which supply resin. NWFP is the major supplier. The production fluctuates from year to year (Table 10.3). A number of medicinal plants are grown in Pakistan forests, the most important being ephedra which is produced in Balochistan. Most of it is consumed by a pharmaceutical factory located in Quetta. *Mazri* is of special note among the minor forest products of Pakistan. It is used for making mats, baskets etc. and for packing purposes. About 34,000 tons are produced annually (Table 10.3). Balochistan produces 90 per cent of the *mazri* and the remaining comes from NWFP.

FOREST COVER AND SOIL EROSION

Great damage is caused to the soils by erosion. Running water and wind are the main agents of soil erosion in Pakistan. Plants check the run-off and act as wind-break as the roots bind the soil particles. Thus by vegetation cover soil erosion is greatly minimized. In Pakistan only 3.8 per cent of the total area is covered with forests.

Aridity prevailing over a large area has made the growth of trees difficult. Over-cutting of trees and over-grazing by animals have destroyed the forests and impeded their regeneration. According to an estimate 14,170 hectares of soils are eroded in Pakistan every year. This is a disturbing situation.

Chapter 11

Agriculture: Problems and Solutions

Agriculture in Pakistan dates back to the Neolithic times. It formed the base of the well known Indus Valley Civilization. Even today agriculture is the mainstay of Pakistan's economy. Starting with stone agricultural tools, today tractors and combines are part of the rural scene. But by and large agriculture in Pakistan continues to be traditional. The common practice is sowing and weeding by hand, field preparation with wooden ploughs, harvesting with sickle and threshing by animal feet. These traditions are age-old. However some fruits of modern science, improved seeds, insecticides, pesticides and fertilizers have reached the nooks and corners of the country. In the field of irrigation Pakistan does not lag behind any country of the world. The present-day agriculture is the outcome of the application of the changing farming technology to the physical environment filtered through the traditional system.

Agriculture is the main contributor to Pakistan's economy though its relative importance has decreased. Its share in the GNP has dropped from 52 per cent in 1950-51 to 24.4 per cent in 1984-85. Agriculture employed 66 per cent of the total labour force in 1950-51 which decreased to 51 per cent in 1984-85 (Table 11.1). The loss in position experienced by agriculture is on account of higher growth registered by other sectors of the economy and not because of a decrease in agricultural production or cultivated acreage. On the other hand both agricultural production and cultivated area have registered a steady increase. Taking 1959-60 as the base year, the production index of major crops was 90 per cent in 1951 and 275 in 1984-85. The total cropped area increased from 13 million hectares in 1950-51 to 20 million in 1984-85. The improvement in the performance of agriculture has been achieved by constant efforts to solve the problems with which agriculture is beset.

Agriculture in Pakistan is facing a number of problems. Some of them are natural while others are man-made. Aridity is the chief natural problem. Topography and soil generally help agriculture but in some unfavourable areas they are impediments. Plant diseases and pests adversely affect agricultural production. Lack of fertilizer and manure, indigenous tools and implements, uneconomic holdings, inadequate marketing facilities and others are man-made problems. The attempt to solve them creates new problems. Irrigation to combat aridity led to the problem of waterlogging and salinity. Introduction of high yielding varieties has exhausted the soils of some useful nutrients.

IRRIGATION TO COMBAT ARIDITY

Irrigation is a very old tradition in Pakistan. Beginning with simple lift irrigation Pakistan has developed one of the most intricate and complex systems of canal irrigation in the world. The fact is that the development of agriculture in Pakistan is largely dependent upon irrigation. About 75 per cent of the total cropped area is under irrigation (1984-85).

Need for irrigation

Rainfall is a critical factor in Pakistan's agriculture. The major part of the country is dry (Fig. 13). The whole of Sindh, most of Balochistan and a large part of the Punjab south of Sahiwal receive less than 250 mm (10 inches) of rainfall. This is the arid region where the potential evapo-transpiration exceeds precipitation by more than two times. North of the arid region, a large part of north Punjab, southern NWFP and northern Balochistan experience semi-arid conditions. There the potential

Table 11.1: Some Parameters of Agriculture in Pakistan in Selected Years

Years	Percentage share of agriculture in GNP	Percentage share in labour force	Production Index (base) (1959-60)	Total Cropped Area (in million hectares)
1950-51	52.0	66.0	90	12.88
1960-61	43.0	59.0	100	14.86
1970-71	36.7	57.6	174	16.62
1980-81	27.9	52.7	249	19.33
1984-85	24.4	50.6	275	19.92

Source: *Economic Survey*, 1986-87, Statistics Table 1.9, 2.2 and 3.1.

evapotranspiration exceeds precipitation but is not twice as great. Humid conditions prevail in the extreme north of Pakistan where the rainfall is 750 mm (30 inches) on the plains and 625 mm (25 inches) on the highlands. In arid and semi-arid regions irrigation is necessary for successful farming. Even in the humid areas the rainfall is not always adequate during the growing season. Year to year variability is high. The coefficient of variability ranges from 30 to 70 per cent. In humid areas it ranges from 30 to 40 per cent and in arid and semi-arid areas from 40 to 70 per cent. The highest variability occurs in a region extending from Jacobabad to Sukkur. Comparatively the monsoon rainfall is more reliable than that from the Western Depressions.

The number of rainy days is a good measure of effectiveness of rainfall for agricultural purposes. Rainfall spread over a sufficiently large number

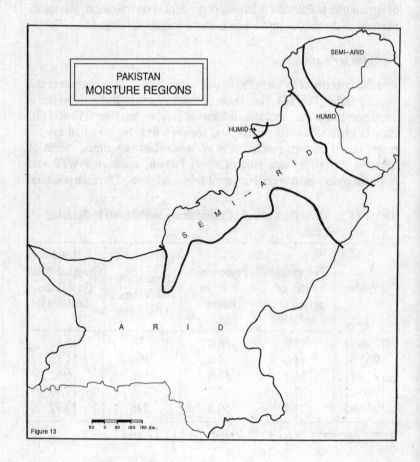

Figure 13

of days is more beneficial for plant growth than heavy downpours of rain coming in a few days. Unfortunately in Pakistan only a small number of days are rainy (Fig. 14). One-third of the country in the south has less than 10 rainy days in a year. Over a major part of the remaining two-thirds the rainy days are less than 20. In the northern areas, largely comprising hills and mountains the number of rainy days exceed 40 but nowhere are they more than 89 (Murree). Such a small number of rainy days is the consequence of a high intensity of rainfall. In Pakistan per rainy day the rainfall varies from 8 mm (Nokkundi) to 26 mm (Wana), when rainfall of 0.25 mm is sufficient for a day to be qualified as rainy. Thus in general, rainfall in Pakistan takes place in heavy showers. Low rainfall coming in heavy downpours within a few days has resulted in the occurrence

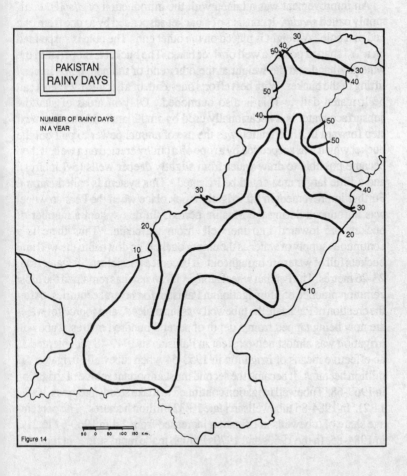

PAKISTAN
RAINY DAYS

NUMBER OF RAINY DAYS
IN A YEAR

Figure 14

50 0 50 100 150 Km.

of long and frequent dry spells. Irrigation during these dry spells becomes necessary over a large part of Pakistan. Thus for assured agriculture supplemental irrigation is a necessity all over the country. Because of these conditions 75 per cent of the cropped area is under irrigation.

Lift Irrigation

Lift irrigation is one of the earliest methods of irrigation practised in Pakistan. In the beginning the water was lifted by hand in a bucket attached to a rope. This could be done only from shallow wells and ditches. It involved a considerable amount of labour and therefore only a small area could be irrigated.

An improvement was attained with the introduction of *dhenkli* commonly called *shaduf*. It consists of a bucket suspended by a rope from one end of a pole. A weight is placed on the other end. The pole is suspended on a 'Y' shaped post at a well or river bank. The bucket is dipped into the water by hand and the weight at the other end of the pole helps in easy lifting of the bucket. With best efforts one-tenth of a hectare (.25 acre) can be irrigated daily. This is also outmoded. Only in areas of shallow subsurface water is it occasionally used by small landholders. The next step forward in lift irrigation was the use of animal power to pull out the bucket which was suspended by a rope on a pulley erected on a well. It then became possible to draw water from slightly deeper wells (5-7 metres), and a little larger area could be irrigated. This system is called *charsa*. Further improvement in lift irrigation took place when the Persian wheel was introduced during the Muslim period. In this system a number of buckets are lowered into the well through a chain. Thus there is a continuous supply of water as the empty buckets go down into the well and buckets full of water are brought out. It becomes possible to lift water from 23-26 metres. The Persian wheel along with *charsa* has remained the most common practice of lift irrigation in Pakistan for several centuries. After the creation of Pakistan, the tubewell was introduced, and sources of water are now being tapped from a depth of several hundred metres. Tubewell irrigation was almost non-existent in Pakistan in 1947-48. It emerged as an effective means of irrigation in 1953-54 when tubewells irrigated .02 million hectares. It became the second most important source of irrigation in 1967-68. Tubewell irrigation continued to make steady progress (Table 11.2). In 1984-85 tubewells irrigated 3.32 million hectares. The percentage share of tubewells in irrigation increased from 2.4 in 1960-61 to 21.3 in 1984-85. In the 1960s and 1970s Punjab made rapid strides in tubewell irrigation, particularly because of the introduction of salinity control and reclamation projects. In the 1980s Sindh, NWFP and Balochistan made notable progress. The development made in Balochistan deserves special mention where from 1979-80 to 1984-85 the area irrigated by tubewells increased by 500,000 hectares. Similarly in Sindh in one year (1981-82) an addition of 700,000 hectares was made in tubewell irrigation. This not only brings out the importance of tubewells but also that of lift irrigation as a whole.

Karez

Karez in an old method of irrigation in Pakistan confined to Balochistan. This irrigation is also practised in Iran under the name of *qanat* and in adjoining Arab countries as *fogarra*. Its place of origin is not known but its distribution covers an area with a close physical similarity.

Karez is a water tunnel or it can be looked upon as a narrow subterranean canal. It starts from the base of the hills and mountains where subsoil water is present. It runs for one or two km underground (sometimes for ten km or more) before it comes out on the surface. The length of the underground journey depends upon the distance between the source of the *karez* and the command area. After coming to the surface the *karez* irrigates the orchards and the agricultural fields. The *karez* throughout its subterranean length is dotted with vertical shafts. The main use of the shafts is to clean and repair the *karez*. If the *karez* is kept in repair and is

Table 11.2: Percentage of Area Irrigated by Different Sources and Total Irrigated Area in Pakistan in Selected Years

Years	Percentage of Area Irrigated by				Area Irrigated (in million hectares)
	Canals	Tubewells	Wells	Others	
1950-51	81.4	—	11.7	6.9	9.25
1960-61	82.5	2.4	8.3	6.8	10.41
1970-71	63.2	21.2	12.2	3.4	10.59
1980-81	74.4	18.9	2.1	4.6	14.90
1984-85	72.6	21.3	1.7	4.4	15.62

Source: *Economic Survey*, 1985-86, Statistical Annexure, Table 3.12, Ministry of Food, Agriculture and Cooperatives, Government of Pakistan, 1986.

not allowed to choke, it may remain running for 100 years or more. The selection of the site for digging a *karez* is done by elderly experienced persons. The digging and repair of *karez* is done by a group of traditional labour. The *karez* is privately owned, usually by a group of persons, and very rarely by an individual. The owners share the water in accordance with the percentage of the share in the *karez* held by them. The problem is that the *karez* water cannot be stopped from flowing, therefore the users must use the water whenever their turn comes irrespective of the fact whether it is day or night.

Karez irrigation is practised only in Balochistan. Within this broad region most of the *karez* are located in Quetta-Pishin Valley, Mastung Valley and favourable areas in Makran. *Karez* irrigation is gradually losing importance. Due to construction of tubewells the water table has dropped and some of the *karez* have become dry. Many *karez* have gone into disuse because of the increasing cost of maintenance and scarcity of skilled labour. *Karez* accounts for about 15 per cent of the irrigated acreage of Balochistan.

Canals

Precursors to canals have been narrow irrigation channels diverted from small shallow streams. They commanded a small area. Such small diversions are still in use in Balochistan and other parts of Pakistan. A small dam is made across narrow and shallow streams and the stored water is used for irrigation. The next step has been the digging of long canals taken off from large rivers. The canals receive water when the level of the rivers is raised by flood. Therefore they are called inundation canals. With advancement in technology it became possible to build weirs and barrages across large rivers. A considerable quantity of water is thus stored in rivers which could be used during the dry period. The canals taken off from the weirs and barrages supply water throughout the year and are called perennial canals.

Inundation Canals

Pakistan has a long history of irrigation canals. Feroz Khan Tughlak dug inundation canals in India for irrigation and colonization. They were laid out in Pakistan up to the middle of the nineteenth century. These canals were seasonal and supplied water only in summer when the donor rivers were in flood. They were thus beneficial for *kharif* (summer) crops. The *rabi* (winter) crops took advantage of the moisture left in the land from the summer flooding. Therefore the emphasis was on growing *kharif* crops.

The inundation canals can only irrigate the flood plains where the land is sufficiently level and slopes downward from the river bank. That is why the network of inundation canals was developed in Sindh and in southern Punjab near Punjnad. A limited number of inundation canals took off from the Upper Indus, Jhelum, Chenab, Ravi and Sutlej. The Bar Uplands were not served by inundation canals as these canals could not rise up 5-7 metre (15-20 feet) high bluffs separating the flood plains and the Bar Uplands. It was after the introduction of the perennial canals that the Bar Uplands were irrigated and heavily colonized.

Perennial Canals

The perennial canals assure the supply of water throughout the year, therefore both the *kharif* and *rabi* crops can be irrigated.

Punjab

It was in 1639 that the first perennial canal in the present-day territory of Pakistan was dug. The credit goes to Ali Mardan Khan. The canal took off from the Ravi River primarily to supply water to the Shalimar Gardens but it also irrigated some agricultural fields which lay in its course. That was the only perennial canal built during the Muslim period. After the first perennial canal dug in 1639, the next was laid out in 1859 namely Upper Bari Doab Canal with its headworks at Madhopur (India). Thereafter other canals were laid out. Sohag Canal, taken out from the Sutlej below Ferozepur was the first colony canal. The Sidhnai Canal in Multan District was a small irrigation project taken out in 1885 from the Ravi. That was followed by a challenging project, the Lower Chenab Canal (1887-92). Its intake is located at Khanki and it irrigates over one million hectares. The Lower Jhelum Canal came next in 1901. It takes off from the Jhelum at Rasul and irrigates 0.4 million hectares of the Chaj Doab. It was followed by the Triple Project (Upper Jhelum-Upper Chenab-Lower Bari Doab Canals). Its construction was started in 1909 and completed in 1917. The Upper Chenab Canal which was constructed first takes off from the Chenab River at Marala at the foot of the Himalayas. After irrigating the upper part of the Rechna Doab, it crosses the River Ravi by an aqueduct near Balloki and becomes the Lower Bari Doab Canal. By the construction of the Upper Chenab Canal the Lower Chenab Canal was starved so the Upper Jhelum Canal was constructed to feed the Lower Chenab Canal. The Upper Jhelum Canal has its intake at Mangla. It runs for a considerable distance parallel to the Jhelum River at the foot of the Salt Range. It irrigates parts of the Chaj Doab and discharges into the Chenab at Khanki to reinforce the Lower Chenab Canal. Thus the canal systems of the Jhelum, Chenab and Ravi have been interlinked.

Until the creation of Pakistan in 1947 there was no irrigation project to irrigate the Sindh Sagar Doab, the interfluve between the Jhelum and the Indus. The Thal project was undertaken soon after the emergence of Pakistan to irrigate that area. A barrage (Jinnah Barrage) has been built across the Indus near Kalabagh. The canals taken out from the barrage irrigate the Thal area. In that area villages and towns have been located at regular intervals. Jauharabad, Quaidabad and Liaquatabad are some of the towns. About 180 miles downstream from Kalabagh, Taunsa Barrage (1953) has been built on the Indus. It irrigates a large area of Muzaffargarh and Dera Ghazi Khan District. A major Kalabagh multipurpose dam project is planned 120 miles downstream from Tarbela Dam. It will irrigate a large area, produce electricity and control floods.

Sindh

The Indus is the only major river which flows through the province of Sindh. It has irrigated, for many years the agricultural fields of Sindh through inundation canals. It was in 1932 that Sindh got its first barrage (Sukkur Barrage). Built on the Indus at Sukkur, it is 4,725 feet long, contains 66 spans, each 60 feet wide and is closed with iron gates 18 feet high. Three canals take off from the right bank and four from the left bank. The command area of the canal is 3 million hectares, of which 2.2 million can be irrigated every year. After independence two more barrages were built in Sindh, Kotri and Guddu. Kotri Barrage at Kotri, close to Hyderabad on the Indus was commissioned in 1959. It contains 44 spans of 60 feet each. Three canals take off from the left bank and one from the right bank. It irrigates 1.11 million hectares. Guddu barrage which was built in 1962 is 10 miles east of Kashmor. Its command area is 1.16 million hectares.

NWFP

It was about a hundred years ago that NWFP got its first canal (the Lower Swat Canal). Then came the Upper Swat Canal. After the creation of Pakistan, Warsak Multipurpose Project was completed near Peshawar on the Kabul River. Canals taken from Warsak Project irrigate 48,000 hectares.

Kurramgarhi is yet another important project completed in NWFP. It is located on the Kurram River at Kurramgarhi. A permanent head in place of a temporary one has been built to provide water to the Bannu Civil Canals. It improves the irrigational facilities of 53,000 hectares and irrigates an additional 61,000 hectares.

Small Dams

Besides large irrigation projects a number of small dams have also been built. They irrigate relatively smaller areas and are located on small streams and command small alluvial areas in hilly regions.They are therefore located in the Western Highlands. Some of them have been built by the Water and Power Development Authority (WAPDA) while others by the Small Dams Organization set up by the Agricultural Development Corporation. Rawal Dam is one of the small dams on the Kurang River. Besides supplying water to Islamabad, it irrigates about 5,000 hectares. Khanpur Dam on the Haro River, irrigating 14,760 hectares in Abbottabad, Attock and Rawalpindi District has been recently commissioned. Tanda, Baran and Gomal are some of the important small dams of NWFP. Balochistan has a number of small dams. The Nari-Bolan project utilizes monsoon flow of the Bolan River to irrigate 9,700 hectares of the Sibi Plains. Narachip Project irrigates 1,300 hectares of Loralai District. Hab Dam in Lasbela District is designed to irrigate 34,000 hectares of Lasbela and Karachi. It was commissioned in 1982.

INDUS WATER TREATY

In 1947, Pakistan was created and the province of the Punjab was divided. Part of it went to India and part to Pakistan. The headworks at Madhopur on the Ravi and at Ferozepur on the Sutlej were in India but many of the canals taken off from them were irrigating agricultural lands of Pakistan.

A number of committees were constituted to deal with the problems arising out of the division of the Punjab. The question of sharing of water between East Punjab (India) and West Punjab (Pakistan) was referred to Committee B. The unanimous agreement of the members of the committee is given in paragraph 15 of the Report which states, 'The committee is agreed that there is no question of varying authorized share of water to which the two zones and canals are authorized.' This agreement was affirmed by the Punjab Partition Committee also which was headed by the Governor of the province. Therefore this problem was not referred to the arbitral tribune appointed to settle the disputes between India and Pakistan arising out of partition. The life of the tribunal ended on 31 March 1948. The very next day (1 April 1948) India stopped the water from flowing in every canal entering Pakistan from India. It was a serious matter. Pakistan took it up with India and an interim agreement was arrived at on 4 May 1948. For a permanent solution of the problem negotiation started in 1952 under the auspices of the World Bank. In September 1960, an agreement was signed which is known as the Indus Water Treaty. Under this Pakistan received exclusive rights of the three western rivers (Indus, Jhelum and Chenab) and India those of the three eastern rivers (Ravi, Beas and Sutlej). There was to be a transitional period ending on 31 March 1970. This was extendable by three more years. During this transitional period India agreed to continue to supply water to Pakistan. During the same period it was expected that Pakistan would construct two storage dams, five barrages, one gated syphon and eight link canals and divert some of the

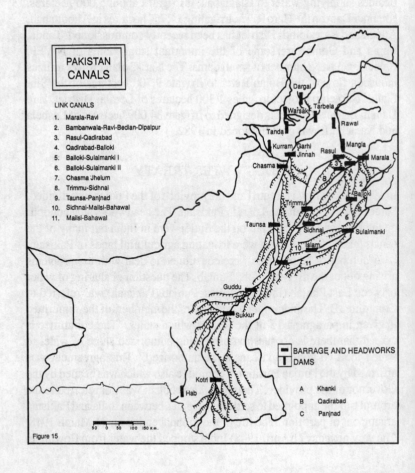

PAKISTAN CANALS

LINK CANALS

1. Marala-Ravi
2. Bambanwala-Ravi-Bedian-Dipalpur
3. Rasul-Qadirabad
4. Qadirabad-Balloki
5. Balloki-Sulaimanki I
6. Balloki-Sulaimanki II
7. Chasma Jhelum
8. Trimmu-Sidhnai
9. Taunsa-Panjnad
10. Sidhnai-Mailsi-Bahawal
11. Mailsi-Bahawal

■ BARRAGE AND HEADWORKS
T DAMS

A   Khanki
B   Qadirabad
C   Panjnad

50 0 50 100 150 Km.

Figure 15

water of the western rivers in the interfluves of the eastern rivers. The construction cost was to be met by aid from USA, UK, West Germany, Canada, Australia and New Zealand. A part of the cost was to be paid by India also. The remaining expenditure was to be met by Pakistan. The replacement works were entrusted to WAPDA. All the replacement work has been completed except Tarbela Dam which is nearing completion. The Tarbela Dam is located on the Indus near Tarbela about 47 km upstream from Attock. It is a multipurpose project designed to store 11.0 million acre feet of water and to generate 2.1 million KW of electricity. It irrigates part of the Potwar Plateau but its main function is to supply water to Chashma-Jhelum Link Canal through which Trimmu-Sidhnai-Mailsi-Bahawal Link System will also be fed. The Tarbela Dam will also feed Taunsa-Punjnad Link Canal. The barrages, Jinnah, Chashma, Taunsa, Guddu, Sukkur and Kotri built on the Indus, will be supplied water from the Tarbela Dam in winter, when the flow is low. The completion of Tarbela Dam has been delayed on account of technical difficulties including some defect in design. Tarbela Dam though not complete is functioning and is supplying water for irrigation and generating electric power. However the silting in the Tarbela Dam is heavy.

The Mangla Dam was completed in 1969. It is a storage dam on the Jhelum with a storage capacity of 5.5 million acre feet. It will be possible in future to raise the storing capacity to 9.6 million acre feet. It supplies water to canals irrigating Chaj and Bari Doabs. The water is also used to generate electricity. Ultimately three million kW of electricity will be generated.

Barrages

The five barrages and a gated syphon constructed under the Indus Water Treaty are the following:

1. *Chashma Barrage*: It is located on the Indus 64 km downstream from Jinnah Barrage and was completed in 1970. It is designed to divert one million cusecs into Chashma-Jhelum Link through which it will irrigate areas served by Sidhnai-Mailsi-Bahawal Link System and also Haveli and Rangpur Canals.
2. *Rasul Barrage*: It is a barrage on the Jhelum 4 km downstream from Rasul weir. It was completed in 1968. Its flood discharge capacity is 850,00 cusecs. It supplies water to Rasul-Qadirabad Link Canal for ultimate supply to Sulaimanki Barrage on the Sutlej.
3. *Marala Barrage* : It is located on the Chenab and was completed in

1969. Its flood discharge capacity is 1.1 million cusecs. It supplies water to Ravi Link Canal and Upper Chenab Canal.

4. *Qadirabad Barrage*: Located on the Chenab 32 km from Khanki weir, it was completed in 1970. Its discharge capacity is .9 million cusecs. It supplies water to Qadirabad-Baloki Link through Rasul-Qadirabad Link.

5. *Mailsi-Syphon*: It is a gated syphon located on the Sutlej near Mailsi. Its purpose is to carry water on the Sidhnai-Mailsi Link across the Sutlej into the Bahawal Canal. The Sidhnai-Mailsi Link gets water from the Sidhnai Barrage.

Link Canals

Link canals are the main carriers of water from the western rivers to the eastern rivers and from the rivers into canals. Important link canals are the following:

1. Rasul-Qadirabad Link carries water from Rasul Barrage on the Jhelum to the Chenab.
2. Qadirabad-Balloki Link is an extension of Rasul-Qadirabad Link by which the water is transferred to the Ravi River.
3. Balloki-Sulaimanki Link connects the Ravi and the Sutlej.
4. Trimmu-Sidhnai transfers water from Trimmu Barrage into the Ravi.
5. Sidhnai-Mailsi takes the same water into the Sutlej.
6. Mailsi-Bahawal Link supplies water to the Bahawal Canal.
7. Chashma-Jhelum Link transfers water from Chashma Barrage on the Indus to the Jhelum River.
8. Taunsa-Punjnad Link carries water from Taunsa on the Indus to the Chenab River to feed the Punjnad canals.

Besides the construction of new links, remodelling of the existing link canals namely Marala-Ravi, Balloki-Sulaimanki and Bombanwala-Ravi-Badian-Dipalpur Link Canal was done.

Thus the Punjab has been interlaced with a network of canals. The loss of the three eastern rivers has been greatly made up. With the Tarbela Dam functioning fully the position will further improve.

WATERLOGGING AND SALINITY

Canal irrigation has not been all blessings for Pakistan. It has created the twin problems of waterlogging and salinity. Perennial canal irrigation was introduced in Pakistan as early as 1859. By the early years of the present century waterlogging and salinity gained such an intensity that remedial measures became a necessity. Since 1912 efforts have been made to tackle the problems. But neither was any comprehensive survey of the affected areas undertaken nor was any comprehensive plan to solve the problem chalked out. It was in 1953-54 that detailed mapping of soils and land use of the Indus Plains was done under the auspices of the Colombo Plan Administration. It revealed that no less than 4.7 million hectares (11.6 million acres) were poorly drained or waterlogged. About 6.5 million hectares (16 million acres) were severely affected. Furthermore .4 million hectares (100,000 acres) of good irrigated land were becoming unproductive every year.

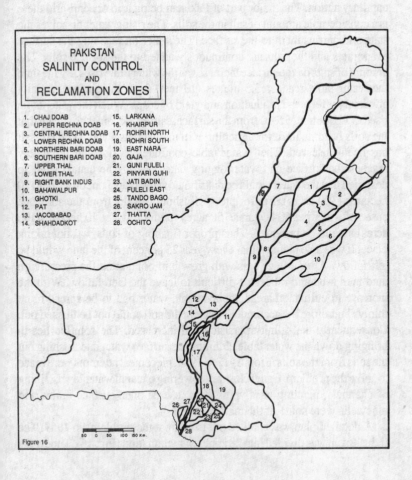

PAKISTAN
SALINITY CONTROL
AND
RECLAMATION ZONES

1. CHAJ DOAB
2. UPPER RECHNA DOAB
3. CENTRAL RECHNA DOAB
4. LOWER RECHNA DOAB
5. NORTHERN BARI DOAB
6. SOUTHERN BARI DOAB
7. UPPER THAL
8. LOWER THAL
9. RIGHT BANK INDUS
10. BAHAWALPUR
11. GHOTKI
12. PAT
13. JACOBABAD
14. SHAHDADKOT
15. LARKANA
16. KHAIRPUR
17. ROHRI NORTH
18. ROHRI SOUTH
19. EAST NARA
20. GAJA
21. GUNI FULELI
22. PINYARI GUHI
23. JATI BADIN
24. FULELI EAST
25. TANDO BAGO
26. SAKRO JAM
27. THATTA
28. OCHITO

50 0 50 100 150 Km.

Figure 16

Inundation canals existed in Pakistan without causing waterlogging or salinity. The canals and fields received water only in one season (summer) when the rivers were in spate. In the winter season the canals remained dry and evapotranspiration was adequate to keep down the water table. With the introduction of perennial canals water has been available throughout the year. The fields are irrigated both during the *kharif* (summer) and *rabi* (winter) seasons. Thus the water seeps to the subsurface throughout the year from the unlined canals and the irrigated fields. This constant supply of water is more than that which can be lost by evapotranspiration. Consequently accumulation of water in the subsurface starts and the water table begins to rise. So long as the water table remains at a depth of 5 metres or more below the surface there is no problem. When the water table rises to 5 metres from the surface the water begins to rise to the surface by capillary action. The major part of Pakistan being arid or semi-arid there is a considerable amount of salt in the soils. The rising water dissolves the salts and carries them to the surface. The water on reaching the surface evaporates and the salts are continuously added to the surface soils. The amount of salts on the surface increases as the water table rises. By the time the water table reaches 3.3 metres (10 feet) from the surface, salinity adversely affects the production and yield of crops. When the water table rises to 1.5 metres (5 feet) from the surface, salinity becomes so severe that the soils become unfit for agriculture. In many areas a white crust of salt has been observed. The water table continues to rise and ultimately reaches the surface and waterlogging takes place. The canals were so designed that the water would be distributed at the rate of one cusec per 120 hectares (300 acres). But for proper flushing of salts from the soils one cusec of water per 60 hectares/150 acres (preferably per 40 hectares/100 acres) should be provided. Thus proper flushing of soils was not taking place. It was also planned that every year 25 per cent of the land would be left fallow. After a few years with growth in population the pressure on land increased and it became difficult to leave the land fallow. With the increase in cultivated areas, the available water had to be spread more thinly. Therefore the accumulated salt in the soil could not be flushed out. Consequently the salinity persisted and increased. The solution lies in bringing down the water table, draining the surface water and flushing out the salts from the soils. From 1912 to 1954, piecemeal attempts were made to solve the problem. Canal closures, lowering of canal water levels, lining of channels, planting eucalyptus trees, use of open surface drains and tubewells were some of the methods used.

A detailed plan was chalked out to combat the problems in 1959. The Indus Basin was divided into 28 zones of reclamation (Fig. 16). Tubewells and drains were to play the key role in reclamation. The tubewells were to pump out water at a rate faster than that of the recharge of the subsoils. Consequently the water table would drop. In case the pumped water was fresh it could be used for irrigation. The underground water over a large part of the Punjab is fresh. The application of heavy doses of pumped water into the fields would flush out the salts. In case the water was saline, it would be drained into the rivers to be diluted. If this was not possible, it would be drained out in some safe area. In Sindh some saline water will be drained into the Manchar Lake. For this 31,000 tubewells and 32,000 miles of drains were planned. The plan was to be executed in phases and was to be fully implemented by 1985. But a recent estimate puts 8 million hectares within 3.3 metres (10 feet) of the subsurface water which is the danger zone for waterlogging. About 3.5 million hectares have been seriously affected by waterlogging and salinity. Only 2.5 million hectares have been protected from this double menace. SCARP has still a long way to go. Furthermore with the tubewells becoming old their maintenance, operation and replacement are becoming costly and difficult.

IMPROVED SEEDS

Improved and good quality seeds can increase the yield of crops by 10 to 20 per cent. Efforts are being made in various agricultural research centres of Pakistan to develop improved varieties. Appreciable success has been achieved particularly in wheat, rice, cotton, maize and gram. Mexi-Pak wheat, Irri-Pak rice and Nayab 78 cotton are most widely known. The chief problem is to popularize, multiply and distribute the seeds to the farmers. The Government is making efforts to achieve this goal. But the success achieved is limited. Quality seeds are sold to the farmers at a subsidized rate. Laboratories have been set up to test the quality of seeds so that certified seeds are distributed among the farmers. Still the farmers are not quite satisfied with the quality of seeds supplied. Improved seeds are not available in sufficient quantity. To meet the demand, seed processing plants were set up recently at Khanewal (Punjab) and Sakrand (Sindh). Two more are being established at Rahimyar Khan and Sahiwal. As a result the improved seed distributed in 1977-87 was 48,420 tons. That increased to 86,390 tons in 1984-85. Punjab consumes 84 per cent of the improved seeds, followed by Sindh (10 per cent). Among crops, wheat accounts for 66 per cent followed by cotton, 23 per cent.

High-yielding varieties require heavy doses of fertilizer and water. These varieties extract nutrients from the soils in large quantities. Therefore after a few years of continuous cultivation of high-yielding varieties the soils start to lose their fertility. Some suitable crop rotation should be developed so that the soils may get sufficient rest and are able to regain lost vitality.

FERTILIZER

The use of manure for increasing crop yield is known from antiquity and has been practised in Pakistan for centuries. Cowdung, oil cake, compost etc. are traditional manures but they are not available in sufficient quantity. A large quantity of cowdung is burnt as fuel and oil cake is too costly to become popular as manure. The answer lies in the application of chemical fertilizers.

In Pakistan chemical fertilizers were consumed in a negligible quantity until 1951-52 (2,000-3,000 nutrient tons). Since then a rapid increase in the use of fertilizers started. In 1960-61, 31,400 tons were consumed which increased to 1,253,000 tons in 1984-85 (Table 11.3). This increase has been achieved after fighting the fear and prejudices that the farmers had developed against chemical fertilizers. The Government had to subsidize the price of fertilizers to popularize them. The subsidy continues but the Government is gradually decreasing it and will eventually withdraw it.

The consumption of fertilizer per hectare of cultivated land has substantially increased from 24 kg in 1974-75 to 63 kg in 1984-85 (Table 11.4). But it is low when compared to some other countries. In 1983-84, USSR consumed 66 kg per cultivated hectare, USA 105 kg, Egypt 360 kg, Japan 437 kg, and Netherlands 789 kg. The consumption in Pakistan was however higher than that in India (39 kg), Iran (42 kg) and Turkey (45 kg). An examination of province-wise consumption (Table 11.4) reveals that Sindh records the highest consumption (92 kg per cultivated hectare) followed by Punjab (61 kg), NWFP, (37 kg) and Balochistan (15 kg).

Table 11.3: Consumption, Production, Import of Fertilizer in Pakistan in Selected Years (thousand nutrient tons)

Year	Consumption	Production	Import
1960-61	31.4	11.5	35.9
1970-71	283.2	233.0	151.0
1980-81	1079.5	439.0	574.0
1984-85	1253.3	1119.0	342.0

Source: *Agricultural Statistics of Pakistan*, 1980 and 1985, Table 70, 74 and 75.

The consumption of fertilizer, though low in Pakistan is not met by local production. In 1984-85 more than 1.25 million nutrient tons of fertilizer were consumed but the production was 1.12 million tons. Therefore about .34 million tons worth 1,393.8 million rupees had to be imported.

The gap between consumption and production is being bridged, but the import is quite heavy because of rapidly increasing consumption (Table 11.3). The soils of Pakistan are deficient particularly in organic matters therefore 75 per cent of the fertilizer consumed is nitrogenous. Phosphates constitute 23 per cent and potash 2 per cent. *Rabi* (winter) crops consume 62 per cent of the fertilizer and *kharif* (summer) crops, 38 per cent.

PLANT PROTECTION

Pests and diseases cause great damage to the crops. It is estimated that every year 10-15 per cent of the crops are destroyed by pests and diseases. Therefore the Government has taken steps to control them. Two measures have been adopted : protective and curative. Sowing of treated seeds is the only preventive measure adopted. The area covered by such seeds is less than 5 per cent of the cropland. Curative measures include aerial and ground spraying. Annually about 5 per cent of the cropped area is covered by ground spraying and 4 per cent by aerial spraying. This shows that a very small area receives plant protection notwithstanding that only the affected area has to be sprayed. For quite a few years the Government provided this service at a highly subsidized rate. In 1980-81 the subsidy was withdrawn for ground spraying in Sindh and Punjab. Aerial spraying continues to be subsidized all over Pakistan.

Table 11.4: Consumption of Fertilizer per Cultivated Hectare in Pakistan in Selected Years

Provinces	1974-75	1979-80	1984-85
Balochistan	5	11	15
NWFP	14	35	37
Punjab	24	55	61
Sindh	32	65	92
Pakistan	24	54	63

Source of raw data: *Agricultural Statistics of Pakistan,* 1983 Tables 59, 70 and 71, and 1985, Tables 60, 70 and 71.

MECHANIZATION

Agriculture in Pakistan is largely dependent upon traditional tools and implements. Wooden ploughs and iron sickles still dominate the scene though tractors and threshers have made great headway. In the meanwhile the debate continues whether to mechanize agriculture or not. The main argument advanced against mechanization is that it results in farm labour unemployment. Machines replace labour, therefore the introduction of machines in the farm turns some labour surplus. It is a matter of concern for a country where unemployment is high. It may be counter argued that if mechanization of agriculture becomes common in Pakistan, a large number of workshops and mechanics will be required for repair and maintenance of farm machinery. Thus a positive avenue for employment of surplus farm labour will open up. Domestic production of farm machinery is very limited therefore the bulk of the machinery and the spare parts have to be imported. A considerable amount of the meagre foreign exchange of the country is spent on this, but it may be pointed out that increasing demand may lead to the establishment of farm machine industries within the country which will absorb some of the surplus farm labour and also save foreign exchange. It is also argued that mechanization will increase the consumption of oil and lubricants in which Pakistan is deficient.

Low yield is one of the important problems faced by agriculture in Pakistan. Some people erroneously think that the use of machinery will increase the yield substantially. The fact is that application of fertilizer, improved seeds, adequate water, insecticides and pesticides improve the yield considerably whereas mechanization helps in the increase of yield to a very limited extent. Tractors play the key role in mechanization. They make possible the use of disc plough, mould-board plough, chisel plough, disc harrow, cultivators and other machines by which the field is better prepared, soils are better pulverized and deep ploughing is possible. Better preparation of land does help the healthy growth of plants.

The tractors not only do the work efficiently but also much more quickly than can be done by slow bullocks. They replace not only the labour force but also the work animals. A survey of agricultural machinery reveals that the tractors had decreased the number of work animals by 56 per cent. Thus the cost of maintenance of tractors and farm machinery can be compensated for by reduction in the number of work animals. The land released from feeding the work animals may produce food for human consumption and raw material for industries.

In this context it is worthwhile to examine the Government policy. In

Warsak Dam and lake in NWFP

Mangla Power House and irrigation canal in Punjab

Primitive irrigation method still in use – the *karez*

A man-made lake for irrigation at Mangla

1952 the Pakistan Agricultural Inquiry Committee discouraged the use of tractors in view of unemployment prevailing in the country. It was estimated that complete mechanization would displace two-thirds of the farm labour force. On the other hand Food and Agricultural Committee of 1960 strongly recommended the mechanization of agriculture. Since then the Government has continuously encouraged mechanization. Import of tractors and other farm machinery is increasing. Loans for purchase of farm machinery are advanced. Pakistan Agricultural Research Council propagates the use of farm machinery in various ways. The result has been that the number of tractors and other farm machinery is continuously increasing. Up to 1975 about 5,000 tractors were imported annually. That increased to 15,000 annually between 1976-80 and 22,000 between 1981-85. The tractors in general are used on large farms. In 1975, the average size of farms using tractors was 22 hectares when the average size of farms in Pakistan is about 4.7 hectares. More than 80 per cent of the tractors were in the Punjab. Besides tractors, tillers, combines, harvesters, threshers, reapers and transplanters are also used. The use of machinery particularly in the development of new agricultural land is now common.

FARM SIZE AND FRAGMENTATION OF HOLDINGS

The subsistence holding in Pakistan is taken to be 5.0 hectares (12.5 acres) at the present level of technology. The average size of farms in 1960 was slightly smaller (4.1 hectares/10.1 acres) than that of the subsistence holding (Table 11.5). This improved to 5.3 hectares (13 acres) in 1972 but became smaller again (4.7 hectares/11.6 acres) in 1980. Similar conditions were observed in owner, owner-cum-tenant and tenant farms. The owner-cum-tenant farm has remained larger than subsistence holdings in all the three censuses, 1960, 1972 and 1980. The average size of tenant farms is the smallest (3.9 hectares).

The average farm size in Pakistan is not much smaller than the subsistence holding. But a closer scrutiny reveals disturbing conditions. In 1960, 77 per cent of the farms were smaller than 5.0 hectares. In 1972 it improved slightly (68 per cent) but deteriorated again in 1980 (74 per cent). Farms smaller than subsistence level covered 32 per cent of the farm area in 1960, 30 per cent in 1972 and 34 per cent in 1980. This indicates that most of the farmers have a hard time trying to get a living from small holdings and have to supplement their income from other sources. Mechanization is being popularized in Pakistan. The Government is encouraging this trend and the landowners are making efforts in this direction. For farming by tractors it is estimated that the minimum size of a farm should be 20 hectares (50 acres). The small size of farms is an impediment in the mechanization of farms. Three per cent of the total number of farms, covering an area of 23 per cent are larger than 20 hectares. This is a dilemma facing Pakistan's agriculture and a solution has to be worked out.

Not only is the size of farms small in Pakistan, but they are also fragmented i.e., a farm is divided into a number of discontinuous plots. The problem is less acute in newly-settled canal colonies. It has gained dangerous proportions in many rain-fed farming areas. For example in Attock and Rawalpindi Districts fragmentation in 12 to 18 parts of a holding of 1-2 hectares is very common.

In Pakistan 58 per cent of the total number of farms are fragmented. The average number of fragments per farm is 3.7. About 5 per cent of the farms are divided into 10 or more fragments. The average size of each fragment is 0.1 hectare in farms of .5 hectare or smaller, and in farms of 20-60 hectares the average size of pieces is 4.8 hectares. Fragmentation is highest in owner-cum-tenant farms (88 per cent) and least in tenant farms (38 per cent). The percentage of owner-fragmented farms is 57.

Fragmentation causes loss of time and energy. Irrigation becomes extremely difficult since water has to flow through land belonging to other persons. Use of tractors becomes difficult as also does the care and protection of the standing crops. Fragmentation of holdings is the result of many causes. One of the important factors is the law of inheritance. The division not only reduces size of farms but also leads to fragmentation

Table 11.5: Number, Area and Average Size of Farms Classified by Tenure in Pakistan, 1960, 1972 and 1980.

Tenure	Number of Farms (per cent)			Area of Farms (per cent)			Average Size of Farms (in hectares)		
	1960	'72	'80	1960	'72	'80	1960	'72	'80
Owner-cultivator	41	42	55	38	39	52	4.1	5.3	4.7
Owner-cum-tenant	17	24	19	23	31	26	5.3	6.8	6.4
Tenant	42	34	26	39	30	22	3.8	4.5	3.9
All farms	—	—	—	—	—	—	4.1	5.3	4.7

Source: *Agricultural Census of Pakistan*, 1960, 1972 and 1980.

because parcels of both good and bad lands have to be shared. Sale of parts of the holding and division of small pieces of farm among tenants also lead to fragmentation.

The ill effects of fragmentation of holdings have been felt for quite a long time. As early as 1920, voluntary consolidation of farms was attempted in the Punjab. This produced no result. An act was passed in the Punjab in 1936 and in NWFP in 1946 under which consolidation was made compulsory if two-thirds of the villagers were in favour of consolidation. Some positive result was produced in the Punjab but in NWFP the progress was negligible. When conditions became critical in Punjab an act was passed in 1952 whereby consolidation was made compulsory. In 1966 Consolidation of Holding Ordinance was promulgated all over Pakistan but it was opposed by many farmers. Consolidation is being done but the progress is far from satisfactory. Only 5 per cent of the farm area was consolidated by 1985.

LAND TENURE AND LAND REFORM

Land Tenure

Land tenure expresses the relationship both legal and customary that exists between the landowner, the tenant, the cultivator and others who have some interest in the land. The owner-cultivator loves the land and takes good care of it. The tenant-cultivator is interested in taking out the best from the land even if in so doing the quality of land is impaired.

Table 11.6: Number, Area and Average Size of Private Farms by Size Groups in Pakistan.

Farm Size	Number of Farms (per cent)			Area of Farms (per cent)			Average Size of Farms (in hectares)		
	1960	'72	'80	1960	'72	'80	1960	'72	'80
Smaller than 5 hectares	77	68	74	32	30	34	1.7	2.3	1.5
5 to 20 hectares	21	29	23	45	46	43	10.2	8.3	6
Larger than 20 hectares	2	3	3	23	24	23	85.9	40.1	72.2

Source: *Agricultural Census of Pakistan*, 1960, 1972 and 1980.

Therefore the land tenure has a direct bearing on the agricultural practice and production. Land tenure in ancient times was communal. Individual proprietorship did not exist. The Aryans who came to this region in 1500 BC introduced the concept of family ownership of land which paved the way for the emergence of individual ownership. At the time of the Moghal advent three land tenure systems were in vogue, namely, village tenancy, family ownership and individual proprietorship. For collection of government dues, tax collectors were appointed who either kept a part of the tax collected as remuneration or were allotted rent-free land. The rent collection later became hereditary which was the beginning of *zamindari* system. The Moghals allotted *jagirs* (rent-free land) as reward to individuals.

During the period of political instability immediately before the extension of the British rule in the Punjab and NWFP persons of influence had acquired large estates. When the British came, they recognized their proprietary rights and they became big landlords. The British also granted large rent-free *jagirs* to individuals who had helped them in conquering the region. The landlords and *jagirdars* could rent land to the tenants. In the eastern part of the Punjab *mahalwari* system was in vogue. In this system the peasants of a village were responsible collectively and individually for the payment of land revenue. The village comprised small peasants.

Most of Sindh was allotted to local chiefs as *jagirs* by the Moghals. The British recognized this right. In northern parts of Sukkur and Shikarpur Districts, *pattadari* system prevailed whereby lands were held by individuals on payment of nominal rent to the Government. Besides, there were *zamindari* and peasant holdings in which the ownership of the land was vested with the state but occupants possessed heritable, divisible and transferable rights as long as they paid revenue to the state. The British introduced *ryotwari* system in which the state, keeping the proprietary rights, leased the land to the tenants-at-will called *haris*. The tenants-at-will paid the rent only for the years that they ploughed the fields. In 1932, with the construction of Sukkur Barrage perennial canals were laid out. The moneyed people purchased the land at high prices and rented them to poor cultivators. Thus a class of big landlords emerged. Pakistan consequently inherited a complex land tenure system. Some of these systems are briefly described below.

Peasant proprietary system is the one in which the landowners are the cultivators. About 50 per cent of the total area of Pakistan is cultivated by owner-peasants.

Mahalwari system prevails in the Punjab and the same system is called *bhaichara* in NWFP. Under this system the land revenue is fixed on the village as a whole. The owners are collectively and individually responsible for the payment of the revenue.

Pattadari system of the Punjab and NWFP is the one in which the land is divided among owners according to some customary formula. Each proprietor manages his own land and pays the revenue fixed on his land. But all the owners are collectively responsible to the state for payment of revenue. In Sukkur and Shikarpur Districts of Sindh land under *pattadari* system was given to Afghan settlers on a nominal rent for a fixed period of time. They had the full rights to manage the land the way they desired and they passed the land to their heirs on their own terms and conditions.

Jagirdari system consists of the award of proprietary right or assignment of land revenue to an individual called *jagirdar* by the Government. Large estates were thus given as reward to individuals for their loyalty to the Government or for doing some work of distinction. Such *jagirdars* wielded great influence and prestige.

Absentee landlordism led to the development of occupancy tenants and tenants-at-will. Under occupancy tenure the occupants have the right of cultivation on payment of a small rent. They are not the owners of land but their right of cultivation is heritable and irrevocable. The tenants-at-will are hired by landlords and have no occupancy rights. It is estimated that about 50 per cent of the cultivated land is held under these two tenures.

Land Reform

The need for land reform has been felt for quite some time. In 1887 the Punjab Tenancy Act was passed which was applicable to NWFP also. The most notable feature of the act was that the tenants who had held the land continuously for twenty years were protected from ejectment. No protection was given to the tenants-at-will except their claim on uncut crop and cost of preparing land which they could not sow because of ejectment. In 1945 Tenancy Law Committee recommended to the Government to grant perpetual rights to the *haris* who had personally cultivated at least four acres of land of the same landlord for a period of eight consecutive years. They could be ejected only if they failed to cultivate the land or pay the rent or on other similar grounds. No action was taken on the report.

In 1950 Sindh Tenancy Act was passed. It gave permanent rights to the tenants (*haris*) who had cultivated at least four acres of land continuously for three years. It abolished *begar* (free services) and various illegal charges. These protections did not help the *haris* because the landlords were strong and the tenants were weak, ignorant and illiterate. From 1950 to 1952 five tenancy acts were passed in the Punjab. Some of the important provisions of the acts are as stated below:

a. A landlord holding more than 100 acres was to keep only 50 acres for self-cultivation and the rest was to be given to the tenants.
b. The share of the landlord in the produce was fixed at 40 per cent and he was also to pay the Government dues in the same proportion.
c. All *jagirs* were abolished except military *jagirs* and those connected with religious and charitable institutions.
d. Tenants could be ejected only if they failed to pay the tax in time or did not cultivate the land, or the landlord wanted the land for self-cultivation.
e. Occupancy tenancy was abolished and the creation of new tenants was prohibited.

These measures failed to be effective because of the strong position of the landlords and the weak position of the tenants. The tenants continued to enjoy concessions of the Government dues and the landlord threatened to withdraw the additional concessions that the tenants enjoyed such as a free plot of land for growing fodder and vegetables, supply of seeds and manure and advancing of funds if need arose. Further, the period of the landlords' declaration was extended again and again.

From 1952 to 1959 at least three tenancy acts were passed in NWFP. The provisions of the acts, though milder were similar to those of the Punjab. The acts like those of Sindh and the Punjab failed to bring any appreciable change in the existing tenure systems.

In 1958, Martial Law was promulgated in Pakistan and in 1959 the following land reforms were introduced·

1. Ceilings to holdings were fixed at 500 acres of irrigated lands and 1,000 acres of unirrigated lands.
2. The tenants had the first claim to purchase the resumed land.
3. The landlords were given compensation through interest-bearing bonds.
4. *Jagirdari* of all types was abolished without any compensation.
5. Tenure of the tenants was granted.
6. Division of land into uneconomic holdings was prohibited.
7. A plan for consolidation of holdings was adopted.
8. A comprehensive plan for land utilization was formulated.
9. Credit facilities were arranged for new landowners.

Contradictory statistics have been issued regarding resumption and allotment under the Martial Law Regulations. According to the first estimate about 2.2 million acres were resumed of which .825 million acres were sold or auctioned. A later estimate puts the area of resumed land at 1.1 million acres and the land disposed of at .496 million acres. In addition 70,000 acres of *jagirdaris* were also resumed. These land reform measures did not break the backbone of the feudal lords nor did they establish the confirmed rights of the peasants. But they did pave the path for future development in this direction.

In 1972, more positive land reforms were introduced. Some of the important features were the following:

1. The ceiling on land ownership was reduced from 500 acres of irrigated land to 150 acres and from 1,000 acres of unirrigated land to 300 acres. Land owned above the permissible limit was to be surrendered to the Government without any compensation.
2. All the resumed land was to be distributed among the tillers free of cost.
3. *Shikargah* (hunting grounds) except those already owned by the Government were taken over by the Government and distributed among cultivators.
4. All lands of the Pat Feeder area (Balochistan) were resumed and distributed among the local poor farmers.
5. Land over 100 acres acquired by a government servant during his tenure of office or two years after his retirement was to be confiscated.
6. All state lands were to be given to landless cultivators or those having smaller than subsistence holdings on easy instalments.
7. Tenants could be ejected only if they failed to give the crop share or rent.
8. The water rate and the cost of seed were to be paid by the landlord.

In 1975, small landowners (owning not more than 12 acres of irrigated or 25 acres of unirrigated land) were exempted from payment of land revenue. The loss in government revenue was to be compensated by raising the rate of taxes on big landowners. Further steps were taken in 1977. The land ceiling was cut down to 100 acres of irrigated land and 200 acres of unirrigated land. Some compensation was given to the persons whose land was resumed and the land was to be distributed among tenants free of charge. By June 1984 over 1.8 million hectares were resumed of which about 1.5 million hectares were distributed among 291,194 persons.

Chapter 12

Agriculture:
Crops and Livestock

Pakistan is a land of subsistence agriculture. Most of the farmers attempt to make the family self-sufficient in food. Therefore the emphasis is on the production of food crops which account for 65 to 70 per cent of the cropped area. The milk and milk-product needs are also generally met by animals kept by the family. Some cash crops are grown to pay tax and to meet other needs. Growing only cash crops and purchasing food from the market is not part of the farm life in Pakistan and therefore even big landlords in general do not do this.

AGRICULTURAL LAND USE

A small percentage of land in Pakistan is cultivated (about 26 per cent in 1984-85). Aridity and rugged topography are the main deterrents to the extension of cultivated area. Still the total cultivated area (net area sown plus current fallow) has increased by about 40 per cent from 1948 to 1985 (Table 12.1). This can only be achieved by bringing under plough the cultivable waste, area not available for cultivation, and forest area. However, the area of all the three categories of land use has increased: cultivable waste by 2.6 million hectares, area not available for cultivation by 3.0 million hectares and forest area by 1.8 million hectares. Therefore the increase in total area cultivated is surprising. The only plausible explanation for this increase seems to be under-reporting and non-reporting in the previous years. From 1948 to 1985 the reported area increased by 10.7 million hectares, whereas during the same period the total area cultivated increased by 7.4 million hectares. It cannot be denied that large areas of cultivable waste have also been put to the plough by extension of irrigation and other measures. At the same time considerable cultivated area has been lost because of waterlogging and salinity. Therefore the increase in the cultivated area has been largely because of better reporting.

Punjab possesses 26 per cent of the land area of Pakistan but 57 per cent of the cultivated area. The leadership of Punjab in cultivated acreage is based upon its vast alluvial plains and extensive irrigational facilities. On the other hand Balochistan, possessing the largest land area (44 per cent) has the smallest cultivated acreage (7 per cent). Vast areas occupied by rugged and lofty hills and mountains and intense aridity with limited irrigational facilities have turned the major part of Balochistan unsuitable for agriculture. Sindh and NWFP occupy third and fourth positions respectively in both total area and cultivated area. Sindh compares closely with Punjab, and NWFP with Balochistan except that Punjab is rainier than Sindh and NWFP than Balochistan.

One notable feature of the agricultural land use in Pakistan is an increase in the area sown more than once. It increased 4½ times from 1947-48 to 1984-85 (from 1.2 to 5.5 million hectares). This has been necessitated by the increase in population and was made possible by an increase in irrigational facilities.

CROPS

Subsistence agriculture is practised by most farms in Pakistan. An attempt is made by the farmer to be self-sufficient in food including milk and milk-products. Some cash crops are also grown from which other needs like clothes, utensils, furniture, payment of taxes, etc. are met. Food crops

Table 12.1: Agricultural Land Use in Pakistan 1947-48, 1969-70, 1979-80, and 1984-85 (percentage of the total area)

Category	1947-48	1969-70	1979-80	1984-85
1. Not available for cultivation	26.2	25.6	26.4	29.2
2. Cultivable waste	11.5	14.4	14.9	14.1
3. Current fallow	5.0	5.9	6.1	6.4
4. Net area sown	13.4	18.3	19.4	19.4
5. Total cultivated area (3+4)	18.4	24.2	25.5	25.8
6. Area sown more than once	1.2	2.8	4.2	5.5
7. Total cropped area (4+6)	14.6	21.1	23.6	24.9

Source : *Agricultural Statistics of Pakistan*, various years and other sources.

grown in excess of family requirements are also sold.   Therefore the emphasis is on the production of food crops.   Food-grains alone account for 56 per cent of the total cropped area, pulses occupy 7 per cent and vegetables about 1 per cent.   In addition edible oilseeds and sugarcane occupy a small percentage of the cropped area.   Thus about 65 to 70 per cent of the cropped acreage goes to the share of food crops.   The major food-grains are wheat, rice, maize and millets (*jowar* and *bajra*) whereas gram, *masoor, mash* etc. constitute the pulses.   The important oilseeds are mustard, rapeseed and groundnut.   The cash crops are cotton, sugarcane, sugarbeet, tobacco and jute.   The cash crops account for 16 per cent of the total cropped area.

There are two cropping seasons in Pakistan namely *kharif* (summer) and *rabi* (winter).   Cotton, rice, maize and millets are some of the

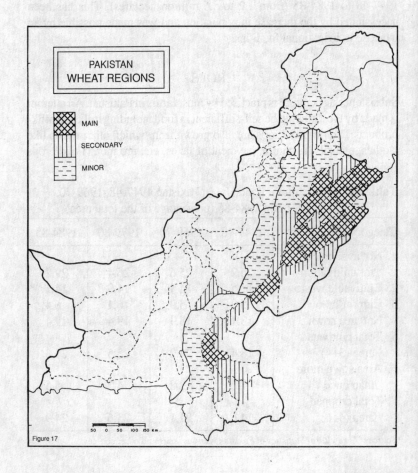

Figure 17

important *kharif* crops. Wheat, gram, *masoor* and rape-mustard are the *rabi* crops.

Wheat

Wheat is the staple food and dominates all crops in acreage and production. It accounts for 37 per cent of the cropped area, 65 per cent of food-grain acreage and 70 per cent of its production. Wheat prefers mild temperature and a small amount of rainfall. Therefore wheat is a *rabi* (winter) crop in Pakistan. It is sown in October-November and harvested in April-May.

Wheat-growing Regions

Wheat is the most extensively grown crop of Pakistan. There is no *tehsil* where wheat is not grown, but the acreage varies widely from one region to another. In general, the acreage is low in the Western Highlands where rugged topography, poor soils, low rainfall, and inadequate irrigational facilities greatly restrict wheat cultivation. On the other hand the Indus Plains with a favourable topography, rich soils and good agricultural facilities have much greater acreage under wheat. Within the Indus Plains there are some areas which grow more wheat than others. A simple method has been adopted to delimit the wheat regions of Pakistan. All those districts are taken as the wheat region where production is not less than minus one standard deviation from the national mean. The region has again been divided into three subregions: main, secondary and minor (Fig. 17). The main region is the one where the production is at least plus one standard deviation. The secondary region is the one where it is at least equal to the mean but less than plus one standard deviation. The minor region is the one where the production is less than the national mean

Table 12.2: Province-wise Area and Production of Wheat in Pakistan for 1971-75, 1976-80 and 1981-85

Area	Area (thousand hectares)			Production (thousand tons)		
	1971-75	1976-80	1981-85	1971-75	1975-80	1981-85
Pakistan	5,935	6,494	7,241	7,222	9,401	11,546
Balochistan	164	159	250	93	177	372
NWFP	651	716	801	515	732	927
Punjab	4,323	4,686	5,169	5,477	6,941	8,237
Sindh	797	933	1,021	1,137	1,551	2,010

Source: *Agricultural Statistics of Pakistan*, 1985, Table 3.

but not less than minus one standard deviation. Some adjustments in the map have been made on the basis of topography, soils and irrigational facilities. Data used is for 1982-83.

The main wheat-growing region of Pakistan is located in the canal colonies. It extends from Sialkot District in the north to Rahimyar Khan District in the south and from Kasur in the east to Sargodha District in the west. It is an extensive plain with rich alluvial soils, watered by canals and tubewells. Outside Punjab, Nawabshah in Sindh is the only district which belongs to the main wheat-growing region. It is also a well-irrigated fertile alluvial plain.

The secondary wheat-growing areas are located on the periphery of the main region. One of them lies to its east in the Punjab comprising Bahawalpur and Bahawalnagar Districts. The other lies to its west, namely Gujrat, Muzaffargarh and Leiah. Attock is the only rain-fed district which belongs to the secondary region. In Sindh, the districts surrounding Nawabshah (the main region) on the north, south and east belong to the secondary region. They are Sukkur, Khairpur, Sanghar, Tharparkar and Hyderabad. These districts are underlain with rich alluvial soils and enjoy facilities of canal irrigation. Nasirabad is the only district of Balochistan which produces sufficient wheat to be grouped in the secondary region.

The minor wheat-growing region comprises the western parts of the Punjab, some districts of NWFP and Dadu District of Sindh. In these areas irrigational facilities and topographical conditions are relatively poor for wheat production.

Area and Production of Wheat

The area under wheat in Pakistan was 7.2 million hectares in 1981-85 (Table 12.2). In 1947-48, it was 4 million hectares. Thus the acreage has increased by 80 per cent. During the last 10 years (1975-85) it has gone

Table 12.3: Province-wise Percentage of Wheat Area under Irrigation in Pakistan, for 1971-75, 1976-80, 1981-85.

Province	1971-75	1976-80	1981-85
Pakistan	70	71	79
Balochistan	54	51	61
NWFP	41	40	37
Punjab	79	81	82
Sindh	86	89	96

Source: *Agricultural Statistics of Pakistan,* 1982, Table 3 and 1985, Table 5.

up by 22 per cent. In this increase all the provinces have made a contribution. Percentage-wise Balochistan is the main contributor (52 per cent) and hectare-wise, Punjab (.85 million hectares).

The expansion in the acreage under wheat in Pakistan has been achieved by extension in net area sown but much more by an increase in area sown more than once. At the same time wheat acreage has expanded at the expense of pulses and oilseed areas. The extension in net area sown more than once has been achieved primarily by an extension in irrigated area (9.3 million hectares in 1950-51 and 15.6 million hectares in 1984-85). Wheat is a winter crop in Pakistan. Winter rainfall is low and variable, therefore wheat does best under irrigation. About 79 per cent of wheat area is irrigated (Table 12.3). The wheat area under irrigation has increased through time. Sindh, which remains the driest in winter has 96 per cent of its wheat land under irrigation. It is only in NWFP where winter rainfall is substantial and the topography makes irrigation in many areas difficult that the acreage of wheat in *barani* areas exceeds that under irrigation.

Production of wheat in Pakistan during 1981-85 was 11.6 million tons which is about 60 per cent more than that produced 10 years back (Table 12.2). Since the creation of Pakistan wheat production has registered an overall increase, with some set-back in years of low rainfall. The increase in production was achieved by an increase in wheat acreage and the yield of wheat per hectare. The yield of wheat per hectare in Pakistan has increased two-fold from 780 kg per hectare in 1951-55 to 1,596 kg in 1981-85. This improvement has been registered in all the provinces (Table 12.4). The increase in yield has been achieved by greater use of fertilizer and sowing of high yielding varieties of wheat. The yield of wheat per hectare of irrigated land is twice that of the unirrigated land. The same is the position with regard to land under high yielding varieties and that under other varieties. Today 90 per cent of the wheat land in Pakistan is given

Table 12.4: Province-wise Yield of Wheat in kg per hectare in Pakistan for 1970-75, 1976-80, 1981-85.

Province	1971-75	1976-80	1981-85
Pakistan	1,217	1,448	1,596
Balochistan	568	1,113	1,475
NWFP	792	1,047	1,155
Punjab	1,267	1,482	1,594
Sindh	1,427	1,662	1,978

Source: *Agricultural Statistics of Pakistan*, 1985.

to high yielding varieties. Though the increase in yield made in Pakistan is impressive but compared to some other countries Pakistan still has to cover a long distance. The yield of wheat in India (1,873 kg per hectare) and in Turkey (1,982) is higher than that in Pakistan (1,596). Compared to Mexico (4,200) and France (6,000) Pakistan is no match.

Self-sufficiency in Wheat

Pakistan is an agricultural country practising subsistence agriculture. Wheat is its staple food. It is in the national interest that the country should be self-sufficient in wheat. But from 1952-53 to 1979-80 Pakistan had to import wheat every year except in 1954-55. In 1979-80 more than two million tons of wheat had to be imported which was 21 per cent of the total production. No import was made in 1980-81 because of a bumper crop in 1979-80. In the subsequent three years the position remained satisfactory and a small quantity of wheat was exported in 1982-83 and 1983-84. But in 1983-84, the production decreased and the country became deficient in wheat again. During 1985-86, two million tons of wheat had to be imported. The wheat position in general has improved with an increase in production. But the population is increasing at a very rapid rate. The increase in production is eaten up by the growing population. Therefore any shortfall in production leads to deficiency. It is difficult to assert that Pakistan has become positively self-sufficient in wheat.

Rice

Rice has been grown in Pakistan since antiquity. Excavations at Moen-jo-Daro (3000 BC) have revealed rice grains in earthen vessels. Rice occupies 10 per cent of the total cropped area and 26 per cent of the important *kharif* crop area. Rice does best in a fairly high temperature and requires a plentiful supply of moisture. Therefore rice is a *kharif* crop (summer) in Pakistan. Rainfall is nowhere sufficient for rice but in the northern and eastern parts where rainfall is relatively heavier it is preferred. Even in that area irrigation is necessary. In all other parts rice is almost exclusively dependent upon irrigation. Rice grows best in soils retentive of moisture. Plain areas with fine textured soils like clay loams are preferred as they retain moisture. An impervious layer at some depth helps in keeping the water from seeping.

Rice-growing Regions

Rice is not grown as widely as wheat. More than 90 per cent of the total acreage of rice is located in the Punjab and Sindh (Table 12.5). The percentage share of the Punjab is steadily increasing. It was 48 per cent in 1971-75 which increased to 55 per cent in 1981-85, whereas that of Sindh decreased from 45 per cent in 1971-75 to 37 per cent in 1981-85. But the production in Punjab during the same period decreased from 45 to 43 and in Sindh from 50 to 45 per cent.

There are two major rice growing regions in Pakistan (Fig. 18). One of them includes Larkana and Jacobabad Districts of Sindh and the adjoining district of Nasirabad in Balochistan. The other is located in north-eastern Punjab and comprises Gujranwala and Shekhupura Districts. They together account for 50 per cent of the total production of rice in Pakistan. Most of the rice grown in Sindh is Irri-Pak and that grown in the Punjab is Basmati. The secondary rice-growing regions are located close to the main regions. Shikarpur, Dadu, Thatta and Badin Districts in Sindh and Sialkot and Okara Districts in Punjab belong to this group. They account for 23 per cent of the rice produced in Pakistan. The minor rice-growing region is also contiguous to the major and secondary regions: Hyderabad District in Sindh, and Gujrat, Sargodha, Lahore, Kasur and Sahiwal Districts of Punjab are included in this category. All the rice-growing areas enjoy excellent irrigational facilities. North-eastern Punjab, where rice is grown has the additional advantage of substantial monsoon rainfall. It is worth mentioning that rice requires such a large amount of water that no rice is grown in the *barani* (rain-fed) areas.

Area and Production of Rice

Rice ranks next to wheat in acreage and production among cereals in Pakistan. It occupies about two million hectares on which about 3.3

Table 12.5: Province-wise Area and Production of Rice in Pakistan for 1971-75, 1976-80, 1981-85.

	Area (thousand hectares)			Production (million tons)		
	1971-75	1976-80	1981-85	1971-75	1976-80	1981-85
Pakistan	1,511	1,883	1,976	2,311	2,960	3,331
Balochistan	38	36	94	36	52	282
NWFP	56	65	70	68	93	112
Punjab	729	1,041	1,088	1,048	1,468	1,433
Sindh	688	741	724	1,159	1,347	1,504

Source: *Agricultural Statistics of Pakistan*, 1985, Table 8.

million tons of rice is produced. The area under rice recorded a steady increase from .93 million hectares in 1949-50 to two million hectares in 1979-80 at which it has stood for some years. The production continues to make an onward march with some set-backs in bad years. Besides an increase in acreage, the increase in yield per hectare has resulted in higher production. The yield of rice increased from 1,513 kg per hectare in 1974-75 to 1,659 kg in 1984-85. Its area has also increased appreciably and that of the *desi* (indigenous) variety has decreased.

Balochistan and NWFP are not important provinces for rice cultivation. They together account for a little less than 10 per cent of the production. Sindh is second to the Punjab in acreage but leads in production (Table 12.5). Its leadership in production was achieved in 1980-81. The

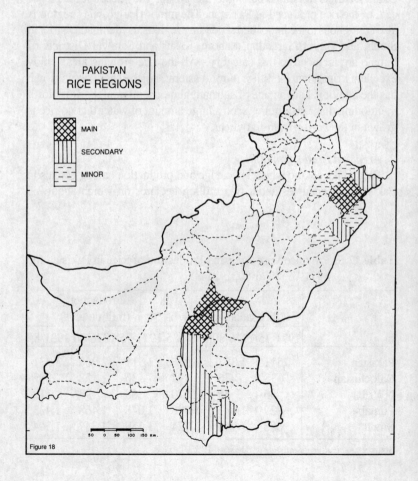

Figure 18

Rice threshing

Livestock

Terraced cultivation

Sugarcane plantations

higher production is the outcome of a greater area given to high-yielding Irri variety. Irri rice was developed in the International Rice Research Institute in the Philippines. It is a high-yielding variety and its acreage is the highest in Sindh. It is a common rice. Basmati is the best variety of rice grown in Pakistan. It is used in the preparation of special dishes and is in great demand in foreign markets. Its highest acreage is in the Punjab particularly north-eastern Punjab. Sindh does not produce basmati rice. Its yield is lower than that of Irri. *Desi* varieties have been grown for a long period of time. Their yield is low and they fetch a lower price, therefore their acreage is gradually decreasing.

Export of Rice

The export of rice recorded a phenomenal increase from a value of Rs. 274 million in 1971-72 to Rs. 1,136 million in 1972-73. The sudden rise in rice export was registered because of the secession of East Pakistan which used to consume the surplus rice of West Pakistan. In the very next year (1973-74) as a single item rice became the leading export of Pakistan. That position was held by rice upto 1983-84, after which it yielded that position to raw cotton. But rice still occupies the second position. Basmati rice mostly goes to the Middle East. Other varieties go to some other Asian countries.

Maize

Maize is a *kharif* (summer) crop in Pakistan. It needs a sufficiently high temperature and a moderate amount of rainfall. It is a food crop but is also used as fodder. It is not a staple food and only some poor families use it as the main food. It does not carry the prestige that wheat and rice do, therefore it is not grown on a large scale. It is a crop which can grow even in poor soils.

Table 12.6: Area, Production and Yield per hectare of Maize in Pakistan, 1971-75, 1976-80 and 1981-85.

	1971-75	1976-80	1981-85
Area (thousand hectares)	633	650	781
Production (thousand tons)	729	812	989
Yield per hectare (kg)	1,151	1,249	1,267

Source: *Agricultural Statistics of Pakistan;* 1985, Table 8.

Maize though grown in many districts, is primarily a crop of the northern part of Pakistan. It is there that rainfall is comparatively heavier and wherever rainfall is insufficient, irrigation facilities are available. NWFP leads other provinces both in area and production. The Punjab comes next. Sindh and Balochistan have a comparatively small acreage under maize.

The acreage of maize in Pakistan is increasing at a slow rate in comparison to that of rice and wheat.

The maize region is not extensive and is confined to the northern part of Pakistan (Fig. 19). In some districts like Abbottabad, Mansehra, Dir and Rawalpindi it is primarily a crop of *barani* regions whereas in other districts maize area under irrigation far exceeds that under *barani*. The main

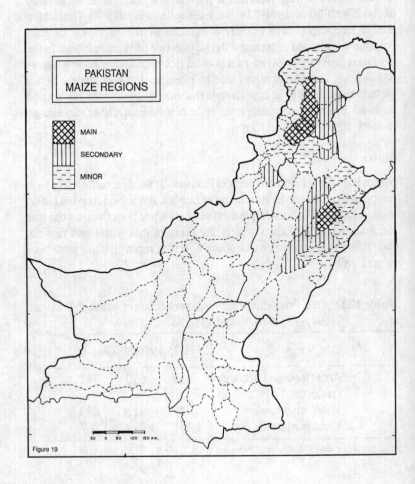

Figure 19

maize-growing region covers only a few districts, namely Swat, Mardan and Peshawar in NWFP and Faisalabad in the Punjab. The secondary region comprises Mansehra, Abbottabad, Bannu and Kohistan Districts of NWFP, and Sahiwal, Toba Tek Singh, Jhang, Multan, Sargodha and Rawalpindi Districts of the Punjab. The minor region includes Chitral and Kohat in NWFP and Gujrat and other districts in Punjab.

The yield per hectare of maize is also much higher in the Punjab and NWFP than in Sindh and Balochistan. The yield in the two northern provinces is about two times more than that in the two southern provinces.

Millet

Jowar and *bajra* are two important millet crops produced in Pakistan. They are the poor man's food and also serve as animal feed. They are *kharif* crops and can be grown in poor soils and are relatively resistant to drought. The acreage of *bajra* is more than that of *jowar*. But the two are rather neglected crops and their acreage and production are on the decline (Table 12.7). Tharparkar in Sindh exceeds all other districts of Pakistan in *bajra* production. Kohat is the only notable district in NWFP.

Jowar is a little more widely distributed than *bajra*. Only two provinces, namely Punjab and Sindh are notable. Again the northern districts are prominent, namely Attock, Rawalpindi, Jhelum and Sargodha. Dera Ghazi Khan Rajanpur and Muzaffargarh in the west, and Bahawalpur Division in the east are also important producers of *jowar*. Dera Ismail Khan is the only important district for *jowar* production in NWFP. In Sindh a number of districts are prominent. Sukkur, Khairpur, Nawabshah, Sanghar and Dadu may be mentioned. Two districts of Balochistan which

Table 12.7: Area, Production and Yield per hectare of *Jowar* and *Bajra* in Pakistan for 1971-75, 1976-80 and 1981-85.

Year	Bajra			Jowar		
	Area (thousand hectares)	Production (thousand tons)	Yield (kg)	Area (thousand hectares)	Production (thousand tons)	Yield (kg)
1971-75	680	327	481	520	317	610
1976-80	627	306	489	467	266	569
1981-85	512	249	489	392	266	575

Source: *Agricultural Statistics of Pakistan,* 1985.

are contiguous to Sindh are of some prominence, namely Nasirabad and Kachhi.

Pulses

Pulses are an important source of protein in Pakistan. Gram, *masoor* (lentil), *mung* and *mash* are the important pulses grown in Pakistan. Among them gram is the most important and accounts for two-third of the total production of pulses in the country. It thrives best in well-drained sandy loams. It is primarily a crop of *barani* areas. More than 50 per cent of the total gram acreage is accounted for by Bhakkar and Khushab Districts of the Punjab. The districts of Mianwali, Leiah and Bahawalnagar are also important. Jacobabad, Sukkur and Shikarpur are prominent in Sindh. Dera Ismail Khan in NWFP and Nasirabad in Balochistan have some importance.

Mung is mostly grown in the Punjab. The major growing area is in the northern districts of Gujrat, Jhelum, Sargodha, Rawalpindi, Mianwali, Bhakkar and Leiah. Kohat, Dir, Swat in NWFP and Kurram Agency are important producers. Tharparkar and Sanghar are the only notable districts in Sindh, and Lasbela in Balochistan.

The distribution of *mash* is very similar to that of *mung*. Sialkot is the leading district. Punjab is the leader in the production of *masoor* also. *Masoor* is more widely distributed than *mung* and *mash* in the Punjab. In Sindh it is largely confined to Hyderabad, Badin, Sukkur, Sanghar and Thatta Districts, and in NWFP Mansehra is prominent. Peas in Pakistan are largely grown in a belt running from Dera Ghazi Khan District through Muzaffargarh, Shikarpur, Jacobabad, Larkana and Dadu Districts. The Punjab is the leading producer of all pulses except peas in which Sindh has the leadership. Pakistan is deficient in pulses and the deficiency is increasing.

Oilseeds

A number of oilseeds are produced in Pakistan. The most important is cotton seed. This is a by-product of cotton and alone constitutes about 60 per cent of the total production of oilseeds in Pakistan. Rapeseed and mustard come next. They produce edible oil. Together they constitute the seventh largest crop of Pakistan in acreage. No area can be specially earmarked as the rapeseed-mustard region. On the other hand groundnut which has recently gained importance is concentrated in a few areas. Rawalpindi Division is by far the most important. Khushab, Mianwali and

Bhakkar are also important. Kohat and Karak Districts in NWFP and Sanghar District in Sindh are other areas. Other oilseeds grown in Pakistan are linseed, castorseed and sesamum. The oilseeds in Pakistan are used for human consumption, animal feed and industrial uses. Pakistan is deficient in edible oil. More than 50 per cent of edible oil consumed in Pakistan is imported.

Sugarcane

Next to cotton sugarcane is the most important cash crop of Pakistan. It is primarily used in making sugar and *gur*. The per capita consumption of sugar has increased from 3 kg annually in 1947 to 11.25 kg in 1982. This quantity is very low as compared to the Western countries where the per capita consumption is over 50 kg per annum. It must, however, be pointed out that the majority of the rural population which constitutes 72 per cent of Pakistan's population depends primarily upon *gur* for sweetening purposes. It is heartening that in spite of an increase in per capita consumption and doubling of the population since 1947, Pakistan has become self-sufficient in sugar which has been achieved by expansion of sugarcane acreage and increase in production. But the buffer-stock is so marginal that bad harvest, an increase in per capita consumption of sugar or population growth will result in a deficiency. There are two planting seasons for sugarcane in Pakistan, February-March (the main season) and September-October. Harvesting is usually done 10 months after planting. Besides the main crop, two ratoon crops are also obtained but with decreasing yield.

Sugarcane-growing Regions

Sugarcane is a tropical crop. It requires plenty of heat but can tolerate frost for a short period. Therefore sugarcane is produced over a wide area in Pakistan from Sindh to NWFP. Sugarcane needs a large quantity of water. Large parts of Pakistan being arid or semi-arid, sugarcane is primarily grown under irrigation. Usually 25-33 irrigations are required, therefore sugarcane does best in the canal colonies. But rainfall is also very helpful and variability in rainfall adversely affects the yield. Sugarcane can be grown in a variety of soils. In texture the soils may range from sandy laoms to clays, but silt loams and clay loams are most suitable as they permit water infiltration and retention. The soils should be well aerated up to a depth of 60 cm. Sugarcane needs soils rich in essential nutrients. It is an exhaustive crop therefore it is difficult for even the most fertile soils to grow sugarcane every year without application of manure and fertilizer. A well-balanced supply of nitrogen, phosphorous and potash is needed. Sugarcane is said to devour potash. It is estimated that 300 to 350 kg of potash per hectare is required (275 to 320 lb per acre). The distribution of sugarcane in Pakistan depends upon these requirements of land, water and soils, and the competition that sugarcane has to face for land from wheat, cotton and rice in particular. Sugarcane is grown over an extensive area in Punjab and Sindh and over a relatively small area in NWFP. Sugarcane is not an important crop in Balochistan. There are three Main Regions (Fig. 20): (i) East central Punjab extending from Gujrat District in the north to Rahimyar Khan District in the south (ii) South central Sindh comprising Nawabshah, Hyderabad and Badin District and (iii) Peshawar and Mardan District of NWFP. They have excellent

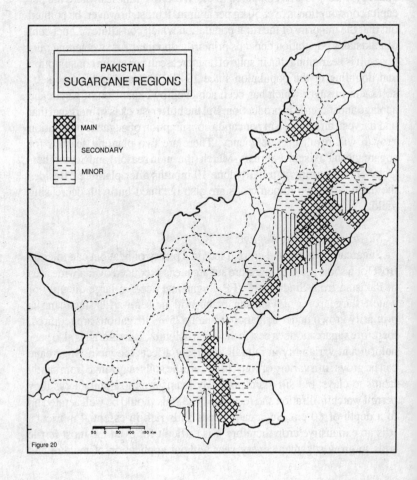

Figure 20

irrigational facilities and rich fertile soils. The Secondary Regions are located adjacent to the Main Region in Punjab and Sindh. They include Shekhupura, Sahiwal, Vehari, Bahawalpur, Muzaffargarh and Leiah Districts in Punjab, and Khairpur and Thatta Districts in Sindh. The Minor Regions are located next to the secondary. In Punjab they are Sialkot and Gujranwala Districts in the north-east and Rajanpur, Dera Ghazi Khan, Mianwali, Bhakkar and Khushab Districts in the west. In Sindh Sukkur, Sanghar and Tharparkar Districts in the east and Dadu Districts in the west belong to the Minor Region.

Area and Production of Sugarcane

The area under sugarcane in Pakistan tripled in 25 years from 1950 (202 thousand hectares) to 1975 (608 thousand hectares). It increased by 50 per cent in the next 10 years (1985: 897 thousand hectares). All the provinces have contributed to the increase (Table 12.9). But area-wise the greatest increase has been registered by the Punjab and percentage-wise by Sindh. The Punjab accounts for 70 per cent of the sugarcane acreage of Pakistan. Sindh displaced NWFP for the second place in 1973-74 and at present accounts for 19 per cent of sugarcane acreage. NWFP comes next with 11 per cent. The share of Balochistan is negligible.

The production of sugarcane in Pakistan has registered a greater increase than the acreage. From 1950 the area increased 4.4 times and the production 4.9 times. The relative positions of the province in production

Table 12.8: Area, Production and Yield per hectare of Sugarcane in Pakistan 1947-85.

Years	Area (thousand hectares)	Production (million tons)	Yield (per hectare in tons)
1947-50	202	6.8	32.9
1951-55	246	7.2	28.7
1956-60	365	10.3	27.7
1961-65	469	15.8	33.6
1966-70	582	22.3	37.5
1971-75	608	21.6	35.6
1975-80	756	28.0	37.0
1981-85	897	33.6	37.5

Source: *Agricultural Statistics of Pakistan*, various years.

remained the same as that in the acreage. The percentage share of Sindh in production was 22 per cent and that of Punjab, 67 per cent. The yield per hectare of sugarcane in Sindh is higher than that in the Punjab (Table 12.9). The yield of sugarcane per hectare in Pakistan is low (37.5 tons). By comparison in Hawaii it is 150 tons, in Java 135 tons, in Peru 100 tons and in Australia 50 tons. In Pakistan the yield has increased since 1960 by about 10 tons. But a much greater increase is possible. Mechanization has been suggested as one measure of increasing the yield. A study conducted in Sindh revealed that the yield on tractor farms was 33 per cent more than that on traditional farms, when the input of the former was 7 per cent higher. Mechanization thus can increase the yield by about 12 tons but will not bring it at par with that of Hawaii or Java. Use of a greater quantity of fertilizer and water, better agricultural practices and sowing of a high yielding variety of sugarcane may produce the desired result.

Tobacco

Tobacco is an important cash crop of Pakistan and an important item of export. But during recent years its acreage, production and export have registered a decline. Tobacco occupied on an average 51,000 hectares in 1971-75. That decreased gradually to 45,000 hectares in 1981-85 (Table 12.10). Along with the decrease in acreage under tobacco, a decrease in production has also taken place. From 81,000 tons annually in 1971-75 it dropped to 74,000 tons in 1981-85. Tobacco is losing ground to other crops in Pakistan.

Table 12.9: Province-wise Area, Production and Yield per hectare of Sugarcane in Pakistan, 1971-75, 1976-80 and 1981-85.

	Area (thousand hectares)			Production (million tons)			Yields (per hectare in tons)
	1971-75	1976-80	1981-85	1971-75	1976-80	1981-85	1981-85
Pakistan	608	756	897	21.6	28	33.6	37.5
Balochistan	–	0.1	–	0.001	.003	.3	33
NWFP	87	93	99	3.4	3.6	3.9	46
Punjab	433	544	628	15.1	20.2	22.7	36
Sindh	88	119	170	3.1	4.2	6.7	41

Source: *Agricultural Statistics of Pakistan,* 1985, Table 13.

NWFP accounts for about 60 per cent of the total area under tobacco in Pakistan and 65 per cent of the production. The share of Punjab is 35 per cent of the area and 31 per cent of the production. Thus 95 per cent of the area and 96 per cent of the production are taken care of by NWFP and Punjab. The remaining 5 per cent of the area and 4 per cent of the production come from Balochistan with Pishin as the leading district.

Mardan and Peshawar Districts of NWFP constitute the Main Tobacco Region (Fig. 21). Mardan alone accounts for 44 per cent of the area and 50 per cent of the production, and Peshawar, 10 per cent of both area and production. The Secondary Region is located in east central Punjab comprising Faisalabad, Sahiwal, Toba Tek Singh and Gujranwala Districts. Pishin District in Balochistan and Mansehra in NWFP also belong

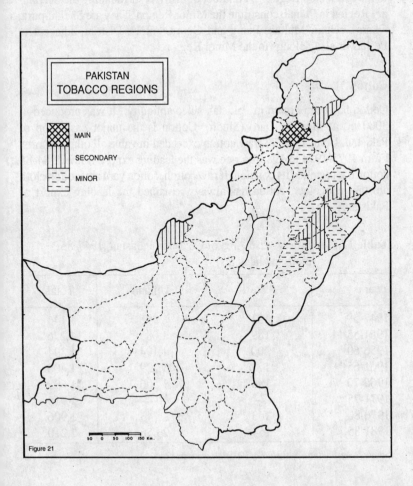

PAKISTAN
TOBACCO REGIONS

MAIN

SECONDARY

MINOR

50 0 50 100 150 Km.

Figure 21

Table 12.10: Area, Production and Yield per hectare of Tobacco in Pakistan in Selected Years

Years	Area (thousand hectares)	Production (thousand tons)	Yield (per hectare in kg)
1971-75	51	81	1,568
1976-80	49	70	1,424
1981-85	45	74	1,639

Source: *Agricultural Statistics of Pakistan,* 1985, Table 18.

to the Secondary Region. A number of districts surrounding the Secondary Region in Punjab constitute the Minor Region. They are Shekhupura, Okara, Vehari, Multan, Jhang and Gujrat. Attock District, adjacent to Peshawar also belongs to the Minor Region.

Cotton

Cotton has been grown in Pakistan since antiquity. It was produced in 3000 BC at Moen-jo-Daro (Sindh). Cotton is the major cash crop of Pakistan. Up to 1972-73, raw cotton exceeded in value all other exports. From 1973-1974 to 1983-84 rice was the leading export. Since 1984-85 cotton has regained its position. If raw cotton, cotton yarn and cotton cloth are taken together, cotton has always remained the leading export of Pakistan.

Table 12.11: Variety-wise Area of Cotton in Pakistan, 1947-85 (thousand hectares)

Year	*Desi*	Upland	Total
1947-50	151	995	1,146
1951-55	189	1,087	1,276
1956-60	200	1,194	1,394
1961-65	171	1,229	1,400
1966-70	186	1,506	1,692
1971-75	—	—	1,915
1976-80	163	1,743	1,906
1981-85	154	2,056	2,210

Source: *Agricultural Statistics of Pakistan,* various years.

Cotton acreage in Pakistan is on the increase. It has doubled, from 1.1 million hectares in 1947-50 to 2.2 million in 1981-85 (Table 12.11). The yield has also registered an increase by more than two times, from 169 kg per hectare in 1947-50 to 343 in 1981-84.

Cotton Regions

Cotton requires a sufficiently high temperature (above 25°C) and moderate rainfall (about 500 mm). Therefore cotton is a *kharif* (summer) crop in Pakistan. Sowing begins in May in Sindh and in June in Punjab. Picking begins by the end of July in the south and continues up to January in the north. Cotton does well in deep friable soils, rich in humus and lime

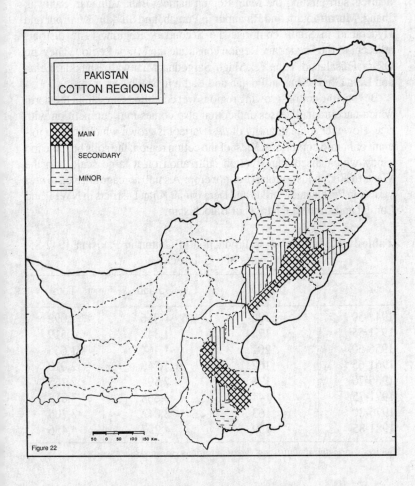

Figure 22

and retentive of moisture. Alluvium laid down by rivers forms good cotton soils. Therefore in Pakistan cotton is grown in the Indus Plains and it loses importance in the Western Highlands. The Indus alluvium is deficient in some nutrients therefore the application of potash and phosphate is required to maintain the fertility. Besides climate, soils and irrigational facilities, economic competition with other crops determines the cotton-growing region. The south-eastern part of Punjab comprising Vehari, Multan, Bahawalpur and Rahimyar Khan Districts constitutes the Main Cotton Region of Pakistan (Fig. 22). The rainfall in the region is less than 250 mm but adequate facilities for irrigation are available. The arid conditions discourage the advent of pests and diseases. Rich alluvium is present to which fertilizer is added to make up the nutrient deficiency. The districts surrounding the Main Region namely Bahawalnagar, Sahiwal, Jhang, Muzaffargarh and Rajanpur in Punjab, and Sukkur, Khairpur and Hyderabad in Sindh comprise the Secondary Region. The districts adjacent to the Secondary Region constitute the Minor Region. They are Okara, Faisalabad, Toba Tek Singh, Sargodha, Mianwali, Bhakkar, Leiah and Dera Ghazi Khan in Punjab and Badin in Sindh.

Beyond the cotton-growing regions wet conditions prevail in the north which encourage diseases and cotton also comes into competition with rice. However some quantity of *desi* variety is grown which is more tolerant of humid conditions. West of the cotton region, the soils become too sandy which discourages cotton cultivation on a large scale. In the Western Highlands cotton is a minor crop. A small acreage is given to *desi* variety in Peshawar, Mardan and Dera Ismail Khan Districts in NWFP and Loralai and Lasbela Districts of Balochistan.

Table 12.12: Variety-wise Production of Cotton in Pakistan 1947-85. (thousand bales of 375 lb each)

Year	*Desi*	Upland	Total
1947-50	126	966	1,092
1951-55	172	1,347	1,519
1956-60	201	1,464	1,665
1961-65	162	1,848	2,010
1966-70	171	2,594	2,765
1971-75	147	3,668	3,815
1976-80	163	3,042	3,205
1981-85	159	4,297	4,456

Source: *Agricultural Statistics of Pakistan,* various years and other sources.

In the cotton-growing regions and in the major part of Indus Plains Pak-Upland cotton (*Gossypium hirstum*) is grown. It was introduced in the territory forming Pakistan in 1914. By 1934-35 more than 50 per cent of cotton acreage of the Punjab was occupied by Upland variety. Today Upland variety accounts for more than 90 per cent of the total cotton acreage of Pakistan. The remaining area is devoted to *Gossypium arboreum* (*desi* variety).

Area and Production of Cotton

The production of cotton in Pakistan is increasing at a rapid rate. In 1947-50, 1.1 million bales of 375 lb each were produced (Table 12.12). Since then in every five-year period, the production registered an increase. It was 1.7 million bales in 1956-60, 2.8 million bales in 1966-70, and 3.2 million bales in 1976-80. It reached 4.5 million bales in 1981-85. The increase in production was achieved by two methods: an increase in acreage and in yield. The cotton acreage in 1947-50 was 1.1 million hectares which increased to 1.4 million in 1956-60, 1.7 million in 1966-70, 2.2 million in 1981-85. Thus while the acreage of cotton increased two times from 1947-50 to 1981-85, the production increased more than four times. This became possible by increasing the yield of cotton per hectare. The yield of cotton lint per hectare in 1947-50 was 169 kg, which increased to 213 in 1956-60, 290 in 1966-70 and 343 in 1981-85. The increase in production and yield has been achieved in Pak-Upland variety of cotton whereas *desi* variety has not registered any notable progress. It has been estimated that 40 per cent increase in yield has been achieved by improvement in irrigational facilities, 40 per cent by application of fertilizer and the remaining 20 per cent by improvement in plant protection, growing of improved variety, etc.

As a consequence of these efforts, in 1979-80 Pakistan, became the fourth largest country in cotton acreage after India, USA and Brazil. In cotton production also Pakistan had the fourth place next to USA, India and Mexico. In yield per hectare it was the sixth after Egypt, Mexico, Turkey, USA and Iran. In yield per hectare Pakistan had a better position than India and Brazil.

LIVESTOCK

Livestock plays an important part in the economy of Pakistan particularly in the agricultural sector. Mechanization still not being common, animals supply the draft power to the farms. The bulk of domestic needs of meat, milk and eggs is met by local supply. Cowdung is an important source of manure. A large tanning industry has developed, using local raw materials. The animals supply leather, skin, wool and hair for export.

It is a matter of concern that such an important sector of economy is in a neglected state. The animals are generally not well fed and are not properly looked after. Pressure on land in Pakistan being great, a small area is given for the production of fodder. Overgrazing is common in dry grasslands and also in village grazing grounds.

Cattle

Cattle are the chief farm animals of Pakistan. They are the main draft animals which are assisted by buffaloes and camels on a limited scale. As suppliers of milk cows are next to buffaloes. As suppliers of meat cattle come after buffaloes and goats.

Cattle in Pakistan belong to the genus *Bos indicus* (Zebu Cattle). The quality of cattle in general is poor but some good breeds are also found though they are small in number. Bhagnari and Dhani have a good reputation as work animals. The short and stout Dhani cattle are found in northern mountains and adjoining areas. Red Sindhi and Sahiwal are well known breeds for milk, and Thari (Tharparkar) for both draft and milk. There is no particular breed developed for beef. Efforts are being made to improve the quality of cattle for which a number of farms have been established. Some of the important ones are at Sakrand, Dadu, Karachi, Mirpurkhas, Bahawalpur, Fazilpur (Dera Ghazi Khan District), Jahangirabad and Jahanian (Multan District), Qadirabad (Sahiwal District) and Rakh Ghulam and Rakh Kishori (Thal). Besides, large farms have been established in Lahore, Sargodha, Multan and Kalabagh.

Table 12.13: Cattle in Pakistan 1972-73, 1979-80 and 1984-85 (in thousands).

Type	1972-73	1979-80	1984-85
Bulls 3 years and above for work	5,758	6,096	6,474
Cows 3 years and above in milk	2,414	2,556	2,714
Cows 3 years and above dry	1,811	1,918	2,036
Others	4,736	5,015	5,325

Source: *Pakistan Census of Agriculture, 1972, Agricultural Statistics of Pakistan, 1985,* Table 116.

Cattle being the work animal every farm requires at least a pair of bullocks. In 1980 there were 6.1 million bullocks (Table 12.13) and 4.1 million farms in Pakistan. In other words a pair of bullocks was not available for every farm. Additionally large farms keep more than two bullocks. This clearly shows that some farms go without work animals. They either borrow or hire draft animals. The condition in 1984-85 had not materially changed though some increase in the number of bullocks (6.5 million) had occurred.

Cows are an important but not the chief source of milk in Pakistan (Table 12.14). The bulk of milk (70 per cent) comes from buffaloes. The cow is the second important supplier (24 per cent). In Pakistan the average daily yield of milk per cow is 3.6 litres. In general 5 per cent of the milk is fed to the calves, 15 per cent is wasted and the remaining 80 per cent is available for human consumption. The lactation period is 250 days and on the average about 33 per cent of milk cows remain dry.

Cattle account for 23 per cent of the total production of meat in Pakistan. It has remained the leading supplier of meat in Pakistan for a long time (Table 12.15). It lost this position to the buffalo in 1979-80. But the competition continues. Buffaloes have a slight edge over cattle. Recently goats have made great headway. In 1983-84 the production of goat meat in Pakistan exceeded cattle-beef and in 1984-85 the goat became the leading supplier of meat. The production of cattle-beef has steadily increased (3.6 per cent annually).

Cattle are an integral part of farms in Pakistan. Every farm desires to be self-sufficient in work animals and milk. Every farmer does his best to have a pair of bullocks and a cow or buffalo for milk. That is why cattle are well distributed in most of Pakistan except for Balochistan, deserts of Thar and Cholistan and rugged and cold Northern Areas where agriculture is practised on a limited scale. Punjab accounts for 55 per cent of the cattle

Table 12.14: Estimated Milk Production in Pakistan 1947-75, 1979-80 and 1984-85 (thousand tons)

Source	1974-75	1979-80	1984-85
Cow	2,156	2,270	2,596
Buffalo	5,743	6,438	7,789
Sheep	25	31	39
Goat	269	336	432
Total	8,193	9,075	10,856

Source: *Agricultural Statistics of Pakistan*, 1983, Table 120 and 1985, Table 117.

Table 12.15: Estimated Meat Production in Pakistan 1974-75, 1979-80 and 1984-85 (thousand tons)

Source	1974-75	1979-80	1984-85
Cattle	182	208	249
Buffalo	175	210	264
Sheep	114	151	198
Goat	151	201	269
Poultry	22	49	99
Total	644	819	1,079

Source: *Agricultural Statistics of Pakistan,* 1983, Table 121 and 1985, Table 118.

population. Sindh and NWFP 20 per cent each and the remaining 5 per cent is shared by Balochistan and Northern Areas.

Buffaloes

Buffaloes are the main source of milk and meat in Pakistan. As work animals they are not that important. Buffaloes are primarily kept for supply of milk. Nili Bar, Kundi and Ravi breeds are well known for producing large quantities of milk. About five million buffaloes in Pakistan produce 7.8 million tons of milk in a year which is more than 70 per cent of the total milk produced in Pakistan. At a time 60 per cent of

Table 12.16: Buffaloes in Pakistan 1974-75, 1979-80, 1984-85 (thousands)

Type	1974-75	1979-80	1984-85
Bulls 3 years and above for work	161	180	202
Females 3 years and above in milk	3,507	3,931	4,414
Females 3 years and above dry	1,674	1,876	2,107
Others	5,047	5,657	6,354

Source: *Agricultural Statistics of Pakistan,* 1983, Table 119 and 1985, Table 116.

buffaloes remain in milk and the rest (40 per cent) remain dry. Their lactation period is 305 days in a year. Per buffalo, 5.4 litres of milk is produced per day.

Buffaloes are large animals. The bulk of the male and the old female buffaloes are slaughtered. Since 1979-80 they have become the leading producers of meat in Pakistan. Buffaloes love water and can not tolerate too much cold. They are heavy animals and live in the plains. Therefore they are primarily animals of the canal colonies of the Punjab. In the eastern part they are particularly important. In the Punjab 75 per cent of the buffaloes are found. Sindh canal areas come next with 17 per cent of the buffalo population. NWFP accounts for 7 per cent and the remaining 1 per cent are found in favourable pockets within the dry rugged areas of Balochistan and cold Northern Areas.

Sheep and Goats

The sure-footed sheep and goats can live in rugged terrain and also in the plains. They can nibble the thin grasses and thus can survive in dry areas. They are therefore widely distributed and are found in hilly areas and also in the plains. They are at home in canal colonies and are also present in desert areas. Environment, inhospitable for cattle and buffaloes can become the abode of sheep and goats. Therefore they are found in abundance in the tribal areas, Balochistan Plateau, Thal, Thar and Cholistan Deserts and also in the well-watered canal colonies of the Punjab and Sindh. The number of sheep and goats has been registering an increase.

Table 12.17: Sheep and Goats in Pakistan 1972-73, 1979-80 and 1984-85 (in thousands)

Sheep and Goats	1972-73	1979-80	1984-85
Sheep			
One Year and above	10,601	15,328	17,900
Less than one year	4,227	6,111	7,137
Total	14,828	21,439	25,037
Goats			
One year and above	10,137	16,420	19,561
Less than one year	5,788	8,533	10,165
Total	15,925	24,953	29,726

Source: *Agricultural Statistics of Pakistan*, 1985 and *Pakistan Census of Agriculture*, 1972.

Their population has doubled from 1972-73 to 1984-85 (Table 12.17). This is inspite of the fact that keeping of goats unless stall-fed is discouraged by the Government. Goat keeping is discouraged because goats are well known for overgrazing and thus accelerating soil erosion. Sheep are kept primarily for wool and meat.

The wool production in Pakistan has doubled from 24 thousand tons in 1972-73 to 48 thousand tons in 1984-85. The wool produced is of poor quality but it is on this that the woollen textile industry of Pakistan is dependent. A small quantity of good quality wool is imported while about 50 per cent of the wool produced in Pakistan is exported. The average yield of wool per adult sheep annually is 1.82 kg. Two clippings are done within a year. Goats along with cattle and buffaloes are the main source of meat in Pakistan (Table 12.15). They supply about 25 per cent of the meat. Sheep are also an important source of meat. Sheep are good suppliers of skin but a poor source of milk.

Chapter 13

Minerals and Power Resources

Pakistan is poor in metallic minerals and power resources but has rich deposits of a few non-metallic minerals. At the time Pakistan was created (1947) only a few minerals were known to exist in the country. Since then with the efforts of Geological Survey of Pakistan and other agencies the existence of some more has been established. Still, the number of major minerals is only 25-30. The quality and quantity of quite a few of them is not known. Their economic feasibility has yet to be ascertained. Many of the mineral deposits are located in inaccessible parts. The infrastructure required for their exploitation does not exist. Therefore mining is a minor sector of Pakistan's economy. It accounts for about .5 per cent of the GNP and the minerals provide a weak base for the industrial development. The Government has taken interest in the exploration and exploitation of minerals. The Geological Survey of Pakistan, functioning since the inception of Pakistan, is responsible for investigation and mapping of mineral deposits. In 1961 Oil and Gas Development Corporation was established to explore, develop, produce, refine, and sell oil and gas. Pakistan Mineral Corporation, established in 1974 is a specialized agency responsible for exploration and marketing of all the minerals. Resource Development Corporation was set up in 1974 to investigate and develop copper mines at Saindak, Balochistan. Gemstone Corporation of Pakistan Ltd. came into being in 1979 to develop gemstone resources. In addition mineral development boards exist at the provincial level. To co-ordinate the work of the various federal and provincial agencies, Mineral Corporation Board has been set up at the federal level. This shows the importance that the Government has given to the mining sector. However some experts feel that there are just too many agencies taking care of a small sector of the economy.

NON-METALLIC MINERALS

Pakistan has rich deposits of a number of non-metallic minerals. Rock salt and limestone are found in a large quantity. Gypsum, barite, magnesite, soapstone, fluorite, marble, China clay, fire clay and Fuller's earth are obtained in sufficient quantity to meet the local demand.

Rock Salt

Rock salt (halite) is used for cooking and preservative purposes and for the manufacture of soda ash, bicarbonate of soda, caustic soda and other sodas for laundry, textiles, tanning etc.

The Salt Range is the main source of rock salt in Pakistan. *Ain-i-Akbari*, written during the reign of the Mughal Emperor Akbar contains a description of the Salt Range. Mining in a planned way was started in 1872. The salt is deposited in the southern escarpment of the Salt Range. Its seams on an average are 20-25 metres thick. Some of the seams are as thick as 90 metres. They are white or pink in colour. There are three important mines namely Khewra, Warcha and Kalabagh (Fig. 23). An extension of the Salt Range across the Indus River exists to the west. That has early Eocene salt deposits. Some of the seams are 100 metres thick. The salt is overlain by gypsum, dolomite and clay. Mining is done at Jatta, Bahadur Khel and Karak.

Table 13.1: Reserves of Principal Minerals in Pakistan

Marble (argonite/onyx)	Very large deposits
China Clay	4.9 million tons
Chromite	Fairly large deposits
Coal	580 million tons
Crude Oil	139 million US barrels
Fire Clay	Over 100 million tons
Fuller's Earth	Fairly large deposits
Gypsum/Anhydrite	350 million tons
Iron Ore	Over 430 million tons
Limestone	Very large deposits
Rock Salt	Over 100 million tons
Silica Sand	Very large deposits
Copper	412 million tons
Dolomite	Very large deposits
Bauxite/Laterite	Over 74 million tons
Barite	5 million tons
Sulphur	0.8 million tons
Soapstone	0.6 million tons

Source: *Pakistan Economic Survey*, 1986-87, Table 8.1.

The total reserve of rock salt has been estimated at over 100 million tons (Table 13.1). The production is steadily increasing, from 163,000 tons in 1947-48 to 573,000 tons in 1984-85. Most of the salt is consumed locally but a substantial quantity is also exported.

Gypsum

Gypsum is an industrial mineral used as a raw material for fertilizer, as a retarder in cement, and as a filler in paper, paints, rubber etc. It is also used in the manufacture of plaster of Paris.

Gypsum is deposited in beds by the evaporation of sea water under arid conditions in the enclosed basins or in the arms of the sea. In Pakistan rich

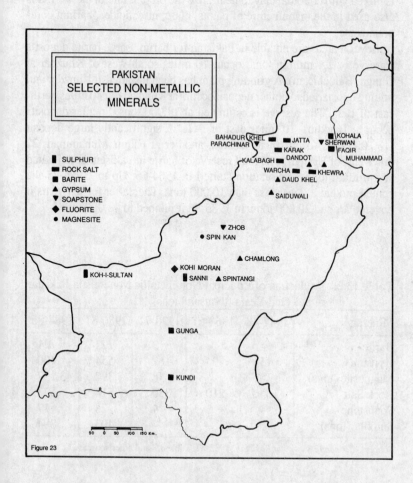

Figure 23

deposits occur in the Salt Range and lesser deposits at Jatta (Kohat), at Rakhi Munh in the foothills of the Sulaiman Mountains west of Dera Ghazi Khan, at Saiyiduwali in Kishore Range, at Spintangi and Chamalong in Marri-Bugti Hills. Most of the gypsum is obtained at present from Khewra, Dandot, and Daud Khel mines in the Salt Range (Fig. 23). The production varies considerably from year to year but a general upward trend has been recorded (Table 13.2). The total reserve is estimated at 350 million tons (Table 13.1).

Barite

Barite (Baryte) is barium sulphate. It is used in oil-well drilling where it is mixed with colloidal clay to neutralize the oil pressure in the well. It is also used in the manufacture of paints, glass, insecticides, barium compounds etc.

Several areas are notable in Pakistan for barite. Large barite deposits (reserve of 1.4 million tons) occur 10 miles south-west of Khuzdar at Gunga (Balochistan). A grinding plant has been installed at Khuzdar and mining has started. Another deposit occurs at Kundi about 40 miles northeast of Bela. The reserve is estimated at 13,000 tons. Smaller deposits occur at Bankhiri, 10 miles east of Bela. A significantly large deposit (130,000 tons) occurs near Kohala, another at Faquir Muhammad, 22 miles east of Haripur. The total reserve of barite in Pakistan is estimated at 5 million tons. Exploitation started in 1964-65. Up to 1974-75 the annual production was less than 10,000 tons. Thereafter for ten years it hovered around 20,000 tons. In 1985-86 it jumped to 42,000 tons.

Table 13.2: Production of Principal Non-metallic Minerals in Pakistan in Selected Years (thousand tons)

Minerals	1947-48	1960-61	1970-71	1980-81	1984-85
Barite	–	–	3	21	21
Gypsum	15	94	167	554	400
Magnesite (tons)	–	–	648	397	3,137
Rock Salt	163	210	350	514	573
Soapstone	–	1	4	28	17
Sulphur (tons)	–	–	–	403	884

Source: *Economic Survey of Pakistan,* 1986-87, Table 8.2 and other sources.

Magnesite

Magnesite contains a high percentage of magnesia (47.7 per cent). It is used in manufacturing magnesium oxychloride, cement, paper pulp, rayon, fertilizer, chemicals, drugs, etc.

In Pakistan magnesite occurs in small quantities in many places from Lasbela to Malakand in the Axial Belt. But the only large deposit is that of Spin Kan near Nisai about 13 miles off Muslimbagh (Balochistan). The annual production is about 3,000 tons which meets the home requirement.

Soapstone

Soapstone (steatite) is a variety of talc. It is put to various uses but in Pakistan it is primarily used as filler in soap, ceramics and face powder. It occurs in a number of localities in the Axial Belt. But the main deposits are located near Sherwan in Abbottabad and this is the main source of soapstone in Pakistan. Small deposits of soapstone are located in Zhob area, and at Safed Koh near Parachinar. The annual production is 22,000 tons and the total reserve is .6 million tons.

Fluorite

Fluorite is used in making steel and glass, in enamelling cooking utensils and in some chemical industry. In Pakistan it has been located about 50 miles south of Quetta at Koh-i-Maran and Koh-i-Dilband and a few other localities nearby. The entire area has been designated as Dilband Flourite District. It has a total reserve of 95,500 tons. A few hundred tons of flourite is mined which meets the local demand.

Sulphur

There are two major sulphur deposits in Pakistan: Koh-i-Sultan and Sanni (Fig. 23). Koh-i-Sultan is located in the Eruptive Zone of western Balochistan about 300 miles west of Quetta. Koh-i-Sultan is an extinct volcano. The lenticular body of the estimated reserve is 738,000 tons at 50 per cent grade. Sulphur extraction was started during World War I but was stopped in 1940. Sanni is located in northern Kirthar about 75 miles southeast of Quetta. The mineralized clay-sandstone bed is 6 feet thick underlying a thin layer of limestone. The reserve is estimated to be 59,000 tons at 45 per cent grade.

Sulphur is the main raw material for sulphuric acid. It is also used in the manufacture of explosives, paints, dyes, rayons, pulp, fertilizer, etc. and in refining petroleum and non-ferrous metals. Sulphur production on a small scale was started in 1971-72 (2,750 tons) but the production since then has decreased (Table 13.2). Home production being insufficient, a substantial quantity of sulphur has to be imported.

Gemstones

A variety of gemstones occur in Pakistan. Emerald, a variety of beryl, is sea green in colour, transparent and highly priced as a precious stone. It is mined at Charbagh-Alburai near Mingora, Swat. Ruby, a transparent deep red variety of corundum, is produced in Hunza. Aquamarine, blue to sea green in colour, white topaz and tourmaline blue are extracted from Dassu, Skardu. Topaz also occurs at Katlong (Mardan). In January 1979 Gemstone Corporation of Pakistan Ltd. was established to help in exploitation and sale of gemstones. Sale points have been established at Hunza, Swat, Peshawar and Rawalpindi.

Limestone

Pure limestone is calcium carbonate but in nature it is invariably mixed with impurities. It is the chief raw material for cement and is also used in the manufacturing of lime, bleaching powder, glass, soap, paper, paints, etc. Pakistan possesses rich deposits of limestone. It is located in many areas but some of them are of greater importance. The Salt Range, the Trans-Indus Salt Range, the Potwar Plateau, and Margalla Hills have several rich deposits of limestone. In this region there are big quantities. The one at Daudkhel is particularly notable (Fig. 24). The limestone deposits of Pezu and Moghalkot of Dera Ismail Khan and those of Kohat and Nowshera and Zinda Pir (Dera Ghazi Khan) are also important. In Sindh, Ganjo Takar limestone in Hyderabad is being used by Zeal Pak Cement. The cement factory at Rohri is utilizing the limestone deposits which extend over 50 miles from Kot Diji to Ranipur. In Karachi the limestone of Murli Hills and that of Manghopir is being used by the cement factories located within the city. Limestone deposits are reported from several areas in Balochistan but those at Harnai are specially large. The reserve of limestone in Pakistan is huge and the production is rapidly increasing. From .34 million tons in 1947 it increased to 6.3 million in 1985-86.

Marble

Marble is primarily used as a decorative stone in the exterior of buildings.

Pakistan has a fairly large reserve of marble of different colours. Some of them compare in quality with the best in the world. Mullagori deposit on Peshawar-Mullagori Road in Khyber Agency has a good reputation (Fig. 24). Its white marble is comparable to the famous marble of Carrara (Italy) and Malirana (India). Marble in colours other than white (grey, yellow and brown) is also available there. At the boundary of Swabi (Mardan District) and Swat, the Gundai Tarko Marble deposits, which are white in colour, are located. Swabi Tehsil has yet another quarry at the Maneri Hills which has white and grey marble of low quality. It is broken into pieces, hence it is used largely as chips. Onyx marble (travertine) occurs in the Eruptive Zone in Chagai area. It is considered to be the result of hot spring

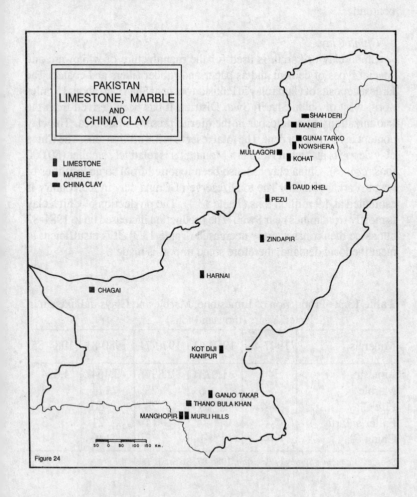

Figure 24

deposition. It is banded in layers of various shades, green, yellow, red and white. Some low quality travertine occurs at Thano Bula Khan.

The demand for marble in Pakistan is on the increase. Its production is consequently increasing (Table 13.3). It was 6,000 tons in 1960-61, 23,000 tons in 1970-71, 114,000 tons in 1980-81 and 122,000 tons in 1985-86. A fair amount of marble is exported.

Clays

Clays are fine-grained material largely composed of hydrous aluminium silicate minerals. They become plastic when wet. Clays are of many types. In Pakistan the important industrial clays are China clay, Fuller's earth and bentonite.

China Clay

China clay or kaolin is used for the manufacture of whiteware and special types of cement and as paper and rubber fillers and coaters.The largest deposits of China clay in Pakistan occur at Shah Deri about 15 miles north-west of Saidu Sharif, Swat District. It has been derived from the kaolinization of the feldspar in the diorite present in the area. The clay content is 16 to 31 per cent. The total reserve is 2.8 million tons. The China clay deposits at Alal in Northern Mountains is relatively smaller (50,000 tons reserve). China clay has also been reported from some localities of Nagar Parkar (Sindh). The total reserve of China clay in the country is estimated at 4.9 million tons (Table 13.1). The production of China clay is mostly from mines near Swat. The production increased up to 1981-82 but since then it has sharply decreased (Table 13.3). It is insufficient to meet the local demand, therefore some import is made.

Table 13.3: Production of Limestone, Marble and Clays in Pakistan in Selected Years (thousand tons)

Minerals	1947-48	1960-61	1970-71	1980-81	1984-85
Limestone	344	1,073	2,897	3,464	4,634
Marble	—	6	23	114	53
Fire Clay	4	15	28	60	77
Fuller's Earth	—	—	14	21	13
China Clay	—	1	8	40	1

Source: *Economic Survey of Pakistan*, 1986-87, Statistics Table 4.1.

Fire Clay

Fire clay is chiefly used in refractories, in the manufacture of potteries and chemicals and as fillers. The main deposits of fire clay have been located both in the eastern and western Salt Range. The western area has better quality of fire clay. It also occurs in the Surghar Range and Kishore Range in the Trans-Indus Area. The total reserve is 100 million tons and the annual production is about 77,000 tons (1984-85) which is sufficient for the present needs of the country.

Fuller's Earth

Fuller's earth is used in oil drilling, foundries and steel mills, oil filtering and clarifying, sealing reservoirs etc. The main deposits of Fuller's earth occur at Ranki and Sebdi Nalas in the southern Sulaiman Range. Huge reserves also occur in Thano Bula Khan in Lakhi Range, 105 km (65 miles) north-east of Karachi. Mining in this area started in 1960. Fuller's earth has also been reported from hills between Sukkur and Kot Diji. Padhrar deposits, 51 km (32 miles) from Khushab are being exploited since 1967. The total reserve of Fuller's earth is very large. Annually over 15,000 to 20,000 tons are produced which meet local demand.

Bentonite

Bentonite has similar uses to those of Fuller's earth. Bentonite occurs in the central Salt Range at Qadirpur-Bhilmor and Bhadrar, in the eastern Salt Range at Rohtas-Dariala, and in the foothills of Azad Kashmir at Bhimber-Mawa Kanch and Samwal-Pothi-Kharota. The total reserve is estimated at 100,000 tons and the annual production is small, ranging from 1,000 to 1,500 tons.

METALLIC MINERALS

Metallic minerals in Pakistan exist in the Axial Belt and in the Eruptive Zone. Iron ore, celestite, copper, manganese, chromite, alumina ore and antimony are known to exist. Only chromite is mined in substantial quantities but difficulties are being experienced. A small quantity of antimony, alumina ore and manganese is also obtained.

Chromite

Chromite is the only metallic ore produced on a commercial scale in Pakistan. It is used to impart hardness and electrical resistance to steel. Bridges and railway carriages are built from steel containing chromite. It is used for the manufacture of engineering tools, stainless steel, etc. It is put as lining in metallurgical furnaces. Chromite has been reported from a number of localities along the Axial Belt of Pakistan where it is associated with ophiolitic suite. It is reported to occur at Harichand, north of Peshawar, at Lasbela in the south, at the flanks of Ras Koh in Balochistan and in South Waziristan. But the main chromite deposits are located around Muslimbagh which is about 120 km (75 miles) north-east of Quetta (Fig. 25). It is from the Muslimbagh mines that chromite is produced.

The reserve is estimated to be fairly large but the quantity has not been established. Mining of chromite from Muslimbagh was started in 1903. Production reached a peak during World War I and again during World War II, after which the production declined. In 1971-72 the production was 34,000 tons. Since then a sharp decline in production has taken place. In the very next year it dropped to 18,000 tons. In 1976-77 the production was 5,000 tons and since 1980-81 it is only 1,000 tons. In Pakistan the local consumption of chromite is nominal. There is no arrangement for refining the ore. Therefore the chromite industry depends upon the foreign market, particularly USA and UK. The export trade has to face competition from other suppliers of chromite like Turkey, the Philippines, South Rhodesia, South Africa, etc. The demand for chromite in the world has recently declined because of a fall in the production of steel. There is keen competition in the world market and Pakistan has failed to compete because of the high cost of production caused by mining with outmoded machinery. The export therefore has virtually ceased since 1978-79. It is unfortunate that the mining of the only metallic mineral produced on a commercial scale is in disarray. Efforts are being made to instal modern machines. With the development of the steel industry it is expected that in the near future chromite mining will get a new life.

Copper

Copper deposits are known to exist in several areas in Pakistan of which some detail is available about Saindak copper deposits. These deposits are located in the Eruptive Zone of western Balochistan about 25 miles north of Koh-i-Tuftan Railway Station (Fig. 25). The Iranian border is 25 km (15 miles) to its west and the Afghan border 42 km (26 miles) to its north. The copper deposits are found in the popularly called Sulphide Valley. It is a desert area and there is a great scarcity of water. The Government has taken interest in Saindak copper. Resource Development Corporation was established in 1974 and was assigned the task of developing the deposits. Mapping, estimation of its reserve, chemical analysis, economic feasibility study, etc. are in progress. The Romanian Government and a consortium of French-Canadian-Yugoslavian Companies have expressed some interest in' its development and exploitation. Recently China has shown interest. There is also a fear that several years of valuable time, rupees in millions, and an immeasurable amount of effort may ultimately go waste. Mining of copper has not yet started.

Iron Ore

Iron ore has been located at a number of places in Pakistan but its commercial exploitation has not started. Low grade ore, small deposits,

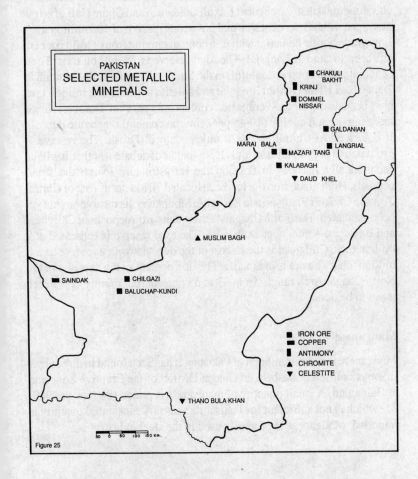

PAKISTAN
SELECTED METALLIC MINERALS

- CHAKULI BAKHT
- KRINJ
- DOMMEL NISSAR
- GALDANIAN
- MARAI BALA
- LANGRIAL
- MAZARI TANG
- KALABAGH
- DAUD KHEL
- MUSLIM BAGH
- SAINDAK
- CHILGAZI
- BALUCHAP-KUNDI

■	IRON ORE
▬	COPPER
▌	ANTIMONY
▲	CHROMITE
▼	CELESTITE

- THANO BULA KHAN

50 0 50 100 150 Km.

Figure 25

location of some of the reserves in inaccessible areas are the main handicaps. The total reserve of iron ore in Pakistan is estimated to be over 430 million tons (Table 13.1).

Kalabagh iron deposits are the largest in Pakistan with an estimated reserve of 309 million tons which is about 72 per cent of Pakistan's total reserve. It is a sedimentary iron ore of low grade with an iron content of 33-34 per cent. It is exposed in a discontinuous belt from Makerwal in the Surghar Range to Kalabagh and Sakesar in the Salt Range. Its economic utilization is still under study. Limonite and siderite deposits with an iron content of 31 per cent have been located at the Marwat Range near Pezu. The total reserve is 12 million tons. Hematite iron ore with 40-45 per cent iron content has been reported at Mazari Tang, Marai Bela and Samana Range in Kohat area. Their total reserves are not known. Hematitic claystone and siltstone occur at Kakul, Galdanian and Chure Gali. It is low grade ore with 20 per cent iron and has a total reserve of 100 million tons. Low grade oolitic hematite with iron content ranging from 9 to 30 per cent has been located at Langrial. The total reserve is 28 million tons. Their economic utilization is doubtful. In the Sulaiman Range at Rakhimunh in Dera Ghazi Khan District limonite and siderite deposits of a million tons have been discovered. Average iron content is 37 per cent. Dommel Nissar has a fairly good quality (40-45 per cent iron content) magnetite deposit. It is located in Chitral about 20 miles south of Drosh. The reserve is estimated to be 6.05 million tons. It is a matter of debate whether it will be economically feasible to develop the infrastructure to tap the small deposits. High grade iron ore has been located 70 km north-east of Chitral Town in Chakuli Bakht area in Zarimure Mountains. Its reserve has not yet been estimated. The North Chagai Arch contains iron deposits at Chilghazi and Baluchap-Kundi near Dalbandin. The total reserve is estimated at 9 million tons. Chilghazi is the largest of the deposits with a reserve of 5.8 million tons. The ore is magnetite. The iron content in the deposits of the North Chagai Arch ranges from 33 to 55 percent, but mining of iron ore is yet to be done.

Manganese

Manganese is a minor mineral of Pakistan. It has been found in three areas in the Axial Belt at Lasbela, in Chagai District of the Eruptive Zone and at Galdanian. A small quantity of manganese is mined (84 tons in 1980-81) which is not sufficient for Pakistan's needs. A substantial quantity is imported. Manganese is primarily used in the steel industry

Antimony

The chief source of antimony is stibnite. It is used as an alloy and in the chemical industry. Pakistan produces a small quantity of antimony (6 tons in 1984-85) from Krinj (Kamalgol) mines, about 20 km (13 miles) north of Chitral Town (Fig. 25). The estimated reserve of antimony in Pakistan is 12,000 tons. Antimony is also reported from Qila Abdullah, Pishin.

Bauxite

Aluminous rocks rather than true bauxite have been established in a number of areas in Pakistan : Muzaffarabad and Kotli in Azad Kashmir, Central Salt Range, Loralai District in Balochistan and other areas. The quality differs widely. The total reserve is estimated to be 74 million tons. The mine at Khakhan-China Spring, Loralai District, was worked from 1955 to 1961. For the last few years the production of alumina ore has been about 2,000 tons annually.

Celestite

Celestite is used in signal rockets and flares, tracer bullets, transportation warning fuses and fireworks. It is also used in the manufacture of strontium compounds, ceramics, luminous paints, plastics, etc. Celestite usually occurs in cracks and cavities of sedimentary rocks. In Pakistan there are two well-known deposits. The largest deposits occur near Thano Bula Khan (Sindh) in limestone (Fig. 25). The content of strontium sulphate is high (84 per cent or more). The estimated reserve is 300,000 tons. Small deposits of celestite occur near Daud Khel in the Western Salt Range. The content of strontium sulphate on an average is 83 per cent and the reserve is about 10,000 tons. In Pakistan a small quantity of celestite is mined (650 tons in 1984-85) which is sufficient for the present needs of the country.

POWER RESOURCES

Pakistan is a small consumer of energy. Per capita energy consumption in Pakistan is 180 kg coal equivalent, which is 11 times less than the world's average consumption. Pakistan consumes two times less energy than Egypt, 3.5 times less than Turkey, 34 times less than UK and 79 times less than that consumed by USA. In spite of such a low consumption Pakistan is not self-sufficient in power resources. The main power resources of

Pakistan are oil, natural gas, hydroelectricity and coal in descending order of importance (Table 13.4). Oil and gas are the main sources of energy in Pakistan. They supply 40 and 35 per cent of the energy respectively. Hydroelectricity supplies 18 per cent and coal 6 per cent. Nuclear energy (.6 per cent) and LPG (.4 per cent) are minor sources. Except for oil all other sources of energy are available within the country. But 64 per cent of the oil consumed is imported which is about 25 per cent of Pakistan's total imports by value. This is a heavy burden on Pakistan's economy. To save foreign exchange a search for alternate sources of energy has been started. Biogas, solar energy and wind may be of some help. But the development of nuclear power will greatly ease the situation. Efforts in that direction are being made.

Coal

Pakistan possesses low quality coal, lignite to sub-bituminous of Tertiary Age. It has low carbon content and has high ash, sulphur and volatile matter. The seams in general are lean, on an average one to three feet thick. Mining started in 1887. The production was .25 million tons in 1948-49 which increased to 1.23 million tons in 1964-65. Since then the production has fluctuated between 1.0 million and 2.0 million tons. The total reserve is estimated at 580 million tons. More than 95 per cent of the coal produced in Pakistan is used in brick kilns. There are three coal provinces, Salt Range, Quetta and Lower Sindh (Fig. 26).

Salt Range and Makerwal-Gullakhel Coal Fields

The coal fields of the Salt Range occupy the southern scarp of the eastern and central ranges covering an area of 260 sq km (100 sq miles).

Table 13.4: Energy Supply in Pakistan (percentage share)

Source	1980-81	1984-85	1985-86
Oil Excluding Export	36.7	40.7	40.2
Gas Excluding Feed Stock	41.6	35.4	35.0
Hydroelectricity	15.8	17.1	18.4
Coal	5.3	5.9	5.5
Nuclear	0.23	0.4	0.6
LPG	0.3	0.5	0.4

Source: *Economic Survey of Pakistan,* 1985-86, Table 8.2, and 1986-87, Table 8.2.

The main coal mines are at Dandot and Pidh. Ara, Chittidand and Dhak Katha are other mines. The coal is of poor quality with high ash and sulphur content. The Makerwal-Gullakhel coal mining area is located in the Trans-Indus Salt Range. The seams are slightly thicker and the coal is of somewhat better quality. A metre gauge line connects the mines with the main railway station.

Quetta Coal Province

The Quetta Coal Province comprises three major coal fields: Khost-Shehrig-Harnai, Sor Range-Degari, and Mach. They are located within 80 km (50 miles) from Quetta. Khost-Shehrig-Harnai is the largest coal field of Balochistan covering an area of 210 sq km (80 sq miles). The coal, though poor is better than that produced in other fields of Pakistan. Shehrig coal in particular has some coking characteristics. This mine is managed by Mineral Development Corporation of Pakistan. They have established a coal washing plant there. The coal on being washed is mixed with high grade imported coal to be transformed into metallurgical coal. Almost 7,500 tons of washed coal will be supplied annually to Pakistan Steel Mill located at Karachi. This field is connected with Zardalu-Sibi Railway Branch.

Sor Range-Degari is an important coal field located 16 km (10 miles) east of Quetta. A metalled road goes from Quetta to Spin Karez and from there a fair weather road goes to the mines. A mile long haulage tunnel has been built by Pakistan Industrial Development Corporation leading to the central part of the field. The coal is sub-bituminous containing ash and sulphur. It is fit for brick kilns and briquetting. It covers an area of 49 sq km (18 sq miles).

Mach Coal Field is located 55 km (40 miles) south of Quetta on both sides of the Sibi-Quetta Railway. A metalled road also passes through the field. The coal is of inferior quality and is located at a shallow depth. The mines are located in low-lying areas, therefore rain water disturbs the mining operations. The field covers an area of 40 sq km (16 sq miles). Besides these three important coal fields coal also occurs at Ab-i-Gum, Ali Gul, Pir Ismail, Ziarat, Duki and other areas of Balochistan. Except for Duki they have small deposits of coal and some of them are not easily accessible.

Lower Sindh Coal Fields

More than 50 per cent of the coal reserves of Pakistan occur in the two Lower Sindh Coal Fields namely Jhimpir-Meting and Lakhra. A third field has been discovered, namely Sonda-Thatta in Thatta District.

Jhimpir-Meting Coal Field is located south of Hyderabad and covers an area of 900 sq km (350 sq miles). It is a relatively small field. Coal occurs at the base of a low limestone hill. The overburden is 15 to 17 metres (50 to 75 feet) thick. The coal is of low quality.

Lakhra coal field is located north of Hyderabad in Dadu District 16 km west of Khanot Railway Station on Dadu-Kotri Section of Pakistan Railways. It has proved reserves of 60 million tons which is about 50 per cent of the total reserve of Pakistan. It is located on a gentle anticline with an overburden of less than 50 metres (150 feet) thick. The coal is lignite.

In 1981 Sonda-Thatta coal field was discovered by the Geological Survey of Pakistan. The field is located on both banks of the Indus River

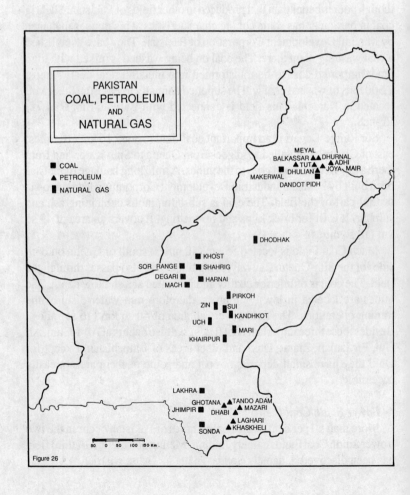

Figure 26

covering an area of 620 sq km (220 sq miles). The coal is said to be of good quality. The proved reserve is 6 million tons.

Petroleum

Pakistan is deficient in petroleum. Up to 1983-84 the domestic production fluctuated between 2.5 and 4.8 million barrels, meeting 11-12 per cent of the local demand. In 1984-85 a breakthrough was achieved when the production reached 9.5 million barrels, 95 per cent increase over that of 1983-84. That year 19 per cent of the oil consumed was met by local supplies (Table 13.5). In 1987-88, the production had already crossed 16.3 million barrels. This became possible with the discovery of new oil fields. However oil continues to be a major item of import by value since 1974-75.

The petroleum products are largely consumed by transport (50 per cent). The bulk is used in running the trucks, buses, automobiles, and aeroplanes. Power, industry, domestic and agriculture are other users in descending order of importance.

Table 13.5: Field-wise Location, Year of Discovery and Production of Crude Oil in Pakistan 1980-81 and 1984-85 (thousand US barrels)

Field	Location	Year of Discovery	1980-81	1984-85
Khaur	Potwar	1915	2	3
Dhulian	Potwar	1935	123	9
Joya Mair	Potwar	1944	181	87
Balkassar	Potwar	1946	280	184
Toot	Potwar	1968	515	925
Meyal	Potwar	1968	2,271	1,895
Adhi	Potwar	1978	57	399
Dhurnal	Potwar	1984	–	2,166
Fimkassar	Potwar	1978	–	10
Khaskheli	Lower Sindh	1981	–	1,161
Laghari	Lower Sindh	1983	–	2,188
Tando Alam	Lower Sindh	1984	–	995
Total	–	–	3,567	9,522

Source: *Energy Year Book*, 1985, Tables 2.1 and 2.2

The geological conditions in parts of Pakistan are favourable for the formation and trapping of oil. Extensive areas are covered with marine sedimentary rocks and there are suitable structural traps for oil. Encouraged by these conditions the search for oil was started in the 1860s and is still continuing. The Americans, the British, the Russians and others have helped in the search. In 1961 Oil and Gas Development Corporation was set up to organize and undertake exploration and development of oil and also its production, refining and sale. The search has been made in the favourable areas of all the four provinces. Seismic survey of the search for oil culminated in the discovery of natural gas. However a number of oil fields have been discovered since 1968 (Table 13.5).

Oil Fields

There are two oil regions in Pakistan: Potwar Plateau and Lower Sind. Potwar Plateau emerged as an oil region in 1915 when Khaur oil field was discovered (Table 13.5). Since then a number of oil fields have been located. Dhulian (1935), Joya Mair (1944), Balkassar (1946), Karsal (1956), Meyal (1968), Toot (1968), Adhi (1978), Fimkassar (1978), Dakhni (1983) and Dhurnal (1984). The production of Khaur, Dhulian, Joya Mair and Balkassar has considerably declined and they are at present minor producers. Dhurnal, Meyal, Toot and Adhi are major producers. Dhurnal started production in 1983-84 with 32,000 barrels and the very next year it made spectacular progress when the production rose to 2.17

Table 13.6: Domestic Production and Total Consumption of Petroleum in Pakistan and the Percentage of Domestic Production to Total Consumption in Selected Years

Year	Consumption (thousand metric tons)	Domestic Production (thousand metric tons)	Domestic Production as percentage of consumption
1949-50	817	99	12
1959-60	2,413	258	11
1969-70	3,820	461	12
1979-80	4,151	479	12
1984-85	6,616	1,278	19

Source: *Economic Survey of Pakistan*, 1980-81 and *Energy Year Book*, 1985.

million barrels. Dhurnal became the second most productive field. Fimkassar is a newcomer (1983-84). It is still a minor producer. Dakhni oil field has yet to go into production.

Lower Indus emerged as an oil region in 1981 when Khashkheli oil field (Badin District) was discovered and in 1982-83 it became a major producer (Table 13.5). Laghari (1983) became the leading oil producer in the country in the very next year after it started production. Tando Alam was discovered in 1984 and became an important producer the same year. Dhabi has also gone into production. Lower Sindh oil region produces 35 per cent of Pakistan's oil. Nari, Tajedi, Mazari, South Mazari and Turk are other fields of Sindh which have not yet started production.

Oil Refineries

There are three oil refineries in Pakistan. Attock Refinery is the oldest and is located at Morga, Rawalpindi. It refines the oil produced in the Potwar Plateau and accounts for about 10 per cent of the total oil refined in Pakistan. The remaining 90 per cent is refined by Pakistan Refinery and National Refinery. Both are located in Karachi. They primarily refine imported oil but now the oil produced in Lower Sindh at Khaskheli, Laghari and Tando Alam is also refined there. Both of them are of equal importance.

Natural Gas

Natural gas is the second most important source of energy, supplying 35 per cent of the energy. The production of gas has doubled in 10 years from 4,957 million cubic metres in 1974-75 to 10,195 in 1984-85. About 95 per cent of the gas is derived from the gas fields and 5 per cent is associated with oil. The industries are the main consumers which utilize 57 per cent of the gas. Among them the fertilizer industry is outstanding with 31 per cent of the gas, followed by domestic consumers (12 per cent) and commercial consumers (3 per cent). The original recoverable reserve was more than 20 trillion cubic feet of which more than 20 per cent has already been consumed. The share of Balochistan in the total original reserve was 65 per cent, 28 per cent that of Sindh and 7 per cent that of Punjab.

The search for oil in Pakistan resulted in the discovery of the gas field at Sui (Balochistan) in 1952. Since then 25 gas fields have been located, 6 in Balochistan, 10 in Sindh and 9 in Punjab. A number of areas are particularly important for gas. Sibi Trough is of special note where Sui, Uch, Zin, and Pirkoh are located (Fig. 26). Upper Sindh has a number of gas fields namely Kandhkot, Khairpur and Mari, while a few are located in Lower Sindh namely Sari/Hundi, Golarchi, Khaskheli and Laghari. In Punjab most of the gas fields are located in the Potwar Plateau and are associated with oil e.g., Meyal, Toot and Dhurnal. Gas at present is produced from three gas fields, namely Sui, Mari and Pirkoh, and from three oil fields, namely Toot, Meyal and Dhurnal. Sari/Hundi and Dhulian have ceased production since 1984-85.

Sui is the largest gas field of Pakistan both in reserve (42 per cent) and production (73 per cent). At the present rate of production it will last up to AD 2000. It has good quality gas with methane content of 90 per cent. It is located in the foothills of Marri-Bugti Hills, Balochistan. The gas is contained in limestone. Sui gas is distributed to Karachi, the most industrialized and populous city of Pakistan by a pipe-line passing through Sukkur and Hyderabad. The gas is transmitted to Lahore by a pipe-line passing through Rahimyar Khan, Multan and Faisalabad. From Faisalabad another pipe-line goes to Rawalpindi, Islamabad, Wah and Peshawar. A pipe-line goes to Quetta from Sui. Pirkoh was discovered in 1977 and was commissioned in 1983-84. It produces 4 per cent of the total gas production. It is located about 100 km north of Sui. Gas from Pirkoh is fed into in the Sui transmission line.

Mari is the second largest gas field of Pakistan with 20 per cent in reserve and 18 per cent in production. The methane content is 73 per cent. Mari gas is primarily used in the production of fertilizer at Dharki, Mirpur

Table 13.7:   Field-wise Production of Gas in Pakistan in Selected Years (million cubic metres)

Gas Fields	1971-72	1974-75	1981-82	1984-85
Sui	2,949	4,363	7,327	7,423
Pirkoh	—	—	—	410
Mari	274	318	1,286	1,876
Sari/Hundi	–	–	71	—
Dhulian	292	247	57	—
Meyal	1	29	352	268
Toot	—	—	18	102
Dhurnal	—	—	—	116
Total	3,516	4,957	9,107	10,195

Source: *Economic Survey of Pakistan*, 1985-86; Statistics Table 5.2

Mathelo and Machigot. A small quantity is supplied to thermal power station at Guddu. Kandhkot gas field was commissioned in 1987. It supplies gas to Guddu Thermal Plant. Meyal, Dhurnal and Toot oil fields in descending order of importance, are located in the Potwar Plateau and produce a small quantity of gas which is fed into the main transmission line. Meyal is the main supplier (3 per cent).

Electricity

At the time of independence (1947) the installed capacity of electricity in Pakistan was meagre (68.8 MW), which was not adequate to meet the local needs. About 10 MW of electricity had to be imported from India (primarily from Uhl River Hydel Plant), therefore efforts were made to develop electric power at a rapid rate. After the commissioning of Rasul hydel plant in 1952 it became possible to cut off the supply coming from India. By 1971-72 the installed capacity increased to 1,862 MW, by 1980-81 to 4,105 MW, by 1984-85 to 5,615 MW and by 1986-87 to 6,653 MW. The increase is phenomenal but the total installed capacity is hardly 50 per cent of the electrical capacity of a large city of a developed country. The per capita consumption of electricity in Pakistan is 33 per cent of that of Turkey and 2 per cent of that of USA and Switzerland. Furthermore the plants do not run to full capacity. The plant utilization factor is less than 50 per cent. The supply of electricity is unable to meet the demand. Load shedding has to be practised every year during the winter season when the hydel power generation is disturbed because of low flow in the rivers. The gap between demand and supply is more than 25 per cent. On the other hand the transmission and distribution losses are 30 per cent. A major loss of electricity is caused by long transmission. Today all the provinces are knit by a national grid. The power is then distributed to different parts of

Table 13.8: Generation of Electricity in Pakistan in Selected Years (million kWh)

Year	Hydel	Thermal	Nuclear	Total
1971-72	3,679	3,789	104	7,572
1980-81	9,043	6,869	150	16,062
1984-85	12,241	10,416	346	23,003

Source: *Economic Survey of Pakistan*, 1985-86, Statistics Table 5.2

the country according to their needs. This system does have some advantages but a considerable amount of power is lost in transmission which has been laid out at a colossal cost and is maintained at an equally heavy cost. Punjab consumes the largest quantity of electricity (56 per cent), followed by Sindh (31 per cent), NWFP (10 per cent) and Balochistan (3 per cent). In per capita consumption Sindh leads (173 kWh), followed by Punjab (144 kWh), NWFP (97 kWh) and Balochistan (31 kWh).

There are three main sources of electrical energy in Pakistan. Hydel (53 per cent) and thermal (45 per cent) are major producers, while nuclear is a small producer (2 per cent).

Hydroelectricity

Hydroelectricity is a major source of energy in Pakistan. Most of the hydel plants of Pakistan are located on the rivers of the northern hilly and mountainous areas where the rugged topography provides a good head for the generation of electricity. A good head makes the water fall from a sufficient height on to the turbine wheel to move it. A regular flow of water is also essential to ensure year-round generation of electricity. But the rivers of Pakistan experience low discharge in the winter season which reduces their power-generating capacity, therefore in the winter season power shortage is generally experienced. A few low artificial falls along the canals have been utilized to develop small hydel plants. According to an estimate made by WAPDA, the hydel power potential of Pakistan is 30,000 MW of which 20,000 MW can be utilized economically. The installed capacity of hydel power plants was 2,898 MW in 1987-88.

At the time of independence there were 2 hydel plants in Pakistan namely Renala and Malakand. Since then several more important hydel plants have been added. Of them Tarbela, Mangla and Warsak are large projects. Tarbela is a magnificent earth-fill dam about 445 feet high on the Indus River (Fig. 27). It is a multipurpose project primarily constructed to supply water for irrigation. But it also produces electricity. Its installed capacity is 1,400 MW. In 1984-85, 7,255 million kWh of electricity was generated with 47 per cent of plant utilization factor. Mangla is another gigantic multipurpose project. It is located on the Jhelum River at a point where the river leaves the mountains. Besides providing water for irrigation, it will generate 800 MW of electricity of which 3,800 million kWh was produced in 1984-85. Its plant utilization factor was 55 per cent. Warsak is yet another multipurpose project designed to provide water for irrigation and for generation of electricity. It is located on the Kabul River about 32 km (20 miles) from Peshawar. Its installed capacity is 240 MW. In

1984-85, 662 million kWh of electricity was produced with plant utilization factor at 55 per cent.

There are a number of small hydel plants in Pakistan. One of them is Renala, located on the Upper Bari Doab Canal. Commissioned in 1925, it is the oldest hydel plant of Pakistan. Its installed capacity is one MW.

Rasul hydel plant utilizes a head of 27 metres between the Upper and Lower Jhelum Canals. Its installed capacity is 22 MW. It was commissioned in 1952, after which the import of electricity from India was stopped. Chichokimallian hydel plant makes use of a seven-metre fall on the Upper Chenab Canal. It is about 45 km from Lahore. It was completed in 1959 with a capacity of 13.2 MW. Nandipur hydel plant is located about

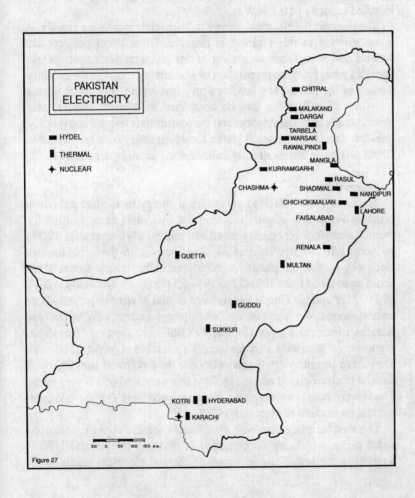

Figure 27

17 km (11 miles) north-east of Gujranwala on the Upper Chenab Canal. It was commissioned in 1963. Its installed capacity is 13.8 MW. Shadiwal hydel plant, with an installed capacity of 13.5 MW utilizes an artificial fall seven metres high on the Upper Jhelum Canal. Malakand hydel plant was constructed in 1938, utilizing the water of Upper Swat Canal with an installed capacity of 16.7 MW which was raised to 20 MW in 1952. The water of Malakand plant is reutilized to turn the turbines of the Dargai Project. This was completed in 1954 with a capacity of 20 MW. Kur-ramgarhi hydel plant takes advantage of the canal taken off from the Kurram River and produces 4 MW of electricity. Chitral is a new hydel plant (1983-84). Its capacity is one MW. As many as 50 units of micro-hydel plants have been developed in remote areas which have a total installed capacity of 0.7 MW.

The demand for electrical energy in Pakistan is increasing rapidly. A quick solution to this problem is required. Giant hydel projects like Tarbela and Mangla are no answer to this problem. Such projects take about 15 years from the preparation of a feasibility report to the commis-sioning of the plant. They involve heavy investment, and return takes a long time. Small plants can be completed in a much shorter time, investment is considerably less and the return starts much more quickly. Pakistan should go for small plants for which many sites are available. China and Japan have gainfully utilized many small hydel plants.

Thermal Power

The contribution made to the electrical energy by the thermal power plants in Pakistan is slightly less than that by hydel plants. In 1984-85, thermal electricty generated was 10,416 million kWh as against 12,241 million kWh by hydroelectricity. The increase in the generation of electricity by thermal plants has been appreciable during recent years, about three times from 1971-72 to 1984-85 (Table 13.8). Guddu unit-IV of 210 MW and the Guddu gas turbines of 400 MW have recently been commissioned. Water and Power Development Authority (WAPDA) and Karachi Electrical Supply Company (KESC) are the two commercial producers of electricity. Besides there are a number of private producers. They have installed small generators for their personal use. The total amount of electricity generated by them is not known but it is very small. The Government is encouraging the private investors to enter into com-mercial production of electricity.

The thermal plants are well distributed over the country unlike the hydel plants which are concentrated in northern Punjab and NWFP. Karachi is the single largest centre of thermal electrical plants in the country. Its six plants produce more than 43 per cent of the total thermal electrical energy of Pakistan. Pipri Thermal Power Station produces 21 per cent and Korangi Thermal Plant 15 per cent of the total thermal energy. Besides Karachi, other stations in Sindh which have large thermal plants are Kotri, Hyderabad, Sukkur and Guddu (21 per cent). In the Punjab large thermal plants are located at Faisalabad (12 per cent), Multan (12.5 per cent), Lahore and Rawalpindi. Outside Sindh and Punjab, Quetta has a large thermal plant producing about 2 per cent of the total thermal electricity of Pakistan.

Nuclear Power

A nuclear power plant has been installed at Karachi with Canadian aid. Its installed capacity is 137 MW. It contributes about 1.5 per cent of the total electricity produced in Pakistan. The supply has sharply fluctuated. From 104 million kWh in 1971-72, it reached its peak in 1975-76 when it produced 610 million kWh. Thereafter the production declined and reached a low level of 2.0 million kWh in 1979-80. Since then the production has steadily increased and was 346 million kWh in 1984-85. Technical difficulties have been the main cause of fluctuation. Another large nuclear plant is being set up at Chashma. Its installed capacity will be 900 MW and it is expected to be completed by 1991.

Solar Energy

Pakistan has an abundance of sunshine all over the country. The length of the shortest day of the year in Pakistan is about 9½ hours. Cloudy days even in the rainiest areas are not many. Continuous occurrence of cloudy conditions interfering with the solar electric generation is rare, therefore conditions in Pakistan are ideal for the development of solar energy. However its economic implications and organizational problems are not easy to solve. The generation of electricity by solar energy is still in its experimental stage in Pakistan.

Starting from 1981 eight plants have been installed and eleven are in various stages of completion, while the feasibility studies for some are under way. It was in December 1981 that the first solar photovoltaic system was commissioned. It is located in Mumniala, a village 60 km from Islamabad. Its capacity originally was 6.8 kWp which was later increased to 8 kWp. The plant supplies electricity to 30 houses and street lights and maintains a storage of 10,000 gallons of drinking water. The storage capacity is to meet three days requirement of the village. Electricity is supplied only for limited hours. The second photovoltaic system is located at Kankoi village in Swat. It was commissioned in June 1983. Its original capacity of 5 kWp has been increased to 60 kWp with the financial assistance of European Economic Community. The power is enough to meet the requirements of 170 houses with two tubelights and one fan for every house, 46 street lights, and fans and lights for three mosques.

Mera Rehmat Khan, a village at a high altitude in Abbottabad District, has a solar electrical plant established with the assistance of UNDP in December 1984. It is a village where snowfall is common in winter but the houses receive electricity from solar energy. Its capacity is 18 kWp.

Commissioned in January 1984, a 20 kWp solar system supplies electricity to two villages of Miro Pediar in Punjab. Recently four solar photovoltaic systems have been commissioned. They are located at Khurkhera (Lasbela District), Malmari (Thatta District), Dittal Khan Leghari (Tharparkar District), and Ghakar (Attock District). In addition four stations are in various stages of completion. They are Dhoke Mian Jeevan (Jhelum District), Nasirabad (Gilgit), Sundus (Sukkur) and Gaiker, (Marri-Bugti area). Solar photovoltaic systems at Patkin (Kharan) and Hoot (Multan) are being set up. Kharan solar project with a capacity of 100 kWp will electrify 4-6 villages.

Biogas

From a demonstration unit in 1974, a national biogas programme was launched in 1980-81. The programme is to go through three phases. In the beginning biogas plants are provided free of cost. In the second phase the beneficiary has to share the cost. In the third phase the beneficiary will bear the whole cost and the Government will provide the technical know-how. The programme has not yet entered the third phase. By 1985, 3,858 family-units were set up, 65 per cent of which were installed free of cost and 35 per cent on cost share basis. The free units are not working well. The biogas is primarily used for çooking. Biofan and biomax for lighting have yet to come in common use. Biogas is still in its experimental stage. Some technical problems involved with the plant remain to be solved. The raw material used is animal waste, primarily cowdung. Its ready supply all the time cannot be guaranteed. Cowdung also constitutes an important manure. If biogas gains popularity and the cowdung is converted into gas the soils of Pakistan which are already deficient in organic matter will further suffer. Biogas plants as they exist today are family-units which are owned by a privileged class. This hardly solves the energy crisis of the rural areas. Further, it is yet to be proved that the benefits derived from biogas plants equal the cost involved. Thus the biogas programme is faced with technical, economic and social hurdles.

Rural Electrification

Rural electricifcation in Pakistan was taken up in right earnest in the second Five-year Plan beginning from 1960. Before that about 600 villages, out of a total of 45,000 villages had electricity (Table 13.9). No village of Balochistan and Sindh had electricity till then. From 1960-80, about 500 villages were electrified every year. By 1986, 48 per cent (21,769 villages) had electricity. In NWFP, 62 per cent of the villages have been electrified, 63 per cent of Sindh, 39 per cent of Punjab and 14 per cent of Balochistan.

The installation of electrically operated tubewells for irrigation and control of waterlogging and salinity has greatly helped rural electrification. Successive efforts for rural development (Village Aid, Basic Democracy, Rural Works Programme, Integrated Rural Development Programme, etc.) have encouraged extension of amenities including electricity to the rural areas. The heavy cost of laying down and maintenance of transmission lines to distant villages with small population is the main impediment in rural electrification. To overcome this, villages within one kilometre of the distribution line and with a population of 1,000 in Punjab and Sindh, and 300-500 in Balochistan and NWFP are selected for electrification. Thus many villages which do not meet these two requirements are left out. To solve this problem generation of electricity by solar energy and biogas has been initiated.

Table 13.9: Number of Villages Electrified in Pakistan

Province	Number of Villages Electrified				Total No. of Villages
	1959-60	1959-60 to 1979-80	1980-81 to 1984-85	Total	
Punjab and Islamabad	100	4,761 2,305	4,910	9,771	25,280
NWFP and FATA	509	2,305	2,101	4,915	7,949
Sindh	—	2,218	1,535	3,753	5,916
Balochistan	—	276	554	830	6,136
Total	609	9,560	9,100	19,269	45,080

Source: *Economic Survey of Pakistan*, 1988-89, Table 4.10 and other sources

Table 13.10: Sectoral Consumption of Electricity in Pakistan in Selected Years (percentage)

Sector	1959-60	1969-70	1979-80	1984-85
Industry	65	46	39	37
Agriculture	11	27	25	17
Domestic	13	10	19	29
Bulk Supply and Public Lighting	8	14	12	12
Commercial	3	3	5	5

Source:- *Economic Survey of Pakistan*, 1981-82 and 1985-86.

Sectoral Consumption of Electricity

Industry, household, agriculture, street lighting and commercial users are the main consumers of electricity in Pakistan in descending order of importance (Table 13.10). Through time the consumption of electricity by all users has increased except street lighting. During the last five years (1981-85) the amount of electricity consumed by street lights has slightly decreased (.5 per cent). The consumption by other sectors has increased by varying amounts. Consequently the percentage share of various consumers has changed. Industry is the largest consumer but its percentage share has sharply decreased from 65 in 1959-60 to 37 in 1984-85 (Table 13.10). On the other hand domestic consumption has been increasing rapidly from 13 per cent in 1959-60 to 29 per cent in 1984-85. This is the consequence of the rising standard of living and expanding rural electrification. The percentage share of agriculture increased markedly from 1960 (11 per cent) to 1970 (27 per cent), but dropped to 17 per cent in 1984-85. The percentage share of commercial consumers has only slightly increased from 1960 to 1985.

Chapter 14

Industries

Pakistan started its life with a weak industrial base. Since then substantial progress has been made but great room for development exists. Manufacturing contributed 8.1 per cent to the GNP in 1950-51 and 19.1 per cent in 1986-87. Industries provided employment to 12 per cent of the labour force in 1951 which increased to 20 per cent in 1961 but decreased to 13 per cent in the 1970s and 1980s. In export, trade manufacturing has registered notable achievements. In 1954-55 manufactured goods accounted for less than 2 per cent of the exports. That gradually increased to 44 per cent in 1969-70 and then to 49 per cent in 1985-86. About 16 per cent of the total exports includes semi-manufactured goods. If this is added, the share of the industries in export becomes more than 65 per cent. Thus manufacturing has made considerable progress in Pakistan's trade to which both private enterprise and government efforts have contributed.

INDUSTRIAL POLICY

The Government of Pakistan spelt out its industrial policy in April 1948, and another after the promulgation of Martial Law in 1958. The two policies were basically the same with small differences.

1. Priority was to be given to industries based upon indigenous raw materials particularly agricultural raw materials.
2. Emphasis was laid on the development of consumer goods industries.
3. Small and cottage industries were to be supported for which Small Industries Corporation was established in 1965.
4. Private enterprise was to be encouraged for which liberal tax concessions were allowed and tariff protection was provided through Pakistan Tariff Commission set up in 1950.
5. Manufacture of arms and ammunition, telephones and wireless equipment, railway wagons, hydel power and any item vital to the security of the country would be undertaken by the Government.

6. The Government would provide financial assistance and help in import of raw materials, technical training and keep a watch on the standard of manufactured goods.

In 1949, Pakistan Industrial Corporation was set up to provide short and long term credit to industries. This was replaced by Industrial Development Bank of Pakistan in 1961. Pakistan Industrial Credit and Investment Corporation (PICIC) was established as a public limited company with the financial support of the State Bank of Pakistan, the International Bank of Reconstruction and Development, the International Co-operation Administration of USA, and a group of private investors of UK, USA, Japan and Pakistan. Its objective was to assist the private sector in the establishment of industries. Industrial Development Corporation was established in 1952 to invest in industries where private capital was shy. Liberal policies were adopted for import of raw materials, machinery and spare parts. Port facilities were expanded. Polytechnic institutes and engineering colleges and universities were established to ensure the availability of technical personnel. Pakistan Council of Scientific and Industrial Research was set up to undertake research primarily to help the industries. Central testing laboratories came up to test the quality of goods imported and produced. Pakistan Standard Institute was set up to improve the quality of local products. A patent office was established to grant patents to inventions and to register industrial designs. Foreign capital was welcomed for investment in industries but investors were to employ Pakistanis both in administrative and technical positions and provide them training facilities. Pakistani nationals were to be given the option to subscribe 51 per cent of all classes of share capital in specified industries and 30 per cent in other industries. In 1954, the local participation was reduced to 40 per cent. In 1959 the condition of local participation was fully withdrawn. The foreign investors could repatriate profit and also the capital. Investment Promotion Bureau was set up in 1959 to attract foreign investment by providing help and facilities in establishing and running the industries. This was the policy followed by the Government until 1971.

Industrial Policy 1972-77

In 1972 a big change in government policy was brought about by adopting the principle of 'Mixed Economy'. Under this principle industrial units belonging to the following basic categories were nationalized:
1. Iron and steel industries
2. Basic metal industries

3. Heavy engineering industries
4. Heavy electrical industries
5. Assembly and manufacture of motor vehicles
6. Assembly and manufacture of tractors
7. Heavy and basic chemicals
8. Petro-chemical industries
9. Cement industries
10. Public utilities: (a) electric generation, transmission and distribution (b) gas and (c) oil refineries.

The Board of Industrial Management was set up to run the nationalized industries. Later the following ten holding corporations were established to distribute the work:

1. Federal Chemical and Ceramics Ltd.
2. Federal Light Engineering Corporation
3. National Design and Industrial Services Corporation
4. National Fertilizer Corporation of Pakistan Ltd.
5. Pakistan Automobile Corporation Ltd.
6. Pakistan Steel Mills Corporation Ltd.
7. Pakistan Industrial Development Corporation Ltd.
8. State Cement Corporation Ltd.
9. State Heavy Engineering and Machine Tool Corporation Ltd.
10. State Petroleum Refining and Petro-chemical Corporation Ltd.

In 1973 vegetable *ghee* industry, in 1974, shipping industry and in 1976, cotton ginning, paddy husking and large flour mills were nationalized. Compensation was paid to the share holders of the nationalized industries at the market value. Measures were taken to broadbase the share, ownership and management of the industries in the private sector.

Industrial Policy 1977 To Date

Martial Law was imposed in July 1977 and soon after, an assurance was given that there would be no further nationalization of industries. The agro-based industries, cotton ginning, rice husking and flour mills were denationalized. Heavy chemicals and cement were opened for development in the private sector. In other heavy and basic industries the extent of participation between private and public sector was determined. In 1978 a presidential order was passed by which it became possible to denationalize the taken-over industries. Accordingly some industries were returned to their former owners.

Incentives in many forms have been given to the private sector to participate in the industrialization of the country. These include fiscal and monetary concessions, liberal import of raw material and machinery, streamlining of investment procedure and legal protection. Incentives have also been provided to overseas Pakistanis to invest in industries. Foreign investment is welcomed and full protection has been granted. Foreign investment is possible with or without local participation. Repatriation of capital and profit is allowed.

An export processing zone has been developed in Karachi over an area of 80.94 hectares. As part of the incentive no import and export duty will be imposed in this zone. Income tax exemption for 5 years is allowed. The infrastructure for setting-up of industries has been provided. Six Pakistani and foreign banks have been allowed to open up branches. So far 76 projects have been accorded sanction of which 15 units have gone into production.

INDUSTRIAL DEVELOPMENT

Industrial development depends upon a number of factors. Availability of raw materials, power, capital, entrepreneurs, technical and managerial skill, market, government policy, and political stability are some of the important ones. Pakistan is rich in a number of agricultural raw materials particularly cotton and sugarcane but is poor in industrial minerals. It is making commendable efforts to improve its energy position. It has a good domestic market for both consumer and capital goods but has to face stiff competition in the world market. The business community migrating from India brought managerial skill and also a fair amount of capital. Later the Industrial Development Bank and other agencies were established to finance the industries. In addition foreign aid and loans were tapped, but a shortage of capital particularly foreign exchange has almost always been felt. Technical skill has been steadily growing with the establishment of technical universities and institutes. Lack of sophisticated technology still exists. The government policy has always been directed towards encouraging the establishment of industries but periodic disturbed political conditions have impeded industrial development. In general the industrial development in Pakistan can be divided into three periods:

Period of Rapid Industrial Growth: 1947-71
Period of Slow Growth: 1972-1977
Period of Fluctuating Growth: 1977 onwards.

Period of Rapid Industrial Growth (1947-1971)

The period from 1947 to 1971 is one of rapid industrial growth in Pakistan though the growth rate was not uniform throughout the period. The pace of development in general increased in the Second Five-year Plan (1960-65). In the Third Five-year Plan period (1965-70) the growth slowed down.

The entrepreneurs who migrated from India had adequate managerial skill and financial resources. Technical know-how was available within the country. A ready home market existed. The raw materials available locally and the foreign exchange earned by the businessman during the Korean War made it possible to develop consumer goods industries like cotton textile, sugar, vegetable *ghee*, cigarette, cement, etc. on a large scale. In the First Five-year Plan period (1955-60) the pace of industrialization continued its onward march and the overall increase in industrial production was 80 per cent as against the target of 60 per cent. Furthermore diversification was started. Plants for the manufacture of fertilizers, dyes, DDT, penicillin, engineering and electrical goods, and steel re-rolling mills came into existence.

In the Second Five-year Plan (1960-65) industries were allowed 23.5 per cent of the total allocation and if the power sector is added to this it increased to 50 per cent. The result was phenomenal. The industrial production was doubled. The existing industries registered a record increase. Some basic industries like sulphuric acid, caustic soda and soda ash provided a new dimension to chemical industries. Pakistan Industrial Development Corporation of the Government entered the scene to establish industries in which the private sector was not interested.

In the ambitious third Five-year Plan (1965-70) the allocation for industrial development was doubled. The emphasis was shifted from consumer to capital goods industries. But the plan met with difficulties in the very first year. A war broke out with India and funds had to be diverted for defence. USA, the main donor, suspended aid. Later political disturbances adversely affected the economic development of the country. In spite of difficulties the pace of industrial development continued though at a slower rate. Some industries like sugar, cement, cigarette, art silk and rayon, caustic soda, soda ash and sulphuric acid registered commendable growth. The overall progress of industries was satisfactory. The annual growth rate of the manufacturing sector was 7.7 per cent in 1950-60 and 9.9 per cent in 1960-70.

Period of Slow Growth (1972-77)

Industrial development in Pakistan greatly suffered because of internal and external forces. In 1971, after a war between Pakistan and India, East Pakistan (Bangladesh) seceded. This placed a heavy economic burden on Pakistan. In the wake of the war, aid was virtually suspended which put a further strain on Pakistan's economy. The new Government pursued the policy of mixed economy. Under the policy the basic industries and a number of other industries were nationalized in three stages. By this measure the share of the public sector in industrial investment increased to 30 per cent. The management particularly the top tier went into some hands which did not have much experience of running industries and the production of some of the industries was adversely affected, at least temporarily. The private sector which was at the vanguard stopped further investment. The private investment in large scale industries was reduced to one-third from 1970-71 to 1976-77. The international market was also not very receptive. The textile industry which was already in trouble suffered further. Consequently the industrial development greatly slowed down. The annual growth dropped from 9.9 per cent in 1960-70 to 5.5 per cent in 1970-80.

Period of Fluctuating Growth (1977 onwards)

In 1977 the Government reversed its industrial policy. Assurance was given that no further nationalization of industries would be carried out. Agro-based industries were denationalized. The private sector was given incentives in more than one form. Foreign investors were also invited and provided many facilities. The activities of the public sector were limited to the completion of on-going projects (Karachi Steel Mills being the largest), erection of traction plants, modernization of the existing plants and the establishment of a few new projects. Out of a total of Rs. 40 billion, Rs. 19 billion was earmarked for the private sector in the Five-year Plan (1977-83). But the private sector did not take the expected interest in investment in industries. The fact is that the investment in the manufacturing sector declined by 24 per cent from 1977-78 to 1981 at 1977-78 prices. In the Sixth Plan (1983-88) Rs. 77 billion was earmarked for industrial investment. The share of the public sector was fixed at 19.5 per cent and that of the private sector at 80.5 per cent. But the growth which had increased to 10.8 per cent (1977-82) dropped to 7.6 per cent (1982-87). The overall growth from 1977 to 1987 was 8.7 per cent.

COTTON TEXTILE

Cotton textile is the largest industry of Pakistan. It provides employment to 50 per cent of the industrial labour force. It is the main contributor to the GNP from the industrial sector. At present it is passing through a difficult period but it is designed to play a very important role in the industrial complex of Pakistan. Abundance of raw cotton produced at home, a sufficiently large local market, and availability of a big labour force are favourable factors which will help restore the cotton textile industry to its prestigious position.

Cotton textile industries of Pakistan made phenomenal progress. In 1948 there were 78,000 spindles and 3,000 looms which produced 6.3 million kg of yarn and 29.6 million sq metres of cloth. About 7 per cent of the cotton produced in the country was consumed by the mills. Therefore plans were made to develop the cotton textile industry so that better economic use of raw cotton is made. By 1955 there were 1.4 million spindles and 23,000 looms. The production of yarn increased to 114 million kg and that of cloth to 326 million sq metres. About 40 per cent of the cotton produced was locally consumed. This onward march of the cotton textile industry continued until 1973-74 when 380 million kg of yarn and 592 million sq metres of cloth were produced. An adverse change occurred in 1974-75. The number of spindles and looms, and the production of yarn and cloth decreased. Since then some recovery in some years has been recorded. But for more than a decade the textile industry has been in trouble.

The problems which the cotton textile industry faces are many. Some of the important ones are that the machinery is old and obsolete. About 34

Table 14.1: Cotton Looms and Spindles in Pakistan in Selected Years (in thousands)

Years	Spindles installed	Spindles working	Looms installed	Looms working
1950	182	182	3	3
1959-60	1,582	1,491	27	26
1969-70	2,397	2,327	31	27
1979-80	3,731	2,841	26	16
1984-85	4,396	3,022	23	10
1987-88	4,330	3,690	16	9

Source: *Economic Survey of Pakistan,* 1988-89, Statistical Appendix, Table 4.4.

per cent of the spindles are 23 years old and 27 per cent are 13 years old. Duty on parts makes replacement costly. The result was that in 1971-72 out of 30,000 looms, 26,000 were working. In 1984-85, 10,000 out of 23,000 looms were working (Table 14.1). The number of spindles continues to increase but the percentage of working spindles decreased from 94 per cent in 1959-60 to 71 per cent in 1984-85. The production of cloth reached its peak in 1970-71. Thereafter the production dropped by 59 per cent in 1984-85. Yarn production has continued to increase. The working capacity of looms fell from 87 per cent in 1971-72 to 43 per cent in 1984-85. High cost of cotton and polyester, lack of interest by entrepreneurs, labour problems, shortage of technical hands, high power cost in Karachi and financial liability and poor liquidity are some of the problems. The Beg Committee reveals that in spite of financial and other help it will not be possible to revive about 45 per cent of the spindles.

Location of Cotton Textile Industry

Karachi has emerged as the largest cotton textile centre of Pakistan (Fig. 28). As the main industrial city Karachi enjoyed the infrastructure at a scale not available at other centres. Labour from all over the country pours into Karachi. The imported machinery is saved from additional transport cost by installation at the port city. Karachi for the same reason has advantages in exporting cotton goods. The disadvantage that Karachi suffers from is that it is not located in the cotton producing area. Another disadvantage is higher power cost. In order to take advantage of the nearness of raw cotton and the market and also in pursuance of government policy, new textile centres have developed in Pakistan. But Karachi continues to be the largest centre.

Faisalabad is the second largest centre. It is located close to the cotton belt of Pakistan. In course of time an infrastructure has been built up. A labour force has been attracted from the surrounding areas which are the most thickly populated parts of Pakistan and the local market is also sufficiently large. Hyderabad is the third largest centre of cotton textile industry in Pakistan. It enjoys the advantage of being located in the cotton area. The market of Sindh is easily accessible and it is not very far from the port. As an important industrial city of Pakistan, Hyderabad has also the infrastructure required and the labour force needed. Apart from these major cotton textile centres, cotton mills have been established in cotton growing areas to tap the local raw material and to serve the local market as far as possible. Such centres are located in Sindh and Punjab. Tando Yusuf, Tando Adam, Tando Muhammad Khan, Khairpur and Gambat

(Khairpur Mirs) are some in Sindh. Rahimyar Khan, Multan, Islamabad (Multan), Burewala, Sargodha, Lahore, Golra (Faisalabad), and Okara are in the Punjab.

Some cotton mills have been established outside the cotton producing area. They are also away from the port. They are located to meet the local demand and also to take advantage of the tax holiday and other incentives given by the Government. These centres are mainly located in Northern Punjab and NWFP and a few in Balochistan. Rawalpindi, Kala (Jhelum), Bhakkar and Liaquatabad are some of the centres in the Punjab. Peshawar, Haripur, Nowshera and Habibabad (Kohat) are in NWFP. Quetta is an important centre in Balochistan. Hab Chowki has also attracted a few cotton mills but that is a virtual extension of Karachi industrial area.

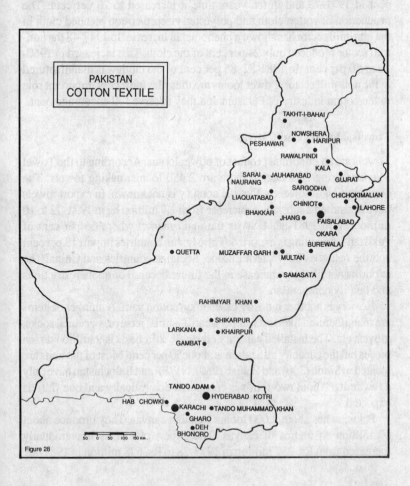

Figure 28

Power Looms (Non-Mill Weaving)

Over the last decade power looms (non-mill looms) made remarkable progress when units of four looms were exempted from excise duty. It is estimated that 60,000 to 70,000 looms are operating in the non-mill sector. This sector has provided jobs directly to 120,000 workers and the number of entrepreneurs is 10,000. The power looms and accessories are locally made. About 4,000 sizing units and 200 finishing units are also operating. It is estimated that the engineering, sizing and finishing units are providing employment to about 60,000 to 70,000 workers. The power looms have also become the saviour of yarn producers. In 1981-82 about 70 per cent of the yarn was consumed by the power looms. There has been a steady increase in consumption of yarn by the non-mill sector. It was about 32 per cent in 1971-72 and in ten years time it increased to 70 per cent. The production of cotton cloth and polyester-viscose/cotton blended cloth in the non-mill sector has shown a phenomenal increase. In 1947-48 the non-mill sector produced only 24 per cent of the cloth. That increased in 1960-70 to 50 per cent. In 1981-82, 85 per cent of the cloth was manufactured in the non-mill sector. Power looms are thus playing a very important role in the cotton industry of Pakistan and they deserve full encouragement.

Towels, Hosiery and Canvas

Towels are an important product of power looms. According to the Towel Manufacturing Association there are 2,450 looms making towels. The consumption of towels within the country is not known. In export towels have registered a substantial increase from 2.7 million kg in 1971-72 to 10 million kg in 1981-82. USA is the main market where 66 per cent of Pakistan's towelling is exported. The Muslim countries import 13 per cent and the rest goes to Western Europe, Socialist countries and China. The export is not likely to increase in the future because of quota restrictions and quality competition.

Hosiery is another industry based upon cotton yarn. A number of items are manufactured like vests, underwear, T-shirts, jerseys, sweaters, socks, gloves, etc. The installed capacity on single shirt basis is 9 million dozen pieces but the capacity utilization is about 50 per cent. Most of the units are located in Sindh (300) and Punjab (250). NWFP and Balochistan have only a few units. About two-thirds is consumed domestically and one-third is exported.

Pakistan has about 2,000 looms weaving canvas. They produce about 60 million sq metres of canvas. The export of canvas has gradually increased from Rs. 257 million in 1977-78 to Rs. 678 million in 1981-82.

WOOLLEN TEXTILE

With one small woollen mill and a number of cottage industries Pakistan produced a small quantity of blankets, carpets, shawls and tweeds at independence (1947). Pakistan had to import worsted and woollen goods worth Rs. 30 million annually. Today with more than 70 large, medium and small units Pakistan has become self-sufficient in hosiery, shawls and carpets. The import of worsted and woollen goods has largely been reduced and carpets and worsted yarns are exported. However the woollen textile industry continues to be relatively small as compared to the cotton textile industry. Pakistan produces a modest quantity of raw wool (48,000 tons in 1984-85). The production of raw wool has been steadily increasing. In the early years Pakistan exported 60 per cent of the total raw wool produced. Today the export has dwindled to less than 10 per cent. On the other hand the import of raw wool is increasing. The import becomes necessary to mix with domestic wool which is of poor quality. The increase in the production of raw wool, reduction in export and increase in import signify the expansion of the woollen textile industry that is taking place in Pakistan. In 1970 Pakistan had 48,000 spindles, which increased to 103,084 in 1982. Of them 61 per cent were located in Punjab, 30 per cent in Sindh, 5 per cent in Balochistan and 4 per cent in NWFP. They together produced 9.1 million kg of wool yarn and 1.5 million kg of acrylic.

The installed capacity of looms in 1982 was 765 of which 616 were working, giving a capacity utilization of 82.5 per cent. The Punjab accounts for 50 per cent of installed looms, Sindh 37 per cent, Balochistan 9 per cent and NWFP 4 per cent. Woollen cloth, suitings, blankets, shawls and carpets are some of the important products of the woollen textile industry in Pakistan. The production of woollen fabrics has doubled from 1976-77 to 1981-82. It was 844,000 sq metres in 1976-77 which increased to 1,733,300 sq metres in 1981-82.

Carpets are both machine-made and hand-knotted in Pakistan. The production of machine-made carpets has increased from 485,000 sq metres in 1976-77 to 615,000 sq metres in 1980-81. The production of hand-knotted carpets is not known exactly. According to an estimate it is 2.50 million sq. metres. Among the woollen textile products carpets have emerged as an export of Pakistan. In 1969-70, Rs. 55 million worth of carpets were exported. That increased to Rs. 2,693 million in 1985-86. Carpets account for about 5 per cent of the total export of Pakistan. Wool spinning and weaving by indigenous methods such as cottage industry is an old practice in Pakistan. It is done in all the provinces. Modern woollen textile industry has also been developed in all the four provinces. Some of the important centres are Harnai and Mastung in Balochistan, Bannu and

Nowshera in NWFP, Quaidabad, Ismailabad, Lawrencepur, Rawalpindi and Sahiwal in Punjab and Karachi, Hyderabad and Larkana in Sindh.

ART SILK

From an importer Pakistan has become an exporter of art silk. The production of art silk in 1951 was only .91 million metres. That increased to 9.3 million metres in 1953 as a result of a ban imposed on import of art silk. It became 32.4 million metres in 1963-64, 270.43 million metres in 1975-76 and 402.23 million metres in 1981-82.

The art silk industry is run by 47,000 looms distributed in Sindh, Punjab and Tribal Areas. The factories in general are small with 6 to 12 looms. Factories with 20 looms are very few in number. The small factories are scattered in many places of which Karachi, Gujranwala, Multan and Faisalabad are specially important. Art silk primarily depends upon imported yarn. About 20 million kg of yarn are imported. The shortage of yarn is met by blended yarn domestically produced. Pakistan has been exporting a significant quantity of art silk.

JUTE INDUSTRY

Jute is an excellent packing material. It is cheap, durable and strong. In Pakistan jute bags are used for packing products like cotton, cotton yarn, cotton goods, rice, carpets etc. Sugar and flour at present are packed in cloth, and cement in paper bags. The demand for jute goods is on the increase. It was 50,616 million tons in 1973-74, and increased to 100,147 million tons in 1981-82. It is estimated that an annual 6 per cent increase in demand will take place during the next few years. It is encouraging to note that in spite of increasing demand, the percentage share of import is decreasing. Imported jute goods accounted for 58.6 per cent of the total demand in 1977-78 which decreased to 44 per cent in 1981-82. This was achieved by the installation of new jute mills and by increasing the capacity of utilization. At present there are 13 jute mills in Pakistan of which 8 were installed after the separation of East Pakistan (now Bangladesh). The capacity utilization which was about 60 per cent in 1973-74 dropped to 44.5 per cent in 1977-78. Thereafter it started to make a recovery. It increased to 70 per cent in 1985. In 1947 when Pakistan was created there was no jute mill in the country, though it was the largest producer of raw jute in the world. Since the jute was produced in East Pakistan (now Bangladesh) it was decided to establish jute mills there. It was in 1964 that the first jute mill was installed in present-day Pakistan at

Kotri near Hyderabad. In 1971 when East Pakistan seceded there were four jute mills in West Pakistan at Kotri, Jaranwala, Muzaffargarh and Gharo near Karachi. By 1985, 13 jute mills were operating with a total production capacity of 120,000 tons. Besides the four jute mills already mentioned the rest are located (Fig. 29) at Karachi, Hab Chowki (Balochistan), Dhabeji (Sindh), on Faisalabad Road 10 km (six miles) from Shekhupura, Noorwala, Jauharabad (Khushab), Muzaffargarh Road (Khushab) and Kabul River Station (Mardan Road, Nowshera). Sanction has already been given for installation of six new jute mills. Two existing jute mills have applied for expansion. Nearness to a port or a market are considerations kept in mind while locating the mills.

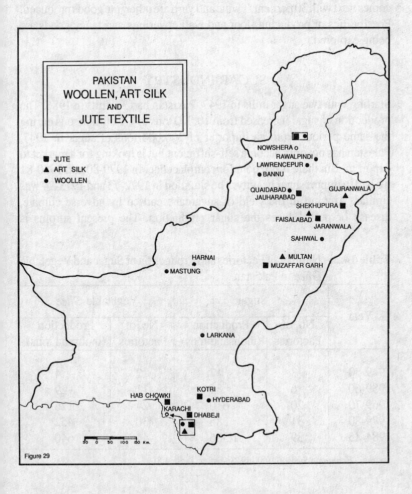

Figure 29

Bangladesh is almost the sole supplier of raw jute to Pakistan. This dependence upon one source is a matter of concern. Immediately after the emergence of Bangladesh the supply of jute to Pakistan was suspended. With great efforts jute was imported from Burma and *kenaf* from Thailand to run the mills yet the production was adversely affected. Attempts have been made with success to grow jute in Pakistan particularly in the Punjab and Sindh. But the jute production is not gaining momentum because it needs good land where it has to compete with cotton, wheat and rice in the Punjab and sugarcane in Sindh. From the farmer's point of view the economic advantage of jute has yet to be established.

The main jute goods produced in Pakistan are sacking and hessian. Sacking accounts for 60 per cent of the jute goods produced. Hessian comes next with 30 per cent. Twine and yarn are other jute goods produced. Possibilities of producing floor and wall coverings and fancy goods are being explored.

SUGAR INDUSTRY

Starting with two sugar mills in 1947, Pakistan had 39 mills in 1986. The production of sugar increased from 10,000 tons to 1.1 million tons during the same period. From an importer of 300,000 tons of sugar in 1947, Pakistan has not only become self-sufficient but is looking for a market to export to. But there is no room for complacence. In 1979-80 and 1980-81 we had to import sugar heavily. The situation in 1972-73 and 1973-74 was similar. Any cut in the yield of sugarcane caused by adverse climate, disease or pest reduces the sugar production. The present surplus is

Table 14.2: Number of Factories and Production of Sugar and Vegetable *Ghee* in Pakistan

Year	Sugar		Vegetable *Ghee*	
	No. of Factories	Production (thousand tons)	No. of Factories	Production (thousand tons)
1949-50	3	17	2	4
1959-60	6	84	11	29
1969-70	20	610	24	126
1979-80	31	586	30	452
1984-85	39	1,306	44	640

Source: *Economic Survey*, 1988-89, Statistics Table 4.5.

obtained with a low per capita consumption of sugar (11 kg per annum as against 55 kg in the western countries). It must however be pointed out that the present-day consumption of 11 kg is several times higher than that in 1947 when it was only 3 kg. In other words the per capita consumption of sugar in Pakistan is increasing and the population is also increasing therefore the surplus can only be maintained by increasing sugar production. Consequently more mills should be established. To feed these mills should not be much of a problem, if only the yield of sugarcane per acre in Pakistan which is very low, is increased. It is 15 tons per acre when it is 90 tons per acre in Brazil and 30 tons in the Philippines. Further, at present 30-35 per cent of cane is crushed for making sugar and the rest is converted into *gur* and other products. With more mills established more

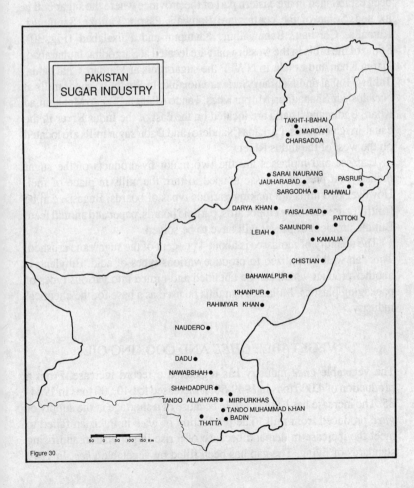

PAKISTAN
SUGAR INDUSTRY

TAKHT-I-BAHAI
MARDAN
CHARSADDA

SARAI NAURANG
JAUHARABAD
PASRUR
SARGODHA
RAHWALI
DARYA KHAN
FAISALABAD
PATTOKI
SAMUNDRI
LEIAH
KAMALIA
CHISTIAN
BAHAWALPUR
KHANPUR
RAHIMYAR KHAN
NAUDERO
DADU
NAWABSHAH
SHAHDADPUR
TANDO ALLAHYAR
MIRPURKHAS
TANDO MUHAMMAD KHAN
THATTA
BADIN

50 0 50 100 150 Km

Figure 30

sugarcane will go to the sugar mills. The recovery of sugar at present in Pakistan is about 9 per cent which can be considerably improved. Sugar in Pakistan is obtained from sugarcane though four mills are equipped to manufacture sugar from beet also. Sugarcane is a product which starts to lose weight soon after it is cut therefore it must be crushed as soon as possible after harvesting. This necessitates the location of sugar mills within the sugarcane growing areas. Fortunately sugar mills can be run by sugarcane bagasse which greatly solves the power problem. The sugarcane crushing season is about 160 days. This does produce some labour problem.

In 1947 there were only two sugar mills, one at Takht-i-Bahai (NWFP) and the other at Rahwali (Punjab). By 1986 there were 39 mills, 18 in Punjab, 16 in Sindh and 5 in NWFP. Most of the sugar mills in Punjab have been established in the eastern part of the province where the sugar belt is located. Some of the centres are Rahwali, Pasrur, Pattoki, Samundri, Kamalia, Chistian, Bahawalpur, Khanpur and Faisalabad (Fig. 30). Some of the mills in the western part are located at Sargodha, Jauharabad, Darya Khan and Leiah. In NWFP the sugar mills at Mardan, Charsadda, Takht-i-Bahai and Naurang Sarai are notable. In Sindh the sugar mills at Nawabshah, Shadadpur, Mirpur Khas, Tando Allahyar, Tando Muhammad Khan, Badin and Thatta are located on the east of the Indus River in the canal-irrigated areas. Larkana (Naudero) and Dadu sugar mills are located on the west of the Indus River.

Bagasse and molasses are the two major by-products of the sugar industry. At present bagasse is used to turn the mills in place of fuel. However two mills are making various types of boards. Bagasse can be fruitfully used to make chipboards, particle boards, paper and animal feed. But the problem of power will have to be solved.

The quantity of molasses is about 4 per cent of the sugarcane crushed. This can well be utilized to produce various types of acid. Ethylene is another product which can be obtained and turned into various types of packaging plastics. Molasses can thus be used as a base for the chemical industry.

VEGETABLE *GHEE* AND COOKING OIL

The vegetable *ghee* industry has registered a record increase. From a production of 4,000 tons in 1949-50, it increased to 640,000 tons in 1984-85. The increase has been possible because of a shortage in the supply of *ghee* produced from milk. The production of *ghee* in Pakistan failed to meet the increase in demand because of a rise in population and rising standards of living. The gap has been filled by vegetable *ghee*. In 1949 there were two units of vegetable *ghee* in Pakistan. That increased to 26 in 1973, when the vegetable *ghee* industry was nationalized. Out of 26 units 23 were taken over. The production was 223,000 tons annually. In 1976 Ghee Corporation of Pakistan was established to look after the industry. The Government has now permitted the private sector to establish vegetable *ghee* industry. In 1984-85, 44 units were operating and they produced 640,000 tons of *ghee* and cooking oil. The main raw material of vegetable *ghee* is edible oil which is not available in sufficient quantity within the country. About 75 per cent of oil consumed by the *ghee* industry is imported. The market for *ghee* is widely distributed all over the country, particularly in the urban areas. *Ghee* industry is, therefore, widely distributed. Karachi, Nawabshah, Rahimyar Khan, Bahawalpur, Multan,

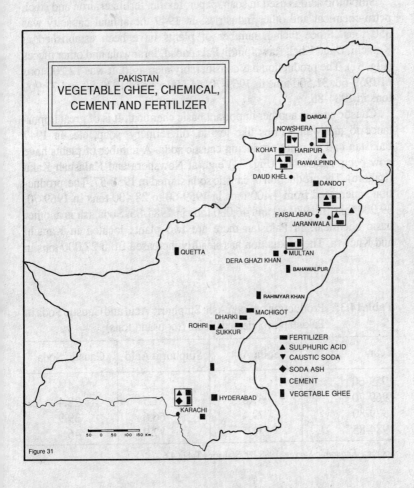

Figure 31

Faisalabad, Nowshera, Haripur and Dargai are some of the important centres where the *ghee* industry is located (Fig. 31).

CHEMICALS

Some of the basic chemicals like sulphuric acid, soda ash and caustic soda are needed by many industries. The basic raw materials like salt, limestone, gypsum and natural gas are obtained in Pakistan in large quantities. Rich deposits of sulphur are present in Koh-i-Sultan (Balochistan) and are awaiting exploitation. Coal and oil are obtained in a moderate quantity. At the time of independence a weak chemical industry existed in the country. Since then appreciable progress has been made.

Sulphuric acid is used in soap, paper, textile, fertilizer, iron and steel, petro-chemical and other industries. In 1949 the annual capacity was 350 tons. Since then a number of plants have been established at Karachi, Daud Khel, Rawalpindi, Faisalabad, Jaranwala and other places (Fig. 31). The production has considerably increased. It was 12,200 tons in 1959-60, 31,500 tons in 1969-70, 66,600 tons in 1979-80 and 77,900 tons in 1984-85.

Caustic soda is another important basic chemical. It is of great importance to many industries like textile, oil refinery, soap, etc. In 1947 Pakistan had no plant producing caustic soda. A number of plants have now been established (Fig. 31) e.g., at Nowshera and Kalashah Kaku (Lahore). The production of caustic soda started in 1956-57. The production increased from 4,400 tons in 1959-60 to 28,400 tons in 1969-70, 39,900 tons in 1979-80 and 46,000 tons in 1984-85. Soda ash is another basic chemical. In Pakistan there are two plants located in Karachi and Khewra. The production has steadily increased from 27,000 tons in

Table14.3:   Production of Soda Ash, Sulphuric Acid and Caustic Soda in Pakistan in Selected Years (thousand tons)

Year	Soda Ash	Sulphuric Acid	Caustic Soda
1959-60	27	12.2	4.4
1969-70	67.8	31.5	28.4
1979-80	79.4	66.6	39.9
1984-85	122.1	77.9	46

Source: *Economic Survey,* 1988-89, Statistics Table 4.6.

Carpet weaving

Women and children cleaning shrimps

National Refinery, Korangi Industrial area, Karachi

One of many fertilizer factories

1959-60 to 122,000 tons in 1984-85. But the demand has outstripped the supply and a substantial quantity of soda ash has to be imported.

FERTILIZER

Pakistan being an important agricultural country requires a large quantity of cowdung, compost and other manures. But they are in short supply therefore chemical fertilizers have gained special importance. The consumption of chemical fertilizers has increased from 31,000 nutrient tons in 1960-61 to 1.25 million tons in 1984-85 (Table 14.4). The increase has been more than three times in 20 years. The production of fertilizer during the same period increased from 11,500 tons in 1960-61 to 1.12 million tons in 1984-85. In other words though the production has been on the increase, it fell short of demand and Pakistan had to import a large quantity of fertilizer. The production of chemical fertilizer in Pakistan started in the 1950s when Pakistan Industrial Development Corportion established two fertilizer factories, one at Faisalabad and the other at Daud Khel (Fig. 31). The factory at Faisalabad went into production in 1957. Its annual capacity was 16,000 tons of superphosphate based upon imported sulphur and rock-phosphate. The ammonium sulphate factory at Daud Khel went into production in 1958. Its annual capacity was 50,000 tons and it utilized local coal and gypsum as raw materials. Natural gas later entered the field as raw material and a plant was established at Multan with an annual capacity of 100,000 tons of ammonium sulphate and 59,000 tons of urea. Since then urea plants have been established at Dharki, Shekhupura, Mirpur Mathelo, Haripur and Machi Got near Sadiqabad (Rahimyar Khan District). A superphosphate plant is at Jaranwala. Nitrogenous fertilizers account for 92 per cent of the total production which is quite understandable as the soils of Pakistan are very deficient in organic matters.

Table 14.4: Consumption, Production and Import of Fertilizer in Pakistan in Selected Years (in thousand tons)

Year	Consumption	Production	Import
1960-61	31	12	36
1970-71	283	133	151
1980-81	1,080	439	575
1984-85	1,253	1,119	342

Source: *Agricultural Statistics of Pakistan*, various years.

CEMENT

The main raw material of the cement industry is limestone. A substantial quantity of gypsum is also required. Pakistan is fortunate in possessing both limestone and gypsum in large quantities therefore there is no dearth of raw material. The domestic market is also sufficiently large. In 1947 Pakistan was an exporter of cement. But with development work starting in Pakistan the country soon became an importer of cement. The annual production of cement has steadily increased from .4 million tons in 1949-50 to 6.1 million tons in 1986-87. The increase in production of cement has not made the country self-sufficient in cement. The gap between demand and supply has not been bridged. But during 1983-86 a marked decrease in import took place.

Pakistan had 5 cement factories in 1947. The number increased to 14 in 1984-85 and to 18 in 1987. They are located at Karachi, Hyderabad, Rohri, Ismailwal (Jhelum), Daud Khel, Dandot and Wah Hattor (Fig. 31). In 1972 the cement factories were nationalized and put under the State Cement Corporation of Pakistan. Since then the capacity of Javedan Cement Factory, Karachi, and Mustahkam Cement Factory, Farooquia, have been expanded by 300,000 tons each. In addition new cement factories have been established at Thatta, Dera Ghazi Khan, Bari Danda (Kohat).

IRON AND STEEL AND ENGINEERING

In the early years of industrialization in Pakistan the emphasis was on the production of consumer goods. However as early as 1955, it was felt that the establishment of basic industry like iron and steel was essential for the economic development of the country. But it was not until 1973 that the foundation stone of the first iron and steel plant was laid with the technical

Table 14.5: Number of Factories and Production of Cement in Pakistan in Selected Years (thousand tons)

Years	No. of Factories	Production
1947-50	–	395
1959-60	6	982
1969-70	9	2,656
1979-80	9	3,343
1984-85	14	4,732

Source: *Economic Survey*, 1988-89, Statistics Table 4.5

and economic co-operation of USSR. It is located in Karachi close to the new seaport of Bin Qasim (Fig. 32). The steel mill covers an area of 7,540 hectares including 3,290 hectares for Steel Township. The raw materials for Pakistan Steel Mill are iron ore, manganese and coking coal. Pakistan imports all these raw materials. Iron ore is already being imported from Australia, Brazil, Canada, India and Liberia and coking coal from Australia. It is expected that Shahrig Coal (Balochistan) after washing will become suitable for the steel mill. This will meet 6 per cent of the need of the mill. The steel mill has two blast furnaces and has a capacity of 1.1 million tons. The plant will produce billets, hot rolled sheets, cold rolled sheets, pig iron, etc.

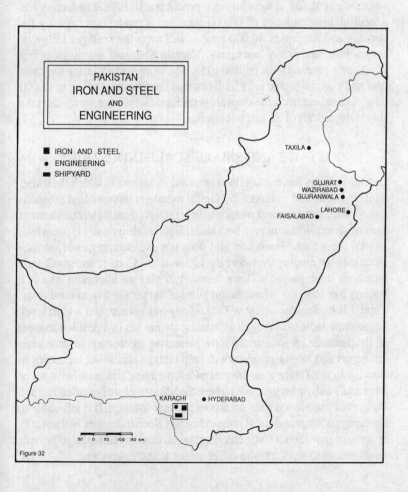

PAKISTAN
IRON AND STEEL
AND
ENGINEERING

■ IRON AND STEEL
● ENGINEERING
■ SHIPYARD

TAXILA ●

GUJRAT ●
WAZIRABAD ●
GUJRANWALA ●
LAHORE ●
FAISALABAD ●

KARACHI ● HYDERABAD

50 0 50 100 150 Km.

Figure 32

Pakistan Machine Tool Factory was established at Karachi in 1968 in collaboration with a Swiss firm. It has grown into a large sophisticated engineering complex. It is manufacturing precision machines and tools for the engineering industry, transmission components and automotive parts. It was in 1968 that the Government gave sanction for a heavy mechanical complex at Taxila. It has been established with Chinese assistance. It started production in 1970. Some of the important items manufactured are sugar mill equipment, cement factory machinery, overhead travelling cranes, road rollers, truck chassis, low pressure package type boilers, etc. Larkana Sugar Mills is using equipment manufactured at Taxila.

Another engineering project, a heavy foundry and forge, was sanctioned by the Government in 1972. This has been established with Chinese assistance at Taxila. It went into trial production in 1976. The factory has a steel melting capacity of 60,000 tons and a production capacity for castings and forging of 46,000 tons. It will meet the needs of railways, automobiles and heavy machinery. Karachi Shipyard and Engineering Works was planned to be built in 1953. The work started during the same year and was completed in 1956. It can build and repair ships up to 12,000 tons. A canal connects the shipyard with Karachi harbour which can take ships with a draft of 22 feet in high tide.

COTTAGE AND SMALL SCALE INDUSTRIES

Cottage industry has been defined as an industrial unit in which the owner himself works and is helped by family members but no hired labour is employed. Craftsmen and artisans have established such units as means of earning on a full-time or part-time basis. Small scale industry is one which employs less than 50 workers and does not use electric power, or uses electricity but employs not more than 20 workers. Cottage and small scale industries have played and are destined to play an important role in a country like Pakistan where the majority of the people live in rural areas. Capital is inadequate and shy. Technology has not reached a high level. Large scale industries though expanding are not yet in a position to meet all the demands for industrial goods. Increasing automation in large scale industries and labour problem will help cottage and small industries to flourish in the future also. Instead of encouraging the establishment of large scale industries in centres where the infrastructure is inadequate and the cost of production rises on account of mal-location, it is advisable to encourage cottage and small scale industries. Such industries will not only absorb the new labour force entering the job market but will also provide employment to workers who suffer seasonal unemployment.

Already cottage and small scale industries provide employment to more than 75 per cent of the industrial labour force of Pakistan. Small industries account for more than 25 per cent of the total capital invested in industries. Rural to urban migration particularly to large urban centres can be appreciably arrested by encouraging cottage and small industries rather than decentralization of large scale industries to unsuitable economic locations. Many by-products of the large scale industries can be gainfully utilized by small and cottage industries. Realizing the importance of such industries the Government established the Small Industries Corporation in 1965. The Corporation provides technical and financial assistance to the cottage and small industries. Training facilities for artisans and technicians have been developed at many centres. Small industrial estates have been

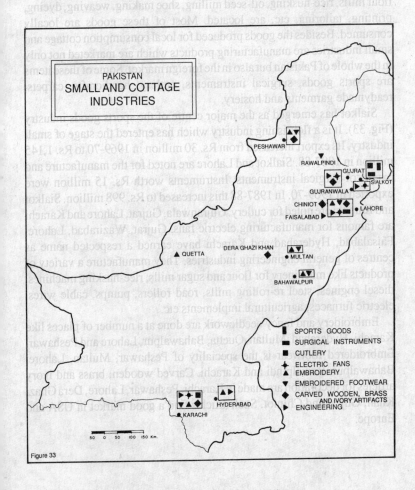

PAKISTAN
SMALL AND COTTAGE
INDUSTRIES

SPORTS GOODS
SURGICAL INSTRUMENTS
CUTLERY
ELECTRIC FANS
EMBROIDERY
EMBROIDERED FOOTWEAR
CARVED WOODEN, BRASS
AND IVORY ARTIFACTS
ENGINEERING

50 0 50 100 150 Km.

Figure 33

established at a number of places like Sukkur, Larkana, Hyderabad in Sindh; Gujranwala, Sialkot, Lahore, Gujrat, Bahawalpur and Jhelum in Punjab; Peshawar, Dera Ismail Khan, Mardan and Abbottabad in NWFP, and Quetta in Balochistan. The Corporation is also providing marketing facilities. The cottage and small industries suffer from high cost of production, lack of standardization, short supply of power and raw materials, inadequate credit facilities and lack of proper marketing facilities.

A web of cottage industries has developed in Pakistan. Blacksmiths and carpenters play a very important role by making and repairing agricultural implements. They also make crude furniture, doors, windows, utensils, etc. Potters play an important part by making pottery in which food in rural areas is mostly cooked. In large villages (central places of higher order) flour mills, rice-husking, oil-seed milling, shoe making, weaving, dyeing, printing, tailoring, etc. are located. Most of these goods are locally consumed. Besides the goods produced for local consumption cottage and small industries are manufacturing products which are marketed not only in the whole of Pakistan but also in the foreign market. Some of these items are sports goods, surgical instruments, cutlery, handicrafts, carpets, readymade garments and hosiery.

Sialkot has emerged as the major centre of the sports goods industry (Fig. 33). It is a flourishing industry which has entered the stage of small industry. Its export increased from Rs. 30 million in 1969-70 to Rs. 1,145 million in 1987-88. Sialkot and Lahore are noted for the manufacture and export of surgical instruments. Instruments worth Rs. 15 million were exported in 1969-70. In 1987-88 this increased to Rs. 998 million. Sialkot and Karachi are noted for cutlery. Gujranwala, Gujrat, Lahore and Karachi are famous for manufacturing electric fans. Gujrat, Wazirabad, Lahore, Faisalabad, Hyderabad and Karachi have earned a respected name as centres of general engineering industries. They manufacture a variety of products like machinery for flour and sugar mills, rice-husking machines, diesel engines, steel re-rolling mills, road rollers, pumps, cable wires, electric furnaces, agricultural implements etc.

Embroidery and fancy needlework are done at a number of places like Karachi, Hyderabad, Multan, Quetta, Bahawalpur, Lahore and Peshawar. Embroidered footwear is the speciality of Peshawar, Multan, Lahore, Bahawalpur, Rawalpindi and Karachi. Carved wooden, brass and ivory articles for decoration are made in Karachi, Peshawar, Lahore, Dera Ghazi Khan, Gujrat and Chiniot. Such articles find a good market in USA and Europe.

Chapter 15

Foreign Trade

The most striking feature of the foreign trade of Pakistan is that it has experienced an unfavourable balance of trade in all years except 1947-48, 1950-51 and 1972-73. The commercial policy of Pakistan is to cut down imports and encourage exports. However not only are exports lagging behind imports, but the gap between the two is also widening. This is a matter of grave concern. The deficit in balance of payment is met by the remittances sent by Pakistanis working abroad and secondarily by loans and grants.

In the first year after independence (1947-48) Pakistan registered a favourable balance of trade because of heavy restriction on imports and a high level of export which occurred incidentally. Encouraged by this situation, the Government announced the policy of Open General Licence (OGL) in August 1948 and heavy import of goods took place. This adversely affected the balance of trade. In 1949 the British pound was devalued by 30 per cent and India followed suit. Pakistan refused to devalue its currency. Thereby a trade crisis developed between India and Pakistan and India restricted trade with Pakistan. At that time 60 per cent of Pakistan's trade was with India. Pakistan revised its trade policy. Open General Licence (OGL) was restricted to certain essential commodities like machinery, drugs, chemicals, minerals, oil, etc. Efforts were made to find new markets for export. In 1950, the Korean War broke out and Pakistan made a good profit by exporting goods worth Rs. 177 million. Pakistan never enjoyed such a heavy balance of export over import in any other year. Import was again liberalized and open General Licence was once again introduced. Heavy over-spending took place and the very next year (1951-52), an adverse balance of Rs. 552 million was registered. The Korean War had also come to an end. In early 1952 the foreign exchange reserve had reached a dangerously low level. Steps were felt necessary to check import and increase export. Open General Licence was restricted in August 1952. Export of cotton was allowed below support price and exporters were compensated by the Cotton Board. Export duty on all exports was reduced and it was abolished on raw wool. These steps did help to reduce the adverse balance of trade but the unfavourable balance continued. By that time industrialization in the country had started and import of capital goods and raw materials could not be cut. Some of the indigenous raw materials which used to be exported were now consumed by local industries.

To boost export Pakistani currency was devalued on 31 July 1955. In the first year after devaluation the desired result was achieved. Export increased considerably. The increase in import was relatively much less. But after the first year exports began to decrease slowly and then sharply. A further boost to the export trade was felt necessary. In January 1958 Export Bonus Scheme was introduced but it was abolished in May 1972. Under the scheme bonus vouchers were issued to exporters of some specified items excluding traditional primary exports. These vouchers were of different percentages of value earned from exports. They could be utilized for importing specified items or could be traded freely in the stock exchange. The Export Credit Guarantee Scheme was introduced in 1962 to cover commercial risk not covered by insurance. In 1964-65 a tax holiday was given to exporters of industrial goods. Export Promotion Bureau was established, and trade delegations were sent to different countries. Participation in international trade fairs and conferences was encouraged. These steps did not produce the desired result because of the liberalization of the import policy. That was necessitated because of the implementation of development plans but unfortunately non-essential luxury goods were also imported by the liberal policy adopted. The foreign

Table 15.1: Export, Import and Trade Balance 1947-48
(million rupees)

Year	Export	Import	Balance
1947-48	444	319	125
1949-50	535	912	− 377
1959-60	763	1,806	− 1,043
1969-70	1,609	3,285	− 1,676
1979-80	23,410	46,929	− 23,519
1984-85	37,979	89,778	− 51,799
1987-88	78,445	111,382	− 32,937

Source: *Economic Survey of Pakistan*, 1988-89, Statistics Table 10.2.

financial assistance which had started to come into the country made it possible to import goods worth more than the foreign earnings. The assistance was more in shape of grants but as the years rolled by the percentage of grants began to decrease and that of loans began to increase. From 1960-61 onward loans exceeded grants every year. In 1973-74 the grant dropped to 10 per cent. Therefore a liberal import policy particularly for non-essential items has no justification.

In 1971 Pakistan had to face the crisis of the secession of East Pakistan (now Bangladesh). Pakistan had to find a market for goods which had been sold to East Pakistan, worth Rs. 923 million (1969-70). Fortunately these problems were easily solved. Even in 1970-71, Pakistan's export was 24 per cent higher than that in 1969-70.

In 1972 a drastic devaluation of the Pakistani rupee (more than 100 per cent) was made under pressure from the International Monetary Fund (IMF) and the World Bank. A favourable impact of devaluation on foreign trade was experienced only in the first year (1972-73) when a favourable trade balance was registered. After that year a worsening position has been experienced. On 9 January 1982, another important measure was taken and that was to delink the rupee from the US dollar. The rupee is now a floating currency. Since the introduction of the managed floating exchange rate system the Pakistani rupee has registered depreciation against all the important currencies of the world. By 1986-87, the total depreciation against the US dollar was 42.9 per cent. This has considerably increased import costs. Unfavourable balance of trade experienced by Pakistan is the outcome of many causes:

1. Inability of Pakistani goods to compete successfully in quality and price in a highly competitive world market.
2. Difficulties faced by Pakistan in crossing the tariff wall of other countries.
3. Quota system introduced by some countries with good buying power.
4. Dependence of Pakistan on other countries for capital goods, sophisticated machinery and tools and spare parts.
5. Heavy import of petroleum.
6. Shortage of food grains, edible oil, tea and other food items. Pakistan has become self-sufficient in wheat but has to import in years of low production.
7. In general a liberal import policy which makes it possible to import non-essential goods with hard earned foreign exchange.

EXPORTS

The exports of Pakistan have registered growth with some fluctuation from 1947-48 onward (Table 15.1). The increase in value of exports was largely because of rise in price rather than increase in volume of export.

Table 15.2: Economic Classification of Exports of Pakistan 1969-70 to 1987-88 (percentage share)

Year	Primary Commodities	Semi-manufactured	Manufactured Goods
1969-70	33	23	44
1974-75	48	13	39
1979-80	42	15	43
1984-85	29	17	54
1987-88	28	20	52

Source: *Economic Survey of Pakistan*, 1988-89 Statistics Table 10.4.

Table 15.3: Ten Leading Exports of Pakistan and their Percentage Share in Total Exports in Selected Years

Position	1969-70	1979-80	1984-85
1st	Cotton Cloth (16)	Rice (17.9)	Cotton Cloth (12.2)
2nd	Cotton Yarn (15.8)	Raw Cotton (14.2)	Raw Cotton (11.5)
3rd	Raw Cotton (13)	Cotton Cloth (10.3)	Cotton Yarn (10.3)
4th	Leather (6.8)	Carpets (9.4)	Rice (8.8)
5th	Rice (5.8)	Cotton Yarn (8.7)	Ready made garments and Hosiery (7.0)
6th	Fish and by-products (3.2)	Petroleum and by-products (7.5)	Leather (6.1)
7th	Carpets (3.1)	Leather (5.4)	Carpets (5.3)
8th	Petroleum and by-products (3.0)	Readymade garments and hosiery (3.1)	Fish and by-products (3.2)
9th	Sports Goods (1.9)	Fish and by-products (2.3)	Surgical Instruments (2.0)
10th	Raw Wool (1.8)	*Guar* (1.4)	Sports (1.8)

Source of raw data: *Economic Survey of Pakistan*, 1986-87, Statistics Table 10.5.

Since 1985-86 a welcome boost in export has been witnessed. Contributory factors have been diversifying goods and markets, improving product quality, simplification of the procedure of export, financial assistance to exporters and other measures.

Traditionally Pakistan has been an exporter of raw material. There were not many manufactured or semi-manufactured goods to be sold. Sport goods, cutlery, leather and others were a few such articles. They had but a small market. Until 1954-55 manufactured goods accounted for less than 2 per cent of the total export. After 1955-56 their percentage began to increase and by 1958-59 the percentage share of manufactured and semi-manufactured goods was more than 50 per cent of the total export. At present the contribution of semi-manufactured and manufactured goods has risen to two-thirds (Table 15.2).

Manufactured goods account for over 50 per cent of the export and semi-manufactured goods about 20 per cent. Cotton-based exports have dominated the export trade of Pakistan. From 1947 to 1952-53 raw cotton had the lion's share. Thereafter cotton goods also entered the world market. Today raw cotton, cotton cloth, cotton yarn, readymade garments and hosiery account for more than 40 per cent of the total export. The first three items have invariably occupied a position among the five leading exports of Pakistan (Table 15.3). Raw cotton goes to Japan, UK and other European countries, cotton yarn to Hong Kong, cotton cloth to East European countries and the Middle East, and readymade garments and hosiery to USA, Europe and the Middle East.

Rice emerged as a major export after the secession of East Pakistan in 1971. Before that East Pakistan used to consume the bulk of West Pakistan rice. In 1973-74 rice became the single largest export item of Pakistan and maintained this position up to 1983-84. Leather, carpets and sports goods are other major exports of Pakistan.

IMPORTS

The import trade of Pakistan registered a steady growth from 1947-48 to 1971-72 when it increased 10 times in 25 years. Since 1972-73 very rapid growth in import has taken place. In 16 years from 1972-73 to 1986-87 imports increased 33 times. Some economic factors have worked behind this rapid growth. In 1972 the Pakistani rupee was devalued by 100 per cent and within one year the value of imported goods was doubled. From 1973 an unprecedented increase in the price of petroleum started to take place and Pakistan had to pay heavily on its purchase. With the introduction of the managed floating exchange rate system in 1982, a marked depreciation of the rupee took place causing a heavy increase in the import bill. However the rapid rate of increase in imports has been checked since 1985-86 with cuts in the import of petroleum, wheat and edible oil.

Pakistan was a heavy importer of consumer goods in the beginning. With industrial development in the country, the composition of imports began to change. Capital goods and industrial raw materials started to gain prominence and by 1960-61, they accounted for 71 per cent of the imports. In 1969-70, capital goods accounted for 50 per cent of the imports and the industrial raw materials, 40 per cent (Table 15.4).

Thereafter the percentage share of capital goods has decreased and that of industrial raw materials has increased. For the last several years industrial raw materials have accounted for 50 per cent of the imports, capital goods 33 per cent and consumer goods 17 per cent. All efforts should now be directed to make cuts in the import of capital goods and industrial raw materials by producing them in Pakistan.

Machinery occupies an important position in the list of imports in Pakistan (Table 15.5). Already in 1954-55 it headed the list. In 1975-76 it yielded the first position to petroleum and its products but machinery continued to occupy the second position. Transport equipment, iron and steel and manufactures and electrical goods have a high position in the import list. They are largely imported from Japan, China, USA and European countries. Petroleum and its products have always remained a major import of Pakistan as the country is deficient in these products. But since 1974-75, they have acquired the leading position among the imports of Pakistan. In 1971-72 petroleum and its products accounted for 7.3 per cent of the imports which rose to 18.3 per cent in 1980-81. Since then a decline in its percentage share has been witnessed. This rise in import

Table 15.4: Economic Classification of Imports in Pakistan
1969-70 to 1987-88 (percentage share)

Year	Capital Goods	Industrial Raw Material	Consumer Goods
1969-70	50	40	10
1974-75	28	49	23
1979-80	36	48	16
1984-85	32	52	16
1987-88	36	45	19

Source: *Economic Survey of Pakistan*, 1988-89, Statistics Table 10.4.

value has largely been on account of a rise in the price of petroleum of which Saudi Arabia and Iran are the main suppliers.

In the early years after its creation Pakistan was self-sufficient in major items of food. But within a few years with a rise in population Pakistan became a net importer of food grains, edible oil, milk, etc. In 1972-73 and 1973-74, Pakistan had to spend large amounts of money on import of food grains, pulses and flour. They accounted for 3 per cent of the import bill. USA is the major supplier. Up to 1971, tea used to come from East Pakistan (now Bangladesh). Since 1971-72, tea has become a major import of Pakistan. Tea accounts for 2 to 5 per cent of the total value of imports. Sri Lanka and Tanzania are some of the important exporters of tea to Pakistan. Edible oil is yet another food product that Pakistan has to

Table 15.5: Ten leading Imports of Pakistan and their Percentage Share in Selected Years

Position	1969-70	1979-80	1984-85
1st	Machinery (non-electrical) (21.6)	Petroleum and Products (22.8)	Petroleum and Products (24.2)
2nd	Iron and Steel and Manufactures (11.0)	Machinery (non-electrical) (11.9)	Machinery (non-electrical) (15.0)
3rd	Transport Equipment (10.4)	Transport Equipment (10.4)	Transport Equiptment (8.8)
4th	Fertilizer (8.9)	Iron & Steel (6.4)	Edible Oils (7.7)
5th	Electrical goods (6.7)	Fertilizers (5.8)	Chemicals (6.2)
6th	Petroleum and Products (6.3)	Edible Oils (4.9)	Iron and Steel & Manufactures (4.4)
7th	Chemicals (2.8)	Electrical Goods (3.8)	Tea (3.9)
8th	Edible Oils (2.3)	Art Silk Yarn (3.2)	Grains, Pulses and Flour (3.2)
9th	Non-ferrous Metals (2.0)	Grains, Pulses and Flour (2.2)	Electrical Goods (2.8)
10th	Drugs and medicines (1.9)	Tea (2.0)	Drugs and Medicines (2.2)

Source of raw data : *Economic Survey of Pakistan*, 1986-87, Statistics Table 10.7

import in a large quantity. It is largely used as raw material for the production of vegetable *ghee*. USA is the main supplier of vegetable oil. Pakistani farmers are using more and more chemical fertilizer for their crops. However, in spite of an increase in the quantity of chemical fertilizer being produced within Pakistan the shortage continues. A heavy quantity of metallic minerals and art-silk yarn constitute other major imports.

DIRECTION OF TRADE

At independence Pakistan carried on the bulk of its trade with India. After 7½ months India raised duties on its exports. In 1949 Pakistan did not

Table 15.6: Direction of Exports from Pakistan in Selected Years (percentage of total exports)

Countries	1970-71	1979-80	1984-85	1986-87
Asia excluding Middle East	44.3	31.9	28.1	28.7
China	4.3	6.2	2.7	0.5
Japan	16.0	7.7	12.0	10.9
Hong Kong	9.0	7.9	2.8	2.8
Middle East	13.5	25.3	20.5	15.2
Kuwait	3.1	2.1	1.0	0.80
Abu Dhabi	0.6	1.3	0.5	0.2
Saudi Arabia	2.4	5.4	6.9	7.1
Dubai	1.2	3.5	4.5	3.4
Iran	0.6	4.4	3.0	1.5
Western Europe	21.8	25.2	27.6	34.0
UK	7.7	4.8	6.7	7.2
Italy	3.7	3.8	4.1	5.8
West Germany	3.1	6.1	5.7	0.7
France	1.8	2.5	2.6	3.3
Eastern Europe	11.7	4.2	5.5	3.7
USSR	4.0	2.2	2.5	2.4
North America	6.1	5.7	11.3	11.3
USA	5.2	5.1	10.4	10.2

Source: *10 Years of Pakistan in Statistics,* 1972-82, Statistics Division, Government of Pakistan, Table 18.3 and *Annual Report,* 1986-87, State Bank of Pakistan, Statistical Annexure, Table 9.2.

devalue its currency along with India and UK. India refused to accept the non-devaluation policy of Pakistan. Thereupon Pakistan decided to diversify its trade relations. First of all, close relations were established with UK and then with other West European countries, Australia and New Zealand. Next to be tapped were USA and Canada. Trade relations with Japan, South-East Asian countries, South America and the Middle East were then developed. Trade was also extended with China, USSR, East European countries and African countries. With India, trade was suspended in 1965. A new agreement was signed in 1978. With Bangladesh a trade agreement was signed in 1974. At present Pakistan has trade relations with many countries, but there are some countries and regions with which the volume of trade is more than with others.

Table 15.7: Direction of Imports into Pakistan in Selected Years (percentage of total imports)

Area and Countries	1971-72	1979-80	1984-85	1986-87
Asia excluding Middle East	23.6	26.6	29.4	31.7
China	2.8	3.1	2.7	3.9
Japan	10.0	11.6	13.4	16.4
Hong Kong	0.7	0.5	0.4	0.3
Middle East	8.0	25.6	26.1	18.0
Kuwait	1.8	10.1	7.9	7.4
Abu Dhabi	1.0	3.2	4.4	1.8
Saudi Arabia	2.6	6.9	10.7	5.3
Dubai	0.2	1.1	0.7	0.8
Iran	1.8	0.2	1.2	1.1
Western Europe	33.5	26.7	22.3	30.3
UK	10.1	6.1	5.9	6.7
West Germany	9.8	4.9	5.8	7.8
Italy	5.5	4.0	2.4	2.8
France	2.2	4.6	1.8	2.6
Eastern Europe	10.3	3.5	1.9	2.6
USSR	2.4	1.1	0.5	0.6
North America	22.1	12.8	13.6	12.0
USA	20.8	12.3	12.3	11.0

Source: *10 Years of Pakistan in Statistics,* 1972-82, Statistics Division, Government of Pakistan, Table 18.4 and *Annual Report,* 1986-87, State Bank of Pakistan, Statistical Annexure.

Asia (excluding the Middle East) leads in trade with Pakistan. Japan is particularly important as its percentage share is the highest. It accounted for 11 per cent of the total exports of Pakistan and 16 per cent of imports in 1986-87. Pakistan suffers from a heavy adverse balance of trade against Japan. China is another country with which Pakistan carries on heavy trade. Exports fluctuate from year to year varying between 3 and 6 per cent. Import remain at about 3 per cent. In some years the balance of trade is in favour of Pakistan while in others it is adverse. Hong Kong is yet another country to which Pakistan makes heavy exports. The import from Hong Kong is comparatively small therefore Pakistan enjoys a favourable balance of trade. Sri Lanka, Bangladesh and Singapore are other Asian countries with which Pakistan has considerable trade. Imports from Sri Lanka usually exceed exports. Trade relations with Bangladesh were established in 1974. The volume of trade is gradually increasing. The trade balance favours Pakistan in some years and Bangladesh in others. With Singapore the exports have not registered any substantial increase but the imports have increased. Pakistan suffers from an adverse balance of trade. Pakistan has established firm trade relations with some of the Middle East countries. In 1971-72 they accounted for 13.5 per cent of the total exports from Pakistan, which increased to 20.5 per cent in 1984-85. In imports to Pakistan the percentage share of the Middle East countries was 8 per cent in 1971-72 which increased to 26.1 per cent in 1984-85. Pakistan enjoyed a favourable trade balance up to 1973-74 after which it has not only faced an unfavourable balance but the gap is increasing. This happened on account of a heavy increase in the price of petroleum which Pakistan imports from the Middle East. Saudi Arabia among the Middle East countries is the largest purchaser of Pakistani goods and the largest exporter of petroleum. Iran is another country with which Pakistan has considerable exports and imports. Dubai is largely an importer of Pakistani goods and Kuwait and Abu Dhabi are largely exporters.

Pakistan has long-standing trade relations with Western Europe. Heavy imports and also heavy exports take place between the two regions. Western Europe accounts for more than 25 per cent of both exports and imports of Pakistan. UK, West Germany, Italy and France are the important countries for trade with Pakistan in descending order of importance. Pakistan suffers from a heavy unfavourable balance of trade with all of them.

Pakistan carries on substantial trade with North America where USA is the most important. The percentage share of USA in exports from Pakistan was 5 per cent for some years which jumped to 10 per cent in 1986-87 but the share in imports dropped from 21 per cent in 1971-72 to

An unmetalled road

The ship of the Desert – the camel

Autorickshaws plying on a busy road

Buses on a hazardous mountain route

12 per cent in 1986-87. Next to Japan, USA enjoys the heaviest favourable balance of trade against Pakistan.

Eastern Europe is yet another notable area for trade with Pakistan. But its percentage share both in export and import is decreasing. USSR is the chief country in this region for trade with Pakistan. With other regions of the world Pakistan's trade is small.

Chapter 16

Transportation

Transportation plays an important role in the economy of a country. Railways and roads are the main arteries of collection and distribution of goods. They also deliver exportable goods to the sea ports and bring imported goods inland. Airlines handle a smaller quantity of cargo but as a means of transport their role is sufficiently important. The transportation network is thus closely linked with the economic development of a country. The more developed the country the better is the network of transport. Pakistan possesses a less developed transportation network.

RAILWAYS

Pakistan had 8,554 km (5,315 miles) of railways in 1947 which increased to 8,875 km in 1986. There has been an addition of only 321 km in 40 years (Table 16.1).

Pakistan Railways have three gauges, broad gauge (5 feet 3 inches wide), metre gauge (3 feet 3 inches wide) and narrow gauge (2 feet 6 inches wide). The increase in route length has been achieved by constructing some broad gauge lines, the most notable being the extension between Kashmor and Dera Ghazi Khan, and another between Mardan and Charsadda. Karachi circular railway has been built to ease the traffic problems of Karachi City. The route length of metre-gauge and narrow-gauge decreased because some of these gauges were converted into broad gauge. For example Jacobabad - Kashmor section has been changed from narrow to broad gauge and Hyderabad-Mirpurkhas section from metre to broad gauge.

The extension work was hampered because of difficulties in maintaining and running the existing railways. The locomotives in Pakistan were run by coal. After the creation of Pakistan coal became a scarce commodity. Pakistan produces only a small quantity of coal of inferior quality. It became increasingly difficult to get coal from India which was the main supplier. Therefore Pakistan had to change its engines from coal to diesel which required money and time. Workshops had also to be remodelled to repair and maintain them. Another problem was the unavailability of railway sleepers in the absence of local supply of wood. Slowly Pakistan Railways switching to concrete sleepers. Before Pakistan Railways was fully rehabilitated, competition came from the road.

The freight carried by the railways increased at a steady rate in the early years after which it has been fluctuating within a narrow margin (Table 16.1). From 1947 to 1960 it increased gradually from 3 million tons to 12 million tons, after that it has fluctuated between 11 to 13 million tons. Railways carry bulky and heavy goods like food grains, cotton, oil and heavy machinery while small consignments have almost become the monopoly of roads. Passenger traffic has registered an increase with some fluctuation from year to year. In 1949-50, 64 million passengers were handled, which increased to 144 million in 1979-80, but dropped to 93 million in 1985-86 as a result of competition with other means of transport.

A railway network has developed only in canal colonies of the Punjab and Sindh. It is in eastern Punjab that the railway network is most extensive. It is here that a number of rivers and associated canals have made possible the development of agriculture and have attracted a large population and many collecting and distributing centres for agricultural products have developed. Many industrial centres have also emerged.

ROADS

At independence roads served more as feeders to the railways. Today they are important competitors of railways both in carriage of goods and

Table 16.1: Pakistan Railways: Route Kilometres, Passengers and Freight Carried in Selected Years

Years	Route km	Passengers (millions)	Freight (million tons)
1949-50	8,554	68	7
1959-60	8,572	121	12
1969-70	8,564	132	13
1979-80	8,817	144	12
1984-85	8,875	95	11
1985-86	8,875	93	12

Source: *Economic Survey of Pakistan*, 1986-87, Statistics Table 6.1

passengers. In 1947, the length of metalled roads was less than that of railways. In 1985-86, metalled roads exceeded railways in length by five times. In 1959-60 railways carried more passengers and handled five times more cargo than roads. In 1982-83 roads handled about three times more cargo and about five times more passengers than the railways. Thus the roads have recorded phenomenal progress. Generally two types of roads are recognized in Pakistan, metalled and unmetalled. The metalled roads have increased from 8,130 km in 1947 to 45,686 km in 1985-86, whereas the unmetalled roads increased from 14,108 km to 61,164 km during the same period. This is in sharp contrast to the small extension of the railways.

Roads can be built and maintained comparatively more cheaply in rugged and desert areas than railways. In many rugged areas construction of railways becomes an impossible task while roads can be laid out. Therefore in many hilly, mountainous and desert areas of Pakistan roads exist where no railway is seen. Northern mountainous areas, large parts of Balochistan Plateau and Cholistan-Thar Desert are such areas. But the areas of densest network of roads and railways coincide because both serve the most productive and most populated parts of Pakistan.

At the time Pakistan was created there was not much vehicular traffic on the roads. But today the roads are packed with trucks, buses, station wagons, jeeps, cars and motorcyles. From 10,000 in 1947, the motor cars, jeeps and station wagons increased to 452,000 in 1985, buses from 4,500 to 62,000 and trucks from 832 to 76,000. Trucks carry goods long distances e.g., between Karachi and Peshawar and between Karachi and Quetta. Trucks and other motor vehicles are very flexible as they can provide door to door service. Transshipment is greatly minimized but it is difficult for them to handle bulky and heavy goods. Therefore for small consignments trucks are competing successfully with goods trains. Buses

Table 16.2: Road Kilometres in Pakistan

Year	Metalled	Unmetalled
1947-48	8,130	14,108
1959-60	14,114	16,740
1969-70	17,483	14,190
1979-80	33,611	62,049
1985-86	45,686	61,164

Source: *Economic Survey of Pakistan,* 1986-87, Statistics, Table 6.1.

are handling heavy passenger traffic for distances which can be covered during the day time. Some buses also ply at night but for long distances and for night journeys trains are still preferred. National Logistics Cell, established in 1978 is performing a great service by transporting grains, edible oil and petroleum to and from Karachi Port.

From Karachi goods are carried by good metalled roads up to Lahore. From there the famous Grand Trunk Road (built by Sher Shah Suri) goes to Peshawar. From Peshawar through the Khyber Pass the road enters Afghanistan. Another important road link is between Karachi and Quetta. It goes through Sibi and the Bolan Pass. An alternate road has been built between Quetta and Karachi via Khuzdar and Bela. This road has become more popular. From Quetta a road goes westward to Zahidan (Iran) parallel to the railway line. A coastal highway connecting Karachi with Bela, Turbat, onward to the Pak-Iran border is greatly needed. This highway, with a proposed length of 603 km is under active consideration by the Government. A metalled road already exists between Karachi and Bela. Another important road project is the Indus Highway connecting Karachi with Peshawar, running through Dadu, Larkana, Dera Ghazi Khan, Dera Ismail Khan, Bannu and Kohat. This will provide transportation to some relatively less developed parts of Pakistan. An important road link has been established with China through Gilgit.

AIR TRANSPORT

In 1947 a small air company, Orient Airways, operated in Pakistan. Two more companies quickly sprang up, namely Pak-Air Limited and the Crescent Airways. By 1952 the two new companies were dissolved. Orient Airways was too small to meet the growing needs of the country. Therefore in April 1955 Pakistan International Airlines (PIA) was established by an Ordinance. Orient Airways was merged with the new company.

PIA has made good progress since its inception. It started its life with a fleet of 15 aircrafts and in 1987 it possessed 44 aircrafts.

PIA services are available to large cities like Karachi, Lahore, Islamabad, Peshawar, Faisalabad, Multan, Hyderabad, Sukkur and Quetta. Some intermediate-size towns have also been linked like Nawabshah, Jacobabad, Mianwali, Bannu, Kohat and Dera Ismail Khan. It also links small places which have transport difficulties like Gilgit, Chitral, Skardu, Zhob, Khuzdar, Panjgur, Pasni, Gwadar, Turbat and Jiwani and important historical places like Moen-jo-Daro. It has wide links outside Pakistan and connects many European countries like UK, Germany, France, Italy,

Russia, etc. It goes to USA and also connects most of the countries of the Middle East and a few African countries. It goes to India, Malaysia, Philippines, Bangladesh, Singapore, Sri Lanka, Thailand, China, Hong Kong and Japan. The result of this expansion has been that the number of passengers and cargo handled by PIA has greatly increased. In 1955-56 PIA carried 1.1 million passengers which more than doubled in five years' time. After a slight set-back during 1971-74 the passenger traffic has steadily increased and was about 4 million in 1985-86. The international traffic has registered a more phenomenal growth. The passenger load factor fluctuates between 55 and 65 per cent.

The progress in cargo handled by PIA is equally remarkable. In 1955-56 only 1,600 tons of cargo was carried and this increased about 7 times in five years (1959-60). In 10 years (1970-71) the increase was three-fold. In another ten years (1970-81), over three times more cargo increase was registered. The international flights carry more cargo than the domestic flights do.

SHIPPING

Pakistan started its life with a frail base in the shipping sector. There were three old ships with a dead weight of 18,000 tons. Almost all the goods from foreign countries were brought on foreign ships and a heavy drain of foreign exchange was taking place. The Government therefore became a member of UK Continent Conference Line. More than 40 ships began to operate. Further expansion of the shipping enterprise was felt necessary. In 1963 a new shipping policy was adopted which among other things sanctioned the purchase of 33 ships. During the same year National Shipping Corporation (NSC) was established. Its ships began to operate on UK-Continent Route and to USA in 1964. In 1965 its ships started to go to Singapore, Hong Kong, China and Japan. In 1966 the Red Sea and the Gulf areas were tapped. By 1970 the Corporation had 31 vessels with a dead weight of 336,931 tons. Besides, there were 40 ships owned by other companies established in Pakistan. These 71 Pakistani ships were handling the entire interwing trade (East Pakistan - West Pakistan) and 14 per cent of the foreign seaborne trade and could carry 6,600 passengers. In 1974, the private shipping companies were nationalized. To manage them the Pakistan Shipping Corporation was established. The National Shipping Corporation continued to function independently. In 1979, the two corporations were merged under the name of Pakistan National Shipping Corporation. Shipping in Pakistan is facing problems. The number of vessels decreased from 71 in 1970-71 to 34 in 1985-86 and the dead weight from 749,000 tons to 595,000 tons. These ships ply on all the important sea routes except Trans-Pacific Route and cater to 20 per cent of the foreign trade of Pakistan by sea.

SEA PORTS

Karachi is the port city of Pakistan. It has existed for more than 250 years. Port Qasim, a new port, has come up about 11 miles east of Karachi port.

Karachi Port

Located west of the Indus Delta on the Arabian Sea coast Karachi Port has served Pakistan since its inception. Karachi has a natural harbour sheltered behind the island of Keamari and a breakwater at Manora. The whole of Pakistan, Azad Kashmir and Afghanistan comprise its hinterland. The story of Karachi goes back to 1720 when a group of merchants moved from Kharak Bunder on the Hab River and established their business at Karachi. It was then a fishing village called Kulachi jo Goth (the village of Kulachi Tribe). Karachi has developed from and acquired its name from this village which turned into an embryo town with the arrival of those merchants. Karachi became an important port under the Talpurs who ruled over it from 1795. In 1838 the port owned 100 boats. The next year (1839) the British acquired Karachi. Charles Napier, the British Governor, expanded the port facilities. He built a lighthouse at Manora and a timber pier at Keamari. He built and improved roads to Kotri, Thatta and Sehwan to connect the port with its hinterland.

In 1952 Karachi Municipality was established and Karachi Port began to receive more attention. The Napier Mole was constructed in 1854. The

Table 16.3: Cargo Handled at Karachi Port in Selected Years (thousand tons)

Year	Import	Export	Total
1947-48	2,216	1,336	3,552
1950-51	2,339	1,190	3,529
1960-61	3,974	1,085	5,059
1970-71	6,379	3,208	9,587
1980-81	11,037	3,617	14,654
1985-86	12,510	3,309	15,819

Source: *Economic Survey of Pakistan*, 1986-87, Statistics Table 6.1

seaward entrance of China Creek was closed. In 1863 Keamari groyne was constructed to protect the harbour from tides and waves. The east pier of this groyne was built after two years. Native Jetty was erected in 1866. Manora breakwater was built in 1877. Up to 1882 there was no dock or pier at the Karachi harbour for ocean-going vessels. In 1882 Mereweather pier, in 1888 Erkin's Wharf and in 1895 James' Wharf were constructed. By 1910, seventeen wharves had been built which were collectively called East Wharf. For management Karachi Harbour Board was set up in 1880 which was replaced by Karachi Port Trust in 1886. In 1861 Karachi was connected with Kotri by a railway line which was extended to Lahore in 1874 and then to Quetta in 1877. Karachi became an important port after World War I. In 1927, 28 berths of West Wharf were built and were equipped with electric cranes. Two more berths were built in 1942-44 and one ship-repairing berth was erected. A shipyard was also established during World War II, and Karachi became an important ship repairing port where 1,000 ships were repaired. After 1947 both East and West Wharf were reconstructed and a bulk oil pier was installed.

A new oil terminal was constructed and the channel was deepened from 30 to 100 feet. With the construction of an oil tanker berth, handling capacity has increased from about 5 million to 10 million tons per annum.

All this development became necessary because Karachi Port had to shoulder increasing responsibilities with the passage of time. In 1947-48 Karachi Port handled 3.5 million tons of cargo and in 1980-81 this increased to 14.6 million tons and in 1985-86 to 15.8 million tons (Table 16.3). The work assigned to Karachi Port has grown beyond its capacity, therefore a master plan for expansion of Karachi Port has been taken up which includes building a hundred more berths. At the same time a new port (Port Qasim) has been established close to the Pakistan Steel Mill.

Port Muhammad Bin Qasim.

In view of the increasing workload of the Karachi Port had to perform, the necessity of a new port was felt. After examining a number of areas, finally a site for the new port was selected at Pitti Creek, close to Pakistan Steel Mill. In June 1973 Port Qasim Authority was established. Besides handling general cargo like rice, cement, etc. the port will have special facilities for handling iron ore, coal and steel mill machinery. In the first phase the port will have 8 berths and 12 more will be added in the second phase. Most of the work on the first phase has been completed and the port has started functioning.

Index

Abbottabad, 20, 65, 95, 97, 106, 107, 121, 148, 149, 168, 190, 216
Abdullah bin Abdullah, 8
Ab-i-Gum, 179
Acid rains, 61
Active Flood Plains, 54, 55, 56
Afghan border, 174
Afghanistan, 21, 39, 231, 233
Aga Khan, 10
Agricultural Development Corporation, 121
Agricultural
   land use, 138, 139
   machinery, 130
   production, 112
   Research Council, 131
Agriculture, 6, 87, 92, 112, 130, 138, 181, 192
Agro-based Industries, 198
Ain-i-Akbari, 166
Alal, 172
Ali Gul, 179
Aligarh Movement, 9
Ali Mardan Khan, 119
Allocations for Industrial Development, 197
Alluvial terraces, 27, 28, 58
Alpine, 53, 158
Alpine forests, 106
Amritsar, 13, 109
Anglo Oriental College, 9
Annual Growth Rate, 76
Antimony, 173, 177
Apabrahmsa, 95
Arabian Sea, 23, 25, 233
Arctic climate, 50
Arid climate, 42, 44, 45
Art silk, 204

Aryan, 6, 7, 93, 95
Asia, 226
   Central, 6
Asoka, 7
Attock, 26, 83, 107, 121, 132, 142, 149, 156, 190
Attock Oil Refinery, 183
Axial Belt, 169, 173, 174, 176
Azad Kashmir, 14, 173, 177, 233

Badin, 98, 145, 152, 183, 208
Bahadur Khel, 166
Bahariawad, 14
Bahawal Canal, 124
Bahawalnagar, 142, 150
Bahawalpur, 14, 28, 29, 60, 83, 142, 149, 153, 158, 160, 208, 216
Baji Valley, 24
Balance of Payments, 217
Balance of Trade, 219
Balkassar, 182
Balloki, 26
Balochi, 93, 94
Balochistan, 12, 19, 24, 33, 35, 39, 40, 42, 45, 57, 60, 65, 83, 95, 96, 97, 98, 101, 102, 103, 104, 105, 106, 107, 109, 111, 113, 117, 118, 137, 139, 143, 145, 146, 148, 149, 150, 152, 155, 156, 162, 163, 165, 168, 169, 170, 174, 177, 179, 183, 184, 186, 191, 201, 202, 203, 205, 210, 213, 216
Baltoro, 20
Baluchap Kundi, 176
Bangladesh, 4, 15, 198, 204, 206, 219, 225, 232
Bankiri, 168

Bannu, 25, 149, 203, 231
Bannu Civil-Canal, 121
Bannu Valley, 22, 87
Baran Dam, 121
Barani, 30, 143, 145, 148, 150
Bari Danda, 28, 67, 123
Barite, 165, 166, 168
Barrage, 65, 110, 120, 123, 124
Bars 29, 55, 56, 119
Basic Democracy, 191
Batala, 13, 14
Batura, 20
Bauxite, 166, 177
Beas, 28
Begar, 136
Bela forests, 105, 109, 111
Bengal, 8, 9, 10, 12, 15
Bentonite, 172, 173
Bet, 28, 29, 55, 65
Betula, 107
Bhadrar, 173
Bhaichara, 135
Bhakkar, 150, 151, 158, 201
Bharat, 98
Bhimber-Mawa Kanch 173
Bikaner Canal, 213
Biogas, 178, 190
Birth rate, 76, 90
Board of Industrial Management, 195
Bolan Pass, 231
Boundary Commission, 12
Brahman, 7
Brahui Range Central, 23
Brazil, 159, 207, 213
British, 1, 6, 8, 9, 12, 13, 97, 182
Buddhism, 7
Buffaloes, 160, 161, 162, 163, 168
Burewala, 201

Cabinet Mission, 12
Canada, 123, 213, 225, 226
Carpets, 203, 216
Carrara, 171
Cash-crops, 140, 154, 156
Caste System, 7
Cattle 160, 161
Celestite, 173, 177
Cement, 212

Central Place Theory, 81
Central Salt Range, 177
Chagai, 19, 23, 24, 84, 171, 176
Chaj Doab, 28, 87, 119, 120, 123
Chamalong, 168
Chaman, 23, 24, 63, 65
Changa Manga, 109
Charbagh Alburai, 170
Charles Napier, 233
Charsa, 116
Charsadda, 208
Chashma Barrage, 65, 87, 123
Chashma Jhelum Link Canal, 123, 124
Chenab River, 26, 27, 28, 54, 60, 119, 120, 122, 124
Chilghazi, 176
China, 63, 175, 188, 202, 222, 224, 231, 232
China Clay, 165, 166, 172
Chiniot, 83, 216
Chistian, 208
Chitral, 14, 21, 41, 86, 94, 106, 176, 177
Chitral Hydel Plant, 188
Chitti Dand, 179
Cholistan, 29, 60, 162, 163
Christaller, 81
Chromite, 166, 173, 174
Climatic Constraints, 63
Climatic Regions, 42
Coal, 1, 26, 67, 166, 177, 178, 179, 180, 210, 213
Complex Mountainous North, 63, 65
Congress, 10, 11, 12
Coniferous forest, 105, 106, 107
Constant Factor Cost, 2
Constituent Assembly, 12
Constitution 10, 12
Continental Shelf, 101
Copper, 166, 173, 174, 175
Cotton, 64, 140, 150, 151, 156, 157, 158, 159
Textile, 197, 199, 200, 203
Crude Birth Rate, 76
Crude oil, 166, 181
Cultivated acreage, 112, 139
Current Account, 4
Cutlery, 216, 221
Cyril Radcliffe, 12

Dadu, 142, 145, 149, 150, 160, 180, 208, 231

Dakhni, 182, 183
Dalbandin desert sands, 35
Dandot Coalfield, 109, 179
Dardic Language, 94, 95
Dargai Project, 188, 210
Dasht, 59, 102
Daud Khel, 168, 170, 177, 210, 211, 212
Deccan Plateau, 8
Delhi, 8
Delta, 29, 56, 86, 109, 233
Dera Ghazi Khan, 82, 149, 150, 153, 158, 160, 170, 176, 212, 216, 231
Dera Ismail Khan, 95, 159, 170, 216, 231
Desertification, 62, 64
Devaluation, 218, 219
Devnagri, 96
Dhabeji, 205
Dhabi, 183
Dhak Katha, 179
Dhands, 29, 102
Dharki, 184, 211
Dhenkli, 116
Dhoro Purna River, 29
Dhoros, 29, 102
Dhulian, 181, 182, 184
Dhurnal, 181, 182, 183, 184, 185
Dilband Fluorite District, 169
Dir, 14, 21, 87, 106, 150
Diwani, 8, 9
Doabs, 28
Dommel Nissar, 176
Duki, 179

Earthquakes, 62, 65, 66
East Central Punjab, 152
Eastern Bengal, 10
East India Co, 8, 9
East Nara, 29
East Pakistan, 2, 15, 147, 205, 219, 221, 223
East Punjab (India), 13, 98, 121
Edible oil, 66, 105, 151, 219, 222, 223
Education, 10, 80, 89
EEC, 190
Electricity, 185, 186, 188, 190, 191
Energy, 67, 177, 178, 189
Environment, 62, 66, 68, 122
Eocene salt, 166
Erosion, 59, 60, 62, 111

Eruptive Zone, 169, 171, 173, 176
European Economic Community, 190
Evapotranspiration, 42, 45, 46, 47, 49, 114, 126
Export, 193, 217, 218, 220, 226, 227

Faisalabad, 68, 69, 79, 81, 82, 83, 97, 156, 184, 200, 204, 205, 208, 210, 211
Faquir Muhammad, 168
Farm Size, 131, 132
Farooquia, 212
FATA, 98
Fazilpur, 160
Ferozepur, 13, 121
Feroz Khan Tughlak, 118
Fimkassar, 181, 182, 183
Firewood, 109, 110, 111
Floating currency, 219
Floating Exchange Rate, 219
Flood Plains, 28, 56, 119
Fluorite, 165, 169
Foreign affairs, 1, 2, 5, 12, 130, 178, 194, 197, 217, 219
Forest, 92, 101, 105, 106, 107, 109, 110, 111, 138
Fort Abbas, 34
Fourteen Points, 11
Fragmentation of holdings, 131, 133
France, 104, 144, 224
Fuller's earth, 165, 166, 172, 173

Galdanian, 176
Gandhi, 11
Ganga, 168
Ganges, 7, 8, 95
Ganji Bar, 28, 56
Ganjo Takar Hills, 27
Ganjo Takar Limestone, 170
Gas, 67, 178, 183
Gemstone, 170
Geological Survey of Pakistan, 165, 180
Ghaggar River, 29
Gharo, 205
Ghee Corporation of Pakistan, 208
Gibbs, 79
Gilgit, 95, 190, 231
GNP, 3, 105, 112, 165, 193, 199
Goat, 161, 163, 164

Godwin Austen, 20
Golarchi, 184
Golra, 201
Gomal, 22, 23, 26, 121
Gond, 6
Goorich, 37
Gorrie, 60
Grand Trunk Road, 231
Guddu, 87, 110, 120, 123, 185, 188
Gujranwala, 12, 69, 83, 109, 145, 153, 188, 204, 216
Gujrat, 82, 87, 95, 109, 142, 145, 149, 152, 156, 216
Gully Erosion, 59
Gurdaspur, 13, 14
Gwadar, 231
Gypsum, 165, 166, 167, 168, 210, 212

Hab, 71, 109, 201, 205, 233
Habibabad, 201
Halite, 166
Hamum, 24
Hamun-i-Maskhel, 24
Haripur, 168
Haris, 134, 135, 136
Harnai, 170
Haro River, 121
Haveli Canal, 123
Hazara Lower Seismic Zones, 65
Hazrat Umer, 8
Heiss, 42
Hematite, 176
Hessian, 206
Himalayas, 20, 23, 119
Hindu Muslim deadlock, 12
Hindu Muslim riots, 10
Hindu Muslim unity, 11
Hindukush, 20, 21, 51
Hindus, 6, 7, 9, 10, 12, 14, 98
Hingol, 24
Hispar, 20
Homogenization, 53, 54, 56
Hong Kong, 221, 224, 226, 232
Hot spring, 171
Hume, 10
Hunza, 95, 170
Hydel power, 106, 67, 186, 187, 188, 193
Hyderabad, 13, 14, 27, 29, 35, 68, 69, 82, 83,
97, 98, 142, 150, 152, 170, 180, 184, 200, 204, 205, 212, 216

Ibn Haukal, 8
IDBP, 194
IMF, 219
Immigration, 98
Import, 217, 218, 221, 222, 223, 225, 226, 227
Index of agriculture production, 121
India, 4, 12, 39, 80, 89, 90, 118, 122, 123, 129, 142, 144, 159, 171, 185, 196, 197, 213, 224, 225
Indian Civil Service, 10
Indian Independence Act of 1935, 10
Indian National Congress, 10
Indian politicians, 10
Indian states, 13
Indo-Aryan, 93
Indo-European, 93
Indo-Pak subcontinent, 6, 8, 9
Indus
    alluvium, 158
    Basin, 127
    Delta, 29, 56, 86, 109, 233
    Lower, 183
    River, 19, 25, 26, 27, 28, 54, 55, 57, 59, 60, 64, 65, 87, 101, 120, 122, 166, 180, 186, 208
    Upper, 119
    Kohistan Seismic Zone, 65
    Plains, 19, 22, 23, 26, 27, 33, 34, 35, 36, 44, 53, 54, 56, 62, 63, 83, 105, 125, 141, 158
    Valley, 6, 29, 87, 95, 112
    Water Treaty, 121, 122
Industrial development, 194, 196
Industrialization, 80, 197, 212, 218
Industries, 193, 195, 197, 198, 214
Insolation, 50
Integrated Rural Development Programme, 191
Intercensal growth, 76
Intermontane valleys, 59
International Monetary Fund, 219
International Rice Research Institute, 146
Inundation canals, 118, 119
Investment Promotion Bureau, 194

Iqbal, Dr. Muhammad, 11
Iran, 39, 44, 117, 129, 159, 223, 224
Iron ore, 166, 173, 175, 213
Irrigated Forests, 109, 110, 11
irrigation, 28, 62, 65, 85, 113, 116, 125
Isa bin Madan, 8
Islamabad, 81, 82, 97, 121, 184, 189
Ismailabad, 204
Ismailwal, 212

Jacobabad, 33, 34, 35, 44, 45, 145, 150, 231
Jagirs, 134, 135, 136, 137
Jahangirabad, 161
Jammu, 20
Jamsukh, 25
Japan, 89, 90, 104, 129, 188, 194, 22, 224, 227
Jaranwala, 205, 210, 211˙
Jarhanwala, 25
Jatta, 166, 168
Jauharabad, 120, 205, 208
Javedan Cement Factory, 212
Jefferson, Mark, 81
Jhelum, 59, 60, 87, 95, 97, 119, 120, 149, 190, 216
Jhelum River, 25, 26, 27, 28, 54, 57, 122, 186
Jhimpir Metting, 179, 180
Jinnah Barrage, 65, 120, 123
Jiwani, 36
Joya Mair, 181, 182
Jute, 140, 204, 205, 206

Kabul, 7
Kabul River, 26, 70, 121, 186, 205
Kachhi, 150
Kakul, 49, 176
Kalabagh, 25, 26, 60, 120, 161, 166, 176
Kala Chitta Ranges, 25
Kalashah Kaku, 210
Kalat, 14, 24, 37, 65, 107
Kalinga, 7
Kallar Kahar Lake, 25
Kalri, 29
Kalt, 42
Kamalgol, 17
Kamalia, 207
Kandhkot, 183, 185
Kanishka, 7

Kaolinization, 172
Karachi, 14, 35, 45, 62, 69, 70, 71, 79, 81, 82, 83, 97, 109, 121, 160, 17, 173, 179, 183, 184, 188, 200, 205, 209, 210, 212, 214, 233
Karachi Shipyard and Engineering Works, 214
Karak, 151, 166
Karakoram, 20, 26, 65, 66
Karezes, 62, 63, 65, 85, 117, 118
Kashmir, 13, 14, 20, 94, 95
Kasur, 83, 84, 142, 145
Katabatic winds, 36, 45
Kathiawar, 8
Katlong, 170
Kaurjos, 63, 65
Keamari, 228, 234
Kech, 24
KESC, 188
Khabeki Lake, 25
Khaderas, 25
Khairi Murat, 25
Khairpur, 27, 149, 153, 201
Khakhan China Spring, 177
Khanewal, 127
Khanki, 119, 124
Khanot Railway Station, 180
Khanpur Dam, 121
Khar Creek, 29
Kharak Bunder, 233
Kharan, 57, 60, 65, 84, 190
Kharif, 64, 119, 126, 144, 147, 149, 157
Khaskheli, 181, 184
Khaur, 181, 182
Khewra, 25
Khojak Pass, 24
Khost Shahrig Harnai, 179
Khowar, 95
Khunjerab Pass, 63
Khushab, 150, 153, 173, 205
Khuzdar, 24, 168
Khyber, 22, 171
Kirana Hills, 27
Kirthar Mountains, 23
Kishore Range, 168, 173
Kohala, 168
Kohat, 22, 87, 107, 149, 151
Koh-i-Dilband, 169

Koh-i-Maran, 169
Kohistan, 65, 87, 95, 97, 106, 149
Koh-i-Sultan, 24, 210
Koh-i-Tuftan, 174
Koppen, 42
Korangi Thermal Plant, 189
Kot Diji, 173
Kotli, 177
Kotri, 87, 110, 120, 123
KPT, 234
Krinj, 174
Kshtriyas, 7
Kulachi jo Goth, 233
Kunar, 21
Kurang River, 25, 121
Kurram, 23, 23, 26, 59, 87, 121
Kurragarhi, 87, 188
Kushans, 7

Labour force, 89, 90, 91, 92, 215
Laghari, 181, 183, 184
Lahnda, 95
Lahore, 11, 47, 69, 79, 81, 83, 97, 109, 145,
    161, 184, 187, 201, 210, 216
Lakhi Range, 173
Lakhra, 179, 180
Land reform, 134, 135
Land tenure, 134
Langrial, 176
Languages, 9, 93, 94, 95, 96, 97
Lar, 96
Large Scale Industries, 214
Larkana, 83, 144, 145, 150, 204, 208, 216
    Sugar Mills, 214
Lasbela, 14, 35, 121, 159, 169, 174, 190
    Plains, 24, 59
Lasi, 96
Law of Inheritance, 133
Lawrencepur, 204
Leiah, 70, 142, 150, 153, 158, 208
Lesser Himalayas, 20, 50
Liaquatabad, 120
Limestone, 23, 58, 170, 177, 184, 210, 212
Link-Canal, 124
Literacy, 3, 80, 97
Lithosols, 58
Livestock, 138, 159, 160
Loralai, 159, 177

Lord Dufferin, 10
Lord Minto, 10
Lower Bari Doab Canals, 88, 119
Lower Chenab Canals, 88, 119, 120
Lower Indus, 29, 183
Lower Jhelum Canal, 119, 187
Lower Sindh, 178, 179, 181, 182, 183, 184
Lower Swat Canal, 120
LPG, 178
Lyari, 70

Mach Coalfield, 179
Machigot, 185, 211
Machinery, 130, 131, 222
Madhopur (India), 119, 121
Magnesite, 165, 168, 169
Mahalwari Syste, 134, 135
Mahmood Ghaznavi, 8
Mailsi Syphon Barrage, 124
Maize, 64, 127, 140, 147, 148
Makerwal, 176, 178
Makrachi, 25
Makran, 8, 19, 23, 25, 65, 118
Malakand, 88, 169
Malir, 70
Malirana, 171
Manchar Lake, 127
Maneri Hills, 171
Manganese, 173, 176, 213
Manghopir, 170
Mangla, 60, 186, 188
Mangla Dam, 66, 87, 102, 123
Mangrove, 109
Manora, 70, 233
Mansarowar Lake, 26
Mansehra, 20, 65, 88, 95, 106, 107
Marai Bela, 176
Marala, 26, 119, 124
Marble, 165, 166, 170, 171, 172
Mardan, 83, 84, 88, 107, 149, 155, 159, 170,
    171, 205, 216
Margalla Hills, 25, 170
Mari, 183, 184
Marine fisheries, 101
Marri Bugti Hills, 168, 184
Martial Law, 136, 137, 193, 195
Marwat Range, 176
Mastung, 24, 118

Mathura, 8
Maurian King, 7
Mazari Tangi, 176
Medicinal plants, 111
Mereweather, 69, 234
Meyal, 181, 182, 184, 185
Mianwali, 150, 153, 158
Middle East, 92, 93, 146, 221, 225, 226, 232
Millets, 140
Mineral Corporation Board, 165
Mineral Development Corporation of
    Pakistan, 179
Mingora, 170
Mirpur Mathelo, 185, 211
Mirpurkhas, 83, 160, 208
Moen-jo-Daro, 144, 156, 231
Moghalkot, 170
Monsoons, 31, 39, 45, 51, 114
Morga, 183
Morley Minto Reforms, 10
Muhammad Ali Jinnah, 10
Muhammad bin Qasim, 8
Muhammad Ghori, 8
Mullagori, 171
Multan, 8, 34, 35, 45, 68, 83, 87, 95, 119,
    156, 158, 161, 184, 190, 201, 204, 208,
    211, 231
Murli Hills, 170
Murree, 20, 39, 41, 49, 50, 114
Muslimbagh, 37, 169, 174
Muslims, 6, 8, 9, 10, 11, 12, 98
Mustahkam Cement Factory, 212
Muzaffarabad, 177
Muzaffargarh, 142, 149,1 50, 153, 205

Nadia, 8
Nagan Range, 23
Nagar Parkar, 172
Nakodar, 13
Nal fault, 23
Napier, Charles, 233
Napier Mole, 233
Narachip Project, 121
Nari, 183
Nari-Bolan, 59, 121
Nasirabad, 142, 145, 150, 190
Nathia Gali, 20
National Oil Refinery, 183

National Shipping Corporation, 232
Nationalization of Industries, 195
Native Jetty, 234
Natural Gas, 178, 183, 211
Naudero, 208
Naurang-Sarai, 208
Nawab Sirajuddaullah, 8
Nawabshah, 34, 83, 142, 149, 152, 208, 209
Nehru Report, 10, 11
Neolithic, 112
Nokkundi, 39, 45, 114, 176
Noorwala, 205
North Chagai Arch, 176
Noshak, 21
Nowshera, 70, 170, 201, 204, 205, 210
NSC, 232
Nuclear, 185, 186, 178, 186, 189
NWFP, 12, 35, 40, 48, 49, 59, 95, 98, 102,
    103, 104, 105, 106, 107, 117, 129, 133,
    134, 135, 139, 142, 143, 146, 148, 149,
    150, 151, 152, 155, 156, 162, 163, 186,
    188, 191, 201, 202, 203, 204, 208, 216
NWFP Canals, 120

Oceanic influence, 45
Official language, 9
ODGC, 165, 182
OGL, 217
Oil, 3, 26, 66, 140, 150, 151, 178, 182, 208,
    210, 219, 222, 223, 234
Oil and Gas Development Corporation, 165,
    182
Okara, 83, 145, 156, 201
Open General License, 217
Ophiolitic suite, 174
Oraon, 6
Orient Airways, 231
Ormara, 36, 45
Ornach, 23
Overseas Employment Corporation, 92
Oxbow lakes, 29
Ozone layer, 61

Pab Range, 23
Pakistan
    Council of Scientific and Industrial
        Research, 194
    Demographic Survey, 76, 77

Industrial Corporation, 194
Industrial Development Corporation, 211
International Airlines, 231, 232
Machine Tool Factory, 214
Mineral Corporation, 165
National Shipping Corporation, 232
Refinery, 183
Resolution, 11
Standard Institute, 195
Steel Mill, 234
Tariff Commission, 193
Railways, 228, 229
Palas, 65
Pamir Plateau, 20
Pandit Kak, 14
Panjora, 21
Parachinar, 37
Parthians, 7
Partition, 11, 12
Pasni, 36, 45
Pasrur, 208
Pat, 29, 137
Pathankot, 13
Pattadari System, 135
Pattan, 65
Pattis, 28
Pattoki, 208
PCSIR, 194
Peasant proprietary system, 135
Perennial canal, 65, 67, 118, 119, 125, 126, 134
Persian, 9, 93, 96, 116
Peshawar, 7, 22, 107, 121, 155, 156, 159, 170, 174, 184, 186, 201, 231
Pesticides, 62, 112, 130
Pests, 123
Petrochemicals, 210
Petroleum, 67, 181, 222
Pezu, 170, 176
pH, 52, 56
Pharmaceutical factory, 111
Philippines, 146, 174, 207, 232
Photovoltaic system, 189, 190
Physiographic divisions, 19, 27
PIA, 231, 232
PICIC, 194
PIDC, 211
Pidh, 179

Piedmont Plains, 27, 28, 57, 58, 87
Pinyari, 29
Pipri Thermal Power Station, 189
Pir Ismail,
Pir Panjal, 20, 57, 59
Pirkoh, 183, 184
Pishin, 59, 155, 156, 177
Plains, 3, 7, 8, 24, 27, 28, 29, 56, 59, 83, 85, 105, 108, 119
Plan:
    Annual, 4
    Colombo, 4, 125
    First Five-year, 4, 5
    Fourth Five-year, 4
    Second Five-year, 4, 191
    Six-year Development, 4
    Sixth, 198
    Third Five-year, 4
Plassey, 8
Playa Lakes, 24
Plebiscite, 14, 15
Pleistocene, 28
Podzolization, 58
Pollution, 62, 69, 70
Poonch, 14
Porali River, 59
Port Qasim Authority, 234
Post and Telegraph, 13
Pothwari, 95
Potwar Plateau, 19, 87, 123, 181
Prakrits, 95, 96
Pre-Cambrian, 27
Primate Distribution, 81
Pulses, 66, 140, 150
Punjab, 8, 12, 19, 29, 39, 40, 45, 46, 65, 83, 94, 95, 96, 97, 98, 102, 103, 104, 105, 106, 107 108, 110, 111, 113, 119, 121, 124, 127, 129, 131, 133, 134, 135, 136, 139, 142, 143, 144, 145, 146, 148, 149, 150, 152, 153, 154, 155, 156, 157, 158, 162, 163, 183, 184, 186, 189, 191, 200, 201, 202, 203, 208, 216, 229
Punjabi, 94, 95, 96
Punjnad, 26, 27, 87, 119, 124
Punjab Tenancy Act, 135, 136
Purushpura, 7

Qadirabad, 124, 161

Qadirpur Bhilmor, 173
Qanat, 117
Qila Abdullah, 177
Quaid-e-Azam, 11, 69
Quaidabad, 120, 204
Quetta, 23, 37, 48, 59, 63, 65,m 83, 94, 97, 107, 109, 111, 169, 174, 178, 179, 184, 230, 231
    Coal Province, 179
    Fault, 65
    Pishin Valley, 119
    Syntaxis, 24
Quota System, 219
Rabi, 64, 119, 126, 129
Radcliffe, Cyril, 12, 13, 14
Rahim Yar Khan, 83, 127, 152, 158, 184, 201, 208, 211
Rahwali, 208
Railways, 13, 228, 229
Rajanpur, 149, 153
Rakh, 105, 108
Rakh Ghulam, 161
Rakh Kishori, 161
Rakhi Munh, 168, 176
Rangpur Canal, 123
Ranipur, 170
Rank Size Rule, 81
Ras Koh, 19, 23, 174
Rasul, 119, 123, 124, 185
Ravi Link Canal, 124
Ravi River, 26, 27, 28, 29, 54, 119, 120, 122
Rawal Dam, 88, 121
Rawalpindi, 20, 25, 68, 69, 83, 88, 95, 97, 106, 121, 132, 148, 149, 170, 183, 184, 204, 210
Razmak, 22
Rechna°Doab, 28, 87
Regosols, 57, 58
Reismann, 79
Resource Development Corporation, 165, 174
Rice, 64, 144, 145, 146, 147, 148, 221
Rill Erosion, 59
Risalpur, 35
Rock Salt, 165, 166, 167, 168
Rohi, 29
Rohri, 170, 212
Rohtas-Dariala, 173

Round Table Conference, 10
Ryotwari System, 134

Sadiqabad, 211
Safed-Koh, 2, 19, 22, 41, 169
Sahiwal, 39, 83, 127, 145, 149, 153, 156, 158, 204
Saidu Sharif, 172
Saindak; 165, 174
Saiyiduwali, 168
Sakas, 7
Sakesar, 176
Sakrand, 127, 160
Salinity, 22, 52, 62, 67, 125, 126, 127, 138, 191
Salt Range, 95, 166, 168, 170, 173, 176, 177, 178
Samana Range, 176
Samundri, 208
Samwal-Pothi-Kharota, 173

Sandal Bar, 28, 56
Sanghar, 98, 142, 151
Sangla, 26
Sanni, 169
Santal, 6
Sapta Sindhu, 7
Sargodha, 26, 39, 83, 142, 145, 149, 158, 161, 201
Saudi Arabia, 223, 224
Sazli, 26
SCARP, 68, 127
Sea Ports, 233
Security Council, 14
Sehwa, 233
Seismic Survey, 182
Seismic Zones, 65
Shaduf, 116
Shah Deri, 172
Shahrig Canal, 213
Shakargarh, 13
Shalimar Gardens, 119
Sheep, 160, 161, 163
Sheet Erosion, 59
Sheet floods, 57
Shahrig Coal, 179
Shekhupura, 204
Sher Shah, 231

Shera Shing, 21
Sherwan, 169
Shikargah, 137
Shikarpur, 134, 135, 145, 150
Shingara, 21
Shipping, 232
Siachen, 20
Siahan Range, 23, 24
Sialkot, 49, 69, 81, 82, 83, 87, 142, 145, 153, 216
Sibi, 33, 34, 44, 45, 63
Sibi Plain, 85, 86, 121
Sibi-Quetta Railway, 179
Sibi Trough, 183
Sidhnai Barrage, 124
Sidhnai Canal, 119
Sidhnai Mailsi-Bahawal Link System, 123, 124
Silk Route, 63
Sindh, 8, 12, 29, 38, 39, 40, 42, 60, 68, 94, 96, 97, 98, 101, 102, 103, 104, 105, 106, 107, 109, 113, 117, 119, 120, 127, 128, 129, 134, 139, 142, 144, 145, 146, 147, 148, 149, 150, 151, 152, 153, 154, 156, 157, 158, 163, 170, 172, 177, 183, 186, 189, 191, 200, 201, 202, 203, 204, 205, 208, 216, 229
    coast, 101
    Industrial Trading Estate, 70
    Kohistan, 85
    Lower, 178
    Sagar Doab, 28, 60, 87, 95, 120
    Tenancy Act, 135
Singapore, 226, 232
Sinkiang, 7
Siraiki, 94, 95
SITE, 70
Siwaliks, 20, 27
Skardu, 170
Small Dams, 121
Small Industries Corporation, 193, 215
Small Scale Industry, 214
Soapstone, 169
Socialist countries, 202
Sohag Canal, 119
Solar Energy, 178, 189
Solar-Photovoltaic-System, 189, 190
Somnath, 8

Sonda Thatta Coalfield, 67, 179, 180
Sor Range Degari, 179
South Africa, 22
South Asia, 22
South India, 95
South Rhodesia, 174
South Waziristan, 85, 174
Spin Karez, 179
Sri Lanka, 223, 226, 232
Steel, 169, 174, 176, 213, 210
Stone age, 6
Stratification, 53
Strontium, 177
Sub-bituminous, 178, 179
Sub-Himalayas, 20
Sudras, 7
Sugarcane, 140, 151, 152, 154
Sui, 183, 184
Sukkur, 27, 83, 87, 97, 120, 134, 135, 142, 149, 150, 153, 173, 184, 231
    Barrage, 110, 120, 123
Sulaimanki, 26, 124
Sulaiman-Kirthar Mountains, 27, 57, 59
Sulaiman Mountains, 19, 23, 65, 108, 168
Sulaiman Range, 176
Sulphide Valley, 174
Sulphur, 166, 170, 172, 179, 210
Surghar Range, 173, 176
Sutlej, 13, 26, 28, 54, 87, 119, 121, 122, 124
Swabi, 171
Swadesi Movement, 10
Swat, 14, 21, 53, 59, 63, 65, 97, 104, 149, 170, 171, 172, 189
Syed Ahmed Khan, 9, 10

Tajedi, 183
Takatu, 23
Takht-i-Bahai, 208
Takht-i-Sulaiman, 23
Talpurs, 233
Tanda Dam, 22
Tando Adam, 200
Tando Alam, 181, 183
Tando Allahyar, 208
Tando Muhammad Khan, 200, 208
Tando Yusuf, 200
Tarbela, 26, 87, 186, 188
Tarbela Dam, 66, 88, 120, 123

Taunsa, 87, 110, 123
Taxila, 214
TDS, 70
Tenancy, 135, 136
Tethys Sea, 19
Thal, 28, 57, 60, 65, 110, 120, 161, 163
Thali, 95
Thanesar, 8
Thano Bula Khan, 172, 177
Thar Cholistan, 57, 65
Thar Desert, 29, 60, 162
Tharparkar, 29, 98, 142, 149, 190
Thatta, 29, 145, 153, 179, 190, 208, 233
Thermal Plant, 185, 189
Thermal Power, 188
Tibbas, 28
Tirich Mir, 21
Toba Kakar Range, 24
Toba Tek Singh, 149, 150, 158
Tochi, 22, 26
Toot, 181, 182, 184, 185
Topography, 28, 52, 53, 57, 62, 84, 87, 105, 113, 138, 141, 186
Towel Manufacturing Association, 202
Traffic Himalayas, 20
Trans Indus, 210
Trans Indus Salt Range, 170, 174
Trimmu, 87, 123
Triple Project, 119
Turbat, 34, 35, 85, 231
Turkey, 80, 129, 142, 144, 174, 177, 185

Uch, 183
Uchchali Lake, 25
Uhl River Hydel Plant, 185
UK, 89, 90, 104, 123, 174, 177, 194, 221, 225, 226, 231
UK Continent Conference Line, 232
UNDP, 190
UNO, 14, 15
Upper Bari Doab Canal, 88, 119, 187
Upper Chenab Canal, 88, 120, 124, 187, 188
Upper Jhelum Canal, 187, 188
Upper Swat Canal, 120, 188
Urbanization, 77, 78, 91, 97
Urdu, 95, 96
USA, 3, 12, 89, 90, 104, 123, 128, 159, 174, 177, 185, 194, 197, 202, 216, 221, 222, 224, 225, 226, 227, 231
USSR, 3, 128, 212, 224

Vaisyas, 7
Varna, 7
Varnasi, 7
Vegetable *Ghee*, 208, 224
Vehari, 153, 156, 158
Vicholi, 96
Village Aid, 191
Vindhyas, 7
Vrachada Apabrahmsa, 96

Wah, 83, 184
Wah Hattor, 212
Wana, 114
WAPDA, 121, 123, 186, 188
Warcha, 166
Warsak, 22, 121, 186
Waterlogging, 22, 62, 67, 125, 126, 127, 138, 191
Wazirabad, 216
Waziristan Hills, 19, 21, 22
West Germany, 104, 123, 224, 225, 226
Western Depression, 31, 39, 40, 45, 48, 51, 113, 114
Western Europe, 202
Western Highlands, 19, 37, 39, 53, 59, 62, 63, 65, 82, 97, 121, 141, 158
Western Himalayas Syntaxis, 65
Wheat, 64, 66, 127, 141, 142, 143, 144, 148, 222
Woollen textile, 203
World Bank, 122, 219
World War, 169, 174, 234

Xerophytic scrub, 108

Zamindari system, 134
Zardalu-Sibi Railway Branch, 179
Zealpak Cement, 170
Zhob, 48, 59, 169, 231
Zhob Valley, 24
Ziarat, 179
Zin, 183
Zinda Pir, 170
Zipf, 81
Zira, 13